S0-AAZ-076

Nunamiut

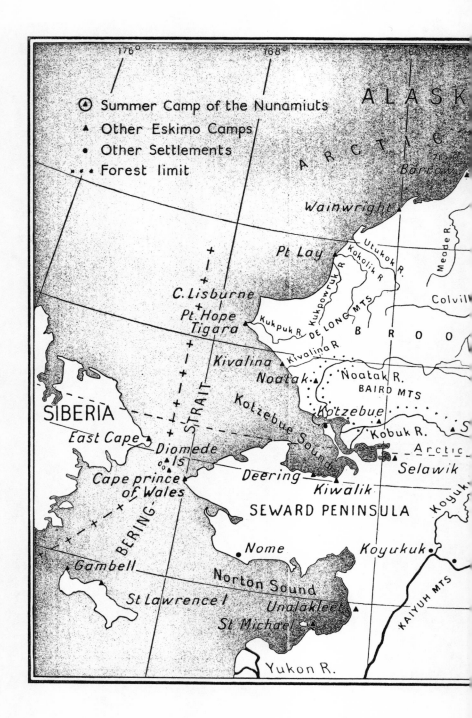

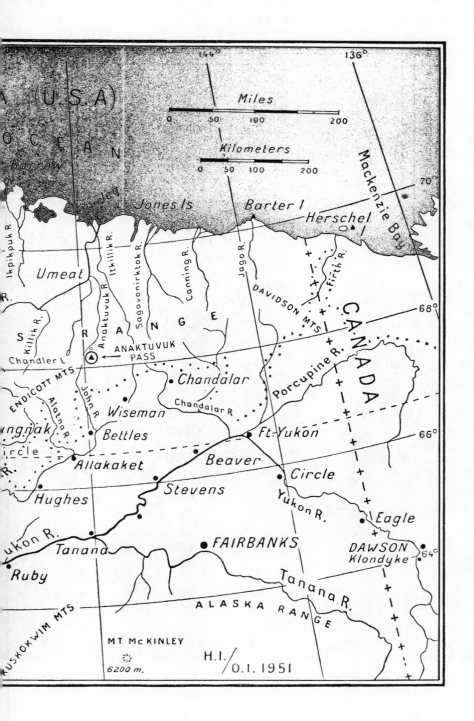

Nunamiuts on the move after caribou. Sledge after sledge, with hunters, women and children, pass through their mountain homeland

HARRISON COUNTY
PUBLIC LIBRARY
105 North Capitol Ave.
Corydon, IN 47112

Nunamiut

AMONG ALASKA'S INLAND ESKIMOS

Helge Ingstad

Preface by Grant Spearman, Curator
Simon Paneak Memorial Museum
Anaktuvuk Pass, Alaska

THE COUNTRYMAN PRESS
WOODSTOCK, VERMONT

Copyright © 1954 by Helge Ingstad

Published in 1951 in Oslo, Norway, in the Norwegian language as
Nunamiut: Blant Alaska Innlands-Eskimoer

First published in the United States of America 1954
Special commemorative edition 2006

All rights reserved. No part of this book may be reproduced in any form
or by any electronic or mechanical means, including information storage
and retrieval systems, without permission in writing from the publisher,
except by a reviewer, who may quote brief passages.

Library of Congress Cataloging-in-Publication Data
Data has been applied for.

ISBN-13: 978-0-88150-761-4
ISBN-10: 0-88150-761-X

Front cover photo of Ingstad Mountain by Grant Spearman
Photo of the author and Simon Paneak courtesy of Helge Ingstad
Cover design by Johnson Design, Inc.

Published by The Countryman Press, P.O. Box 748, Woodstock,
Vermont 05091

Distributed by W. W. Norton & Company, Inc., 500 Fifth Avenue,
New York, NY 10110

Printed in the United States of America

10 9 8 7 6 5 4 3 2 1

To Anne Stine

Barnes & Nagler   3/11/73

06-3041
0-30

Preface

It is not often that a person, a
people, and a place become so
closely linked as have Helge Ingstad and the Nunamiut people of Anaktuvuk Pass, Alaska. It is a bond forged in the late
summer of 1949, when Ingstad first arrived at nearby
Tulugak Lake to spend several months with this then still
nomadic people. It was renewed in the fall of 1989, when he
returned at the invitation of the community to be celebrated
for his contributions to the documentation and preservation
of their cultural heritage, and will continue far into the future
with the official naming of a local mountain in Ingstad's
honor, slated for the early fall of 2006.

Norwegian by birth and a seasoned adventurer and author,
Helge was the first outsider since Diamond Jenness, back in
1913–14, to live among the Nunamiut for an extended period of time, and the first to write about them in depth. In the
course of his nine-month stay over the winter of 1949–50, he
compiled a wealth of films, photos, and recordings that he
drew upon in writing his well-regarded book *Nunamiut:
Among Alaska's Inland Eskimos*. First published in America in

1954, his work quite literally brought these remarkable people to the attention of the world at large, and to the scientific community in particular. Over the past six decades, dozens of researchers in many fields, ranging from biology and botany to geology, anthropology, and archaeology have been drawn to these people to learn both from and about them. Virtually every one, myself included, read Ingstad's book as part of their preparation for coming here.

Now in 2006, a special commemorative edition is being prepared, and in the wake of some 28 years of research and residence in Anaktuvuk, I have been given the privilege of writing a preface to this new edition of Helge's wonderful book. In many ways it has been a great pleasure to reread *Nunamiut* from cover to cover with fresh eyes, and to take it in once again as a whole, rather than in the discrete packets of ethnographic nuggets that I have periodically mined from its pages for so many years. From that full rereading comes to the fore not only an appreciation of what Ingstad accomplished as a storyteller and documentarian, but also the depth of his regard for the Nunamiut people themselves.

For his part, Helge was one of those classically "vagrant Vikings," to borrow a term from famed explorer Peter Freuchen. He combined an insatiably adventurous spirit and wanderlust with a highly educated mind and a curiosity about the world that led him to distant lands, to live among indigenous peoples, and ultimately to find his way into the Norwegian pantheon of adventurers and explorers. The life he lived is one for the books, in every sense of the word.

Born on December 30, 1899—the next-to-last day of the 19th century—Helge Ingstad grew up in a middle-class family in the coastal town of Bergen in the southwestern portion of what would soon become the independent nation of

Norway. At the time, however, it was still part of Sweden—still a sore point to any Norwegian worth his lutefisk.

Lived among the towering, fjord-cut wilderness of forested, steep-walled mountains and deep narrow waters, Ingstad's early years were typical of the times. It was an active outdoor life, of hiking and skiing, hunting and fishing, the kind of existence that since Viking times had yielded generation upon generation of tall, proud, athletic young men, strengthened and hardened by the demands of the Norwegian landscape and weather. Helge was no exception. Handsome and well-built, he grew into early manhood with a taste for adventure and a strong desire to travel.

Yet, being a dutiful son, Ingstad complied, however reluctantly, with his father's wishes—which in his society and times was little less than a command—to advance his education. Leaving Bergen, he moved to Oslo to attend the University and take a degree in law, following the example of his grandfather, who was himself a noted professor of Norwegian jurisprudence.

Degree in hand, Ingstad relocated to the town of Levanger, and by all accounts built a prosperous and successful law practice. But within a few years, he grew worried that his dreams of adventure would remain only that: dreams. Thus, in an act that must have shocked—though perhaps not totally surprised—his family, Ingstad sold his practice and set out for the New World, ending up in the remoteness of northern Canada, where he spent the next four years, from 1926 to 1930, living as a hunter and trapper around the eastern shore of Great Slave Lake. During this period, he lived for a time among the caribou-hunting Chipewyan Athapaskan inhabitants of the area, learning much about their ways, absorbing their lore, and, without knowing it, laying a valuable groundwork for his stay among the Nunamiut a quarter century later.

Returning from his Canadian sojourn, Ingstad wrote a best-selling book, *The Land of Feast and Famine*, and through a combination of his newfound notoriety, familiarity with the Arctic, and legal background, he was called to serve his country in the coming years in a pair of prestigious posts, first as Norwegian Governor of East Greenland (1932–1933) and as Governor of Spitzbergen, from 1933 to 1935.

In 1936, inspired by ancient stories he had heard nearly a decade before among the Chipewyan Athapaskans, he returned to North America and eventually mounted an expedition into northern Mexico in pursuit of a so-called "lost tribe" of Apaches, who had reportedly fled into the rugged Sierra Madre range to escape reservation life several decades before.

Though Ingstad was unsuccessful in his search, his experiences resulted in another well-received book, *The Apache Indians: In Search of the Missing Tribe*, published in 1939. That same year, World War II broke out, and within months his life, like those of his countrymen, was profoundly impacted by the Nazi invasion of Norway in 1940.

The war years, under German occupation, were spent as a representative of the Norwegian Red Cross and—secretly—as a liaison with the Resistance, activities that won him the respect of all Norwegians. Practical and passionate fellow that he was, despite the grinding oppression of the times, Ingstad also found time to marry a very attractive young archaeologist named Anne Stine Moe and to start a family, as well as to write another book and a play.

After the war, while visiting the States with his wife and young daughter in 1949, Ingstad learned about the existence of a little-known group of inland Eskimos who inhabited the nearly inaccessible Brooks Range of Arctic Alaska. Once again his adventurous spirit got the better of him and before the year was out he was living among them and experiencing the life of a nomadic hunter of caribou.

Upon returning to Norway, Ingstad completed *Nunamiut: Among Alaska's Inland Eskimos*, and this is how the Nunamiut know and remember him: as a tall, silver-haired man who spent the better part of a year sharing their lives, recording their stories and songs on tape and their activities on film, and writing a popular book that brought them a flood of attention that has yet to diminish.

Even today, more than a half century later, few of the Nunamiut are fully aware of Ingstad's broader renown, stemming from his 1960 discovery of a Norse settlement at the site of L'Anse aux Meadows. Located on the northern tip of Newfoundland, this site definitively established that the Vikings had reached and settled the New World some 500 years before Columbus. Over the next several years, Ingstad's wife Anne Stine oversaw the excavation of the site, and firmly established the Ingstads' prominent positions in the fields of history and science.

For many years Helge Ingstad was arguably the reigning "grand old man" of Norwegian adventurers and explorers, and nearly every youngster of a certain age avidly read his books and idolized him. With his passing in March 2001, he stepped off into the great beyond to join his countrymen and predecessors Roald Amundsen and Fridtjof Nansen. Honored with the full pageantry of a state funeral, Ingstad's was, by any standards, a life well lived. As he remarked in an interview with the Norwegian Television News a couple of years before his death: "I came into the world at the right time. I got to do everything. I have it in me like wealth, the experiences and the people."

Clearly he had a knack for arriving at the right time, from the day of his birth to the day in early September 1949 when he stepped from Andy Anderson's bush plane onto the eastern shore of Tulugak Lake. Little did he know that he was walking into one of the most pivotal moments in the history of the Nunamiut people.

A scant ten weeks before, the last two independent bands of Nunamiut, the Tulugak and Killik peoples, had loosely joined together, thereby—and without fully realizing it at the time—taking the first tentative step in a decade-long process that eventually led to the establishment of a village and the end of their traditional nomadic ways.

What an exceptional group of people he had found himself among! There were only seven families—65 men, women, and children who were the last inland-dwelling remnants of a once much more numerous folk. Until the closing decades of the 19th century, the Nunamiut had been perhaps the premier caribou-hunting society in northern Alaska. Caribou were not only the focus of their existence, but the very foundation of their economy as well, providing them with meat, fat, and marrow for food; and skins for clothing and shelter; while bones and antlers were the raw materials for a wide variety of tools and implements.

Estimated to have numbered between 1,000 and 1,500 people at its peak, Nunamiut society consisted of a number of extended family-based bands who occupied and seasonally utilized most of the larger river valleys that cut the northern face of the central Brooks Range, between the Nigu and Sagavanirktok Rivers.

Theirs was an ancient way of life, but between the 1890s

and 1910 they saw their once-thriving society shattered and winnowed by a combination of newly introduced diseases and recurrent bouts of famine, the latter brought about by the collapse of the caribou herds upon which they depended. Their only recourse was to move coastward, where marine resources were plentiful, trapping remained good, trading posts were well stocked, and communities like Barrow and Wainwright offered access to mission schools for their children.

By far, the majority of surviving Nunamiut elected to rebuild their lives along the coast, but a small, hardy handful of traditionally minded people, led by the seven family patriarchs (Ahgook, Hugo, Kakinya, Mekiana, Morry, Paneak, and Rulland), now joined together at Tulugak Lake, determined to return inland to reestablish their former way of life, and succeeded in doing so, a short 15 years prior to Ingstad's arrival.

As Helge alighted from the plane and looked into the friendly yet curious faces of this small community, a tall handsome man of about his age strode forward, picked up his backpack, and said in slightly accented English "You come," and led him to his home, a domed, caribou-skin tent. It was a fateful and fortuitous moment when Ingstad first met Simon Paneak, and one that, oddly enough, would resonate nearly 40 years later when he returned to revisit the Nunamiut. But in this moment, Helge was glad to be so graciously taken in by this man with a cordial smile.

He wrote of that first day's end: "Before creeping into my sleeping bag I stood for a while looking out over the tents, whose inhabitants were now under their caribou skins. The fog had cleared; the broad valley came into sight, plunged into darkness and the mountains stood out blackly as they ran away into the distance. Above them a few stars gleamed among hurrying clouds. A new world. A new life." (p. 21)

Over the next several months, until his departure in late May of 1950, Ingstad lived what many, myself included, would consider the experience of a lifetime, to live among the last band of nomadic caribou hunters in Arctic Alaska, and to be largely accepted as one of them.

To be sure, in the early weeks of his stay, they kept a close and benevolently watchful eye upon him, until the Nunamiut felt assured he was an able hand in the Arctic, and wasn't some sort of inept Humpty Dumpty prone to getting himself into trouble. Now it was largely a matter of orienting him to the landscape and imparting some of the finer points of caribou hunting—Nunamiut style—so that he was unlikely to become lost or inadvertently spoil other men's hunting prospects.

Together they shared good times and bad, births and deaths, feasts and hunger, friendships, songs, and stories of the old days. They hunted together, traveled together, and endured the bitter cold and darkness of winter as one. Well, maybe Helge got a bit stronger dose of the cold than the Nunamiut did. They lived in wonderfully warm caribou-skin tents and all he had was one cold canvas wall tent. He had to be one tough customer to get through minus 40- and 50-degree winter weather in that thin-skinned cotton cocoon, for wall tents are far from windproof, and wind is a constant in the passes of the north-central Brooks Range. It doesn't take too much imagination to appreciate what a pleasure it must have been for him when, as he noted, one spring morning for the first time in many long months, his water pail remained unfrozen overnight.

When asked once if he had approached his sojourn here as a scientific expedition, he replied: "No, no, not at all. I just approached them as one human beside another, nothing else.

I just came down and we became friends, and that was all"
(personal communication, 1989). Yet there can be no doubt
about the thoroughness of Ingstad's preparations and the collection of data. This was no will-o'-the-wisp trip, or some
exotic lark. By this time of his life, Helge Ingstad was 50 and
fit, and a veteran adventurer. His upbringing and years
among the Chipewyan Athapaskans in Canada had prepared
him for the cold, taught him the skills of hunting, and how to
respect and to get along with native people. He was also an
accomplished writer and knew his business in terms of
recording his experiences, both photographically and with
the written word, and in the end the data he recorded here
have proved invaluable, not only to the scientific community
but in many ways to the Nunamiut themselves.

What he accomplished during his nine-month stay is
impressive, even by today's standards. First, he penned a
wonderfully readable book about a group of people for
whom he grew to possess the greatest respect and affection,
bringing them to life as individuals for readers everywhere,
while vividly capturing many of the sights and sounds and
sometimes even the scent of the land and its inhabitants.

Set against a backdrop of traditional lore, Ingstad's
account often employs even contemporary activities and sit-
uations as convenient avenues by which to highlight additional aspects of the old ways and beliefs, thereby enfolding
the reader within an evocative atmosphere of how things had
once been.

Nunamiut is a cumulative treasury of ethnographic information that anthropologists and archaeologists like myself
have turned to repeatedly as we delve ever deeper into and
elaborate upon much of what Ingstad was the first to record.

His photographs, both color slides and black-and-white

prints as well as his color 16mm film, are incredibly valuable documentary materials that record the waning days of an ancient way of life that was destined to disappear forever in less than a decade's time. No more the nomads, by 1960 the Nunamiut had become tethered to an increasingly sedentary community and were securely anchored in place.

Interestingly, perhaps Ingstad's most significant contributions, in the realms of folklore and ethnomusicology, remained largely obscured from view until 40 to 50 years later, when his recordings of stories and songs began to be published. It is, I believe, fair to say that had he not collected this material when he did, it might never have been collected at all, and any parallel effort today is not likely yield nearly as rich a harvest. These materials, in particular, are destined to remain the definitive record of these two very important aspects of Nunamiut culture.

Where he also broke new ground at the time was by bringing along a new technology, one only recently developed and refined in wartime Germany: the introduction and use of a tape recorder to record songs and stories. This, in particular, was no easy task, as he was about 300 miles beyond the nearest electric outlet, and batteries were still heavy and primitive and subject to the effects of extreme cold. The only solution was to have a small (and they weren't so small in those days) kerosene- or gasoline-powered generator flown in. Over the course of a few weeks, he recorded dozens of stories, and nearly 200 songs until it gave out. As he recalled: ". . . it should have been more but the motor was tired of working, and the eskimos [sic] were very clever with their fingers, and Ahgook, an old wise hunter he wanted to take it apart and put it together again to try to fix it, but the motor was dead, you know" (personal communication, 1989).

Helge initially approached Dr. Knut Bergsland, a highly regarded linguist, to transcribe and work on the texts, before eventually putting them aside for nearly two decades. In 1985 aided by financial support from the North Slope Borough Commission on History, Language and Culture and the Alaska Native Language Center at the University of Alaska, Fairbanks, Bergsland traveled to Anaktuvuk Pass to work with elders to complete this work. This renewed effort resulted in the publishing of a book, in 1987, entitled *Nunamiut Stories*, which was published by the North Slope Borough with the assistance of the Alaska Native Language Center.

The song tapes were turned over to Dr. Eivind Groven, a Norwegian ethnomusicologist who, in 1955, issued a thick but obscure report entitled "Eskimo Melodies from Alaska, Helge Ingstad's collection of Nunamiut recordings, Studies on the Tonal Systems and Rhythms." There the matter lay for better than a quarter century, until, encouraged by the successful publishing of his *Nunamiut Stories* book, Helge once again approached the North Slope Borough about publishing the Groven report and went to some personal expense to have it translated into English, and the musical scores transcribed.

Although this particular project never came to fruition, Helge pressed on, and in 1998 a double compact disc set entitled *Songs of the Nunamiut: Historical Recordings and Transcriptions of an Alaskan Eskimo Community* was issued by the Norwegian publishing house Tano-Aschehoug. Though hardly a best-seller on Amazon.com, it is, to researchers, an invaluable compilation of songs, most sung by men and women now long gone, and it pleases the Nunamiut to no end to be able to hear their voices once again. It is a very special and concrete link to their past.

Until Diamond Jenness published his memoirs of the winter of 1913–14, spent among a small group of expatriate Nunamiut families overwintering along the Beaufort Sea coast in his 1959 book *Dawn in Arctic Alaska* (University of Minnesota Press), Ingstad's book was the very first to deal with them exclusively, in detail, and one of the very earliest works to present a group of people so that we could see them, at times, as individual personalities operating within a cultural tradition. *Nunamiut* is clearly a fun, informative, and enjoyable book to read.

What is not quite so evident to the reader, however, is the degree to which the trappings of modern life, or at least what passed for them in those days and in that place, had already made very real inroads into everyday Nunamiut life.

For years I have found it both endlessly amusing and oddly enlightening to know, as Paneak's son Roosevelt once shared with me, that at the time of Ingstad's visit his father possessed both a house cat and a regular subscription to *Time* magazine. Look as one may, you will find no mention of either in Helge's book.

If there is to be any criticism here, it would be that the impression a casual reader comes away with is of the Nunamiut sounding a bit more "old school" than they actually were at the time. To be fair, I think Ingstad told things pretty straight, but because his primary focus was clearly upon recording, preserving, and presenting their traditional lore, certain more contemporary aspects of their lives, which evidently held less interest for him, tended to recede into the background in the course of his narrative.

Still, it cannot go unremarked that long before Helge came among them in the fall of 1949, they had already taken upon themselves some rather cosmopolitan airs. Photographs from the 1920s and early 1930s show some of the young Nunamiut men, such as Ingstad's good friend Kakinya, in the shank of the century and the height of his youth, sporting the most stylish of round-framed, tortoise-shell sunglasses (which Kakinya still wore when I knew him in the 1970s and 1980s), an old wool Irish motoring cap, wool riding breeches—also known colloquially as "fart bag pants"—and puttees.

Some of these images were taken by the redoubtable Kakinya himself, with his own Eastman Model 1A Pocket Kodak, now in the possession of the Roosevelt Paneak family. From remote trading posts as far afield as Barrow, Fort Yukon, Old Crow, Canada, Bettles, and Shungnak, Kakinya mailed his film into Mr. Kodak for processing and picked the prints up again months later by dog team or boat. To think of a people so remote, living the lives of nomadic caribou hunters within a couple of decades of the beginning of the 20th century carrying cameras to record their own snapshots, fairly takes the breath away.

Paneak, more so than most, was quite a worldly man, literate in both spoken and written English, and during the war years even owned a large, battery-operated, multiband, mahogany-veneered Zenith radio that he used to track the progress of the conflict as well as to listen to the broadcasts of Tokyo Rose, The Voice of America, and G. I. Jill (Metzger, 1983:54).

Again, to be fair, in winter—when Helge Ingstad spent the majority of his time with them—the Nunamiut were fully furred up and looked and traveled and lived much as they had for more than the previous century and a half, at least. Under these circumstances, they carried an impressive air of the past about them. There is no obscuring the fact that they were still caribou-hunting nomads traveling by dog team and sled and living in skin tents and moss houses, not air-conditioned gypsies rolling down Route 66 in aluminum Airstream travel trailers. But then again, they were not exactly refugees fresh from the Paleolithic either, as some of the Nunamiut felt they had been made to appear.

What they were, of course—and what they still are today—is a group of exceptionally friendly and open-hearted people caught up in an era of rapid and disorienting change, and doing their best to cope, sometimes not as well as either they, or the rest of us, would wish for them. But they continue to confront these challenges as they always have, with determination and resourcefulness.

While Helge's book provides the reader with a fascinating look into the tradition-rich past of the Nunamiut, it also offers us a point of departure from which to broaden our perspective and turn our attention to gain a glimpse at how the Nunamiut saw Ingstad during his stay.

As one might expect, perceptions within the community vary. To the children of the time, like his special little friend Alasuq—who appears on the original cover of the book—and her cousin Uyarak, Helge was a wonder the likes of which they had never seen before, a man so tall, with such white hair who lived in a flimsy old canvas wall tent and traveled mostly on cross-country skis, rather than by dog team, sled, or snowshoes. They recall him as the perfect person to pester, to descend upon him en masse with their little friends, in what Helge affectionately referred to as a "charming robber-band," then getting into his stuff, and into his hair, until he felt compelled to summon up some artificial ferocity and chase them away, only to welcome their return in a day or two.

HARRISON COUNTY
PUBLIC LIBRARY
105 North Capitol Ave.
Corydon, IN 47112

To the young men, once they assured themselves that he was no particular impediment to either their courting or hunting activities—being a faithfully married man, and at age 50 no spring chicken—generally got on well with him, although, given the language barrier, most communication was limited to smiles, waves, and pleasant nods. In terms of hunting, people recall him being far more interested in traveling the country with his camera than with a gun, although he did from time to time take rifle in hand and participate in hunts, bringing in fresh meat to be shared in camp.

To the women of all ages, Ingstad was keen competition for gathering willow to heat their homes and cook their meals. I suspect that some more generous souls came to the conclusion that it was easier to feed him and warm him up from time to time than to constantly have to outcompete him for firewood. The Nunamiut are, after all, a very practical people, and in the firewood collecting department, he was outclassed and overmatched, and knew it.

To the elders he was, to some extent, a source of income, as he paid for the recording of stories and songs. Often, though certainly not exclusively so, his largesse was focused upon those, like Paneak, Mekiana, and to a lesser extent Kakinya, who could speak some English and were therefore easier for him to work with. This, predictably and inevitably, led to a sense of favoritism, especially in such a small community, where a commodity as incredibly scarce and desirable as cash money was at stake. So his reputation inevitably rose or fell among certain individuals based upon its disbursement.

In short, Helge Ingstad made a handful of very close friends, and most people liked him, in a general sort of way. Inevitably, there were a small number of others who didn't, but that is life in a small community, native or nonnative. It is fair to say that overall he was held in good regard, as reflected by the fact that a local mountain at the summit of the pass was called after him and continues to be to this day. As he describes in his book at the time of his approaching departure in the spring of 1950: "We were sitting in the tent, talking a little bit about my departure. Paniaq said "We will give you the mountain which stands at the beginning of the Giant's Valley. It shall bear your name and we will remember you." Then he added, in a manner-of-fact way: "Our people remember such things for many generations."

There is, of course, a little bit more to the story, as this was a gesture rooted in traditional practice, where particular locations commemorate individuals most closely connected with that place. Ingstad's close association with the mountain originates from his favorite—and frequent—pastime of cross-country skiing up Sisuqhaagvik—a large, steeply sloping and gently curving chute on the mountain's western face—and swiftly shussing down its course to the nice long run-out at the bottom. It was a scene that the Nunamiut saw replayed time and time again, and in their minds indelibly linked him to the mountain, which in turn led to their naming it after him. Consistent with Paneak's words, over the past 60 years they have remembered it well and are poised to make the name official and permanent.

After his departure, Ingstad kept in periodic touch with the community for a few years, occasionally writing to Paneak and even sending over about a dozen pairs of cross-country skis for the youngsters, which in the normal course of events ended up as firewood to heat tents and cook food. In 1954, he sent copies of his book to Paneak, but gradually a consensus grew in the community that the book, with its strong orientation toward the lore and atmosphere of the traditional past, made the Nunamiut seem a bit more of the "ancien regime" than they saw themselves to be. It was a feeling that stems from the fact that they are, by nature, a very adaptive and forward-looking people, who take great pride not only in their past, but also in their ability to take to new technologies and circumstances like ducks to water. Consequently, Ingstad's book engendered a bit of annoyance in the ranks, and there the matter rested, scarcely a burning issue, but certainly a mild lingering peeve, for many years, until early in 1980, when Paneak's son Roosevelt contacted Helge about the possibility of securing copies of his photos, film, and recordings for the community.

Roosevelt—who was a youngster during Helge's stay and remembered him vividly—was, like his father, a student of his own culture, and already possessed an impressive pedigree for traveling to search out Nunamiut material in foreign lands, including a trip to Japan. One day he broached the idea of contacting Helge about his materials. At the time, I was working for the North Slope Borough School District in the process of collecting photos, tapes, maps, and publications pertaining to the Nunamiut in a pilot project aimed at developing a history and culture curriculum. Together we proposed a trip to which he generously agreed, and for years ever after Roosevelt reveled in the surprise and then delight in Helge's voice when he answered the fateful phone call that began: "Hello, this is Anaktuvuk calling . . ." Thus in early March, we flew to Olso and were graciously hosted in the Ingstad home, where for the better part of a week we sorted through his pictures, marveled at the living-room window's view across the valley to the Holmenkollen ski jump venue, and passed the evenings in conversation, sipping

xviii   PREFACE

sherry, captivated as Helge regaled us with stories and inci-
dents that, regrettably but understandably, had found no
place in his book.

Upon our return, Roosevelt and I were able to bring with
us the first installment of dozens of black-and-white photographs, followed not long after by larger prints, nearly a hundred color slides, a copy of the half-hour, 16mm color film,
and copies of Ingstad's dozens of hours of audiotaped recordings. Housed at the village school, these materials were wonderfully received by the community and formed the foundation of a collection that eventually led to the construction
and establishment of the local museum in 1985 and 1986.

Over the years, one of the more popular museum pro-
grams has been to contact old, long absent friends who
played important and helpful roles in the early years of the
community, and bring them back to the village to meet once
again and be honored for their contributions to the lives of
the people of Anaktuvuk. The inaugural event, in the summer of 1987, was the return of Sig Wien, pioneer Arctic bush
pilot, the man who first made air contact with the Nunamiut
in 1943, and who helped Helge arrange his trip north.

The second and more ambitious venture was Helge's
return, which took place over the span of several days in
November 1989, some 40 years after he had first come
among them. As he subsequently wrote of his experience:

> In 1989 I really set out for Alaska again, and from
> Fairbanks I flew into the mountains. They were
> expecting me—a crowd of children and adults came
> towards me and the joy of reunion was great. But hav-
> ing walked a short distance, the scene changed radically
> from the old picture I had in my mind. Instead of a

camp in the wilds with tents and dogs, I now saw a
modern village, with large houses and small, and practically none of the good things of life which modern
man considers essential seemed to be lacking. The village had a school and a large village hall, it had elec-
tricity, telephones and television. Where there had
once been dogs, there were tractors and noisy snow-
scooters. And the village had regular air contact with
Fairbanks. I was told that the profit from the great oil
occurrence off the coast had made all this possible.
(N.D.:vi)

And as before, a man with a cordial smile, this time
Paneak's son Roosevelt, strode forth to take Helge, his
daughter Benedicte's husband Edwin, and their son Eirik
into his home. There Ingstad was tearfully reunited with
Paneak's widow Susie, and then went to visit with and pay his
respects to his old friends Paneak, Kakinya, Hugo, Morry,
Ahgook, Mekiana, Rulland, and many others he once had
known, now at rest in the village cemetery. Over the next few
days, he toured the town marveling at the changes. In one
particularly poignant moment, Paneak's younger daughter
Jenny accompanied Helge into the low willows flanking the
runway to find and stand for a while at his old campsite, from
all those years before. In the school auditorium, the community gathered to feast and then to watch his color film and to
view his slides, to present gifts and to hear him speak and give
gifts in return. With a flourish, he pulled from his pocket a
colorful kerchief that he presented to Simon's widow Susie, a
gift he had intended to give her upon his original departure
in 1950, but had forgotten in the hustle and bustle of getting
his gear loaded into the plane. Now after 40 years with the

kerchief gathering dust in his desk drawer, Ingstad made good on his intention.

Of his impressions he later wrote: "A cultural collision—an ancient culture with roots in the far distant past had to give in to modern civilization. My thoughts go back to the Eskimos with whom I had lived in the mountains. The people who had kept ancient traditions alive in their minds and day-to-day lives. I can still see in my mind's eye Simon Paneak sitting in his tent, surrounded by listening Eskimos as he told the story of the raven who brought daylight to man, or about the northern lights where football was played with human skulls. The people lived off the land, they lived with it in good days and bad, they owned practically nothing—but they were very close to one another, they were happy. Now the Nunamiut have almost everything the heart may desire—but I wonder, I wonder . . ." (N.D.: vii)

The community into which he flew in the fall 1989 was at once a part of, and yet in some ways so very far from, the community he first came to join in the fall of 1949. Without a doubt the spirit and hospitality of the people remained undiminished, as his warm welcome amply illustrated, and the broader physical landscape is much as it has been for thousands of years. But in America 40 years is 40 years, and, as observed in the film *Field of Dreams*, "America has rolled by like an army of steamrollers. It's been erased like a blackboard, rebuilt, and erased again, but baseball has marked the time." Well, anyone who has ever been to Anaktuvuk would have substituted basketball, the Nunamiuts' favorite sport, but the principle is the same.

Where once stood a robust patch of 20-foot-high willow covering better than 400 acres, less than half remains, and even that remainder is regenerated growth, for between 1949 and 1965 every last original willow had gone up in smoke, root, branch and stalk, to heat people's homes and cook their meals. In its place lay the village site and a mile-long airstrip designed to accommodate aircraft as big as the C-130 Hercules cargo planes, and flanked by huge gravel extraction pits and access roads.

Likewise, where once small, scattered clearings among the formerly forestlike welter of willows hosted a smattering of caribou-skin tent camps—each one complete with storage racks, a couple of sleds and 10 or 20 dogs—there were now sod houses, plywood shanties, and modern ranch-style homes, a modern $6 million school complete with computers and a swimming pool, a post office, a plane terminal, police and fire stations, satellite TV dishes, and the bewildering array of heavy equipment required to keep the town running.

Even now, a decade and a half after Ingstad's last visit, the village continues to be transformed. A huge, 300,000-gallon water tank now rises and dominates the skyline next to the creek, and nearly every home is hooked up to flush toilets and running water. The industrial section of town, to the south of the school and flanking the runway, houses a modern water treatment plant, a newly upgraded power plant, more warehouses, and a totally redone tank farm, complete with oil and gas pumps such as one would find at any contemporary service station. New modern houses continue to be constructed, new streets plotted and built. A huge chunk of hillside on the very outskirts of town was sacrificed to the gods of progress in order to build a 2.5-mile-long road north to establish a new 5-acre sanitary landfill.

Changes reach far beyond the city limits as well. Today, many of the mountains and side valleys that Helge explored on ski and afoot are either part of, or surrounded by, Gates

of the Arctic National Park and Preserve. By virtue of its reputation as America's premier wilderness park, Gates is growing increasingly popular with recreational enthusiasts who
seek to test themselves in the big leagues of Arctic adventure
travel. By virtue of Anaktuvuk's location, ease of access, spec-
tacular scenery, and regular, affordable air service direct from
Fairbanks, it has become the primary port of entry for park
visitors. Additionally, for those of a less adventuresome
stripe, there are now two commercial travel companies offering internationally advertised package tours of the village, all
of which bring in an average of 1,200 outside visitors per
year.

Even further afield, oil and gas production companies have
been running a web of exploratory seismic lines throughout
the northern foothills just beyond the park boundary and not
too many miles past Tulugak Lake itself. Promising results
already indicate that a number of test wells will be drilled in
the area over the next two to three years. While these developments will at least temporarily offer the opportunity for
local employment, and perhaps even direct access to long-
term supplies of natural gas to heat people's homes, rather
than the very costly diesel stove oil used now, there will be
tradeoffs. If, in fact, commercially viable quantities of gas are
actually found out north, the development will inevitably be
accompanied by a network of support roads and feeder
pipelines that are destined to fundamentally alter the landscape and impact the free movement of wildlife, caribou in
particular. Cheap heat, however desirable, may yet turn out
to be far more costly that anticipated, and in ways other than
dollars.

Of nearly equal, yet more immediate, concern is the sustained presence of commercial guided hunting operations

that have established foothills base camps and conduct hunts on state lands beyond the northern approaches to the main Anaktuvuk valley. Villagers have grown increasingly alarmed about the impact of the hunters and their aircraft traffic upon the fall caribou migrations, which over the past several years have been quite spotty and utterly unpredictable. In response to their concerns, the Alaska State Board of Game has imposed unprecedented restrictions on the guiding operations in order to more closely examine the issue.

From a social and cultural perspective, the changes have been breathtakingly dramatic as well, beginning with a population increase from the original 65 to more than 320 today, and still growing by leaps and bounds.

Although there are many outside influences at work here, arguably the enduring force of change over these many years has been education. The gathering of the last nomadic families at Tulugak Lake in 1949 was largely motivated by the desire of farsighted elders to give their children the opportunity for schooling. At the time of Helge's arrival, surviving photos show children gathered into a small, white canvas wall tent, with school lessons delivered by Simon Paneak and Homer Mekiana assisted by visiting scientists like Robert Rausch.

As the years wore on, the process of settling into a permanent village, while propelled by the establishment of a post office and the building of a trading post and a log church along with the dependability of regular air service, was ultimately capped by the construction of a permanent State of Alaska school building in 1960. Once that was in place, attendance became mandatory, and the days of families with school-age children taking off for weeks or months at a time to hunt and trap afield were brought to a screeching halt.

While parents certainly welcomed this avenue for their youngsters to become conversant with the modern changing world, they have also come to see, in time, that it is fundamentally altering the ancient link between elder and youth so vital to their society and the transmission of its cultural knowledge and values.

Today, with their children and grandchildren deeply enmeshed in the Western educational system, parents and current elders wistfully recall their own youth, when the stories of the old days—some of the very ones recorded that Helge recorded—were recounted to them by their own elders, building and maintaining that strong, durable bond to a rich cultural tradition and a primary venue of teaching in its own right.

This is not to say that today's young people have been wrenched free of their cultural moorings, but they are certainly growing up in a dramatically different world than their parents did, and the path to finding a comfortable and sustainable balance of old and new will be every bit as difficult to navigate as the one their forebears trod in the very early days.

The Nunamiut are, ultimately, an engaging and enduring group of people. Their hunting ethic remains strong, and the songs, dances, and drumming of the old days continue, along with other traditions, to be passed from generation to generation. Some things will never be erased, like their sense of identity, and the ties to the land and the wildlife that have sustained them for centuries, but all cannot remain as it once was, so it will be fascinating—and, one must surmise, sometimes uncomfortable—to see how it all sorts out in the long run.

Better, perhaps, that Helge Ingstad never lived to see, or hear about, the full impact of some of these most recent developments before he took flight, but I suspect that before he finally did leave us, he often reflected upon his time spent here so long ago, treasuring the memories of his friends and adventures, and taking great satisfaction in knowing ". . . I have it in me like wealth, the experiences and the people."

How lucky he was. How fortunate we are to have had him share it with us.

Grant Spearman
September 2006

Grant Spearman is curator of the Simon Paneak Memorial Museum located in the Nunamiut Inupiat village of Anaktuvuk Pass, Alaska. Originally trained as an archaeologist, he has worked and lived in northern Alaska for nearly 30 years.

REFERENCES

Groven, Eivind, 1955, Eskimo Melodies From Alaska (Helge Ingstad's collection of Nunamiut recordings) Studies of Tonal Systems and Rhythms.

Ingstad, Helge. *Nunamiut: Among Alaska's Inland Eskimos.* New York: W. W. Norton & Co., 1954.

Ingstad, Helge. *The Land of Feast and Famine* (reprint). Montreal: McGill-Queens University Press, 1992.

Ingstad, Helge. *Songs of the Nunamiut: Historical Recordings and Transcriptions of an Alaskan Eskimo Community.* Edited by Sigvald Tveit, Transcriptions by Eivind Groven. Tano-Aschehoug (double CD set of recordings), 1998.

Ingstad, Helge. *The Apache Indians: In Search of the Missing Tribe* (reprint). Lincoln, NE: University of Nebraska Press, 2002.

Ingstad, Helge. Unpublished preface to unpublished English version of Eivind Groven book on Nunamiut songs, n.d.

Ingstad, Helge. Interview with Grant Spearman in Anaktuvuk Pass, November 1989 (personal communication).

Jenness, Diamond. *Dawn in Arctic Alaska*. Minneapolis: University of Minnesota Press, 1957.

Nunamiut Unipkaanich: Nunamiut Stories, told by Elijah Kakinya and Simon Paneak. Collected by Helge Ingstad with the help of Homer Mekiana; Edited and Translated by Knut Bergsland, with the help of Ronald W. Senungetuk and Justus Mekiana: North Slope Borough Commission on Iñu-piat History, Language and Culture, Barrow, Alaska, 1987.

Metzger, Charles R. *The Silent River: A Pastoral Elegy in the Form of a Recollection of Arctic Adventure*. Los Angeles: Omega Books, 1983.

CONTENTS

ILLUSTRATIONS

DRAWINGS
(by Paniaq, except those *)

ILLUSTRATIONS 11

SONGS

Nunamiut

HARRISON COUNTY
PUBLIC LIBRARY
105 North Capitol Ave.
Corydon, IN 47112

CHAPTER 1

Toward the Blue Mountains

Not long before we crossed low over the Yukon, a bear came into sight over a mountain ridge—one of those bulky Alaskan bears. He was taking it easy, enjoying the cool air of late summer, stopping now and then to survey the endless wilds spread out below him. Then, catching sight of us, he rose on his hind legs and sniffed in the direction of our plane with forepaws raised. Suddenly he dropped back, hurriedly made off with a comical rolling gait, and vanished behind a rock.

Far beneath us the Yukon glided by, a blue-grey furrow through green woods and brown hills, ploughing its way forward in endless windings to lose itself in scattered gleams in the far distance. Here and there were wooded islands, some resembling great green ships with slender bows. Such was the mighty river that winds its way through the countryside for nearly 2,000 miles and is the thoroughfare of the men of the wilds.

Wilderness lay on every side. It is a land of rich woodlands, wild mountains, and glittering rivers. No town defaces it, no

soot soils it. Only here and there are traces of man: a lonely
trapper's hut beside a lake, a gold-mining camp with heaps of
sand, a river-borne canoe.

Our course was set for the Brooks Mountains, which stretch
like a huge wall for 500 miles across the country from west to
east and are among the wildest and least-known parts of Alaska.
The central region is called the Endicott Mountains, and there
lay my goal: a small group of Eskimos called the Nunamiuts,
who live quite alone in the heart of the range. My intention was
to settle among them, live their life, and try to get a picture
of their culture. I wanted, for many reasons, to find out about
them, not least because they live *inland*. There were many
indications that among them it would be possible to come to
closer quarters with some of the main problems of Eskimo
study.

My first information about this group was obtained at Juneau,
but when, on subsequent journeys in northern Alaska, I tried
to obtain further details, the result for a long time was dis-
couraging. Even in Alaska few knew of the existence of this
people.

I travelled long and far in search of information, and when
at last I came to Fairbanks, I met Sig Wien, and he was the
man. Sig Wien is a burly fellow of Norwegian origin, quiet
and taciturn. He and his brothers, Noel in particular, were
among the first to use aircraft in northern Alaska. Now they
have a fair-sized company which carries on air transport of all
kinds over the region farthest north. Their planes carry supplies and mail to trading stations, trappers' huts, gold miners,
Indians, and Eskimos. Sig Wien knows Alaska as few men do.
He is at home in the remotest corners of the wilds. He flies
northward to the inland Eskimos in the Brooks Mountains
several times a year.

Sig Wien spoke of them warmly, gave me useful hints, and
was willing to arrange air transport at once. I got my equipment

The Eskimo Paniaq, a matchless hunter and splendid story-teller

A caribou bone affords a good meal

The Anaktuvuk Pass in the Brooks Mountains. In the foreground Raven Lake, with the Nunamiuts' camp just visible

together, and early in September 1949 we set off northward.
I planned to spend the winter in the mountains, but how the
Nunamiuts would receive a stranger was an open question.

A bluish mountain massif rose in the north and its outlines
grew sharper as we steered toward it. Valleys, ravines, shining
rivers, and rows of peaks appeared. We followed the John
Valley, with the river below us and steep cliffs on both sides,
and the hillsides were beautiful, with deciduous trees in yellow or flame-red, with dark brown undergrowth spreading up
the slopes. And then, all at once, we were north of the forest
limit. About us were naked mountains and yellow moraines;
along the river were scattered strips of willow.

It grew foggy, and the pilot was not pleased. He had all possible respect for trips into these difficult mountains, where
wind and weather change so suddenly and where it is hard to
find a plane if an accident occurs. But the fog grew thicker
still. It laid itself like a carpet, almost to the ground. The steep
mountain slopes on both sides were gone. We were forced to
fly lower, along the valley at a height of fifty or sixty feet. Below
us we had glimpses of river and water and rock; at one point
a caribou started away. We were approaching the watershed.

"Keep a lookout on your side," cried Andy, the pilot, "and
sing out if you see a big rock or a heap of stones."

I stared till my eyes ached.

We crossed the watershed and entered the Anaktuvuk Pass,
the gateway to the vast lower-lying tundra north of the mountains, and to the Arctic Ocean. The hills were lost in the fog.
We could only catch glimpses of the earth racing past, veiled
in mist. A lake came into view, and Andy said: "A few more
miles."

I breathed a sigh of relief. But suddenly he turned the plane
round and began to fly back south. He said nothing.

This was too bitter a blow. "Put me down by that lake down

there," I cried, "and I'll get along to the Eskimos somehow."
Andy hesitated for a moment and then again turned north.

Suddenly we were over another lake. "Raven Lake (*Tulu-gaq*)," Andy said laconically and laid the plane over. We were going down.

As we steered in toward the bank, I caught a glimpse of a cluster of tents up on the slope. People came running at full speed out of the mist. Before we reached land they were all by the water, a small party of skin-clad Eskimos on a beach.

I landed, and met smiles and curious looks from hunters, women, and a pack of children of all ages. I greeted each of them separately. They were tall, strong people with the wiry agility characteristic of mountain dwellers. Open, friendly faces; gleaming white teeth. The children crowded round me without shyness and chattered away in Eskimo with a boldness I rarely saw in the half-civilized Eskimo children on the coast. They were all dressed in caribou-skin anoraks, splendidly edged with the skin of wolf and wolverine.

I carried my things ashore, and the hunters lent a hand. Andy shoved off, the engine started up, and the plane vanished into the murk. I was left there among the Eskimos on the shore of Raven Lake.

A tall handsome fellow took my rucksack, motioned with his head toward the settlement, and said: "You come." This was Paniaq, who was later to become my special friend. I took to him at once; there was a comfortable placidity about him, and his smile was cordial.

We moved up toward the tents in scattered groups. "You speak English," I said.

"Three men can speak a little. Learnt it once, hunting on the coast. All the others speak only Eskimo, so you learn the language," he said, smiling.

We were met by a vast number of dogs straining at their

chains, barking and yelping full-throatedly. Here were the tents, a dozen in all, queer dome-shaped habitations shaped like snow huts. Smoke rose into the air from crooked chimneys. In the neighbourhood of each tent were stagings of willow sticks, where hides and large slabs of caribou meat were hanging out to dry. Several heavy sledges stood about in the heather.

We stopped at one of the tents, and Paniaq held open the door—a large hanging bearskin. I sat on the floor, and the tent was soon crammed full. On the threshold, with their backs to the bearskin, sat three young girls, continually putting their heads together and giggling as young girls do.

There was plenty of room in the tent, and it was very pleasant there, with sweet-smelling willow boughs, and caribou skins on the floor and everything in good order. Apart from these things, there were so many new impressions that I could not take in all the details. I noticed the curious construction of the tent, the many curved stakes on which the caribou skins rested, the pale eyes in a caribou head flung down by the stove, a face or two which stood out from the rest, a girl's smile. And I wondered what the Eskimos were thinking.

A man appeared in the doorway with one fist full of caribou tongues. I was told that he had just come back from hunting and that the tongues were a present for me by way of welcome.

It was clear that nothing was to be said about my affairs for the present. First we must eat. The tent was filled with a strong odour issuing from the cooking-pot on the stove. The meat was laid on a plate, and we attacked it. I felt myself at home; there was much to remind me of the years in which I lived among Indian caribou hunters in northern Canada.*

A dirty rag was passed round, and we wiped the fat from our hands. One or two of the hunters began to clean their teeth by drawing sinews through them. I lit my pipe and felt

* Cf. the author's book *Land of Feast and Famine,* Knopf, New York, 1933.

happy. Many of them followed the rising smoke with glances
that could not be misunderstood, but no one begged. I passed
the tobacco round; their faces brightened and homemade
willow-wood pipes were brought out.

Now, I thought, it's time, and I said that I had come into
the mountains to live with them through the winter, perhaps
till next summer; I wanted to get an idea of the Nunamiuts' life
now and in former times. I added a few pleasant words, and
that was that.

After my words had been translated, there was silence for a
few moments. Then Paniaq said genially: "This is the first
time a white man has wanted to spend the winter with us. But
it's all right. We Eskimos are not the sort of people to turn
anyone away. You can pitch your tent here, and when the winter comes I'll lend you dogs and a sledge."

Words were one thing; the atmosphere of which I was
conscious was another. It gave me a pleasant feeling that I
was welcome.

Soon we were talking of hunting and of caribou, the beast
that is always in their thoughts. No one asked where I came
from, or wanted to know anything about life in the south. The
conversation was continually interrupted by jokes and laughter.
There is a real joy of living in these simple people, whose only
world is the mountains and who are so poor—who, in fact,
often do not know whether they can get food enough to support life. They are so delightfully natural in their ways, in
every tone of their voices, in every little movement; one never
notices anyone trying to assert himself, and they always have
a ready smile. A cheerful atmosphere of human kindness filled
the tent. We broke up, and I pitched my own tent on a spot
covered with caribou moss, close to a pretty stream which ran
between green willows.

Before creeping into my sleeping bag I stood for a while
looking out over the tents, whose inhabitants were now under

their caribou skins. The fog had cleared; the broad valley came into sight, plunged in darkness, and the mountains stood out blackly as they ran away into the distance. Above them a few stars gleamed among hurrying clouds. A new world. A new life.

My Tent Is
Pitched

I woke suddenly and looked
sleepily around. I stared at the
tent cloth, and it was some time before I realized that I was
in a mountain world in the far north of Alaska, among Eskimos. It was morning, with a gleam of sun. The fresh scent of
the willow boughs which covered the floor tickled my nostrils.
Outside I heard the stream rippling past, clear as a bell.

I looked toward the tent door. A group of smiling children's
faces peeped in, all framed in the bristling wolfskin which
edged the hoods of their caribou-skin cloaks. Their teeth were
white and shining.

"Hello," I said. They did not wait to be pressed, but slipped
in as quick as stoats and sat down among my things. Their
eyes were everywhere; they seemed to be drinking in every
little detail of the tent. There were two girls of between eight
and eleven years and a boy of about three.

They could not speak a word of English, but I learned that
the girls' names were Uyarâq and Alasuq. The last-named had
a broad, beaming smile which exposed teeth so white and so
perfect that I have seldom seen the like. The boy's name was

Ayaqiujaq, a glum, sturdy child, not so talkative as the girls.

They followed my dressing with deep interest, babbling away all the time. Then, their curiosity temporarily satisfied, they disappeared.

Outside, there was a clear autumn morning; the sun lay low over the mountains, and in the valleys there were still dark patches. Just below me were the dome-shaped tents of the Eskimo camp; the smoke curled slowly from their chimneys. The dogs lay half-asleep in the heather. On a staging could be seen the red gleam of large, newly cut slabs of caribou meat hung up to dry. A woman came along, bent double under a huge load of wood; she threw it down in front of one of the tents and began to swing an axe like a man.

The camp was prettily situated on a slope leading down to Raven Lake. A loon was swimming about in the lake. Behind was a wide pass, with undulating plains and heaps of moraine in brown and grey, shining rivers and lakes. It ran from south to north, and through it I had a view of steep mountains on the other side.

Anaqtûwak is what the Eskimos used to call this pass, which is so wide that it can almost be called a plateau. It lies about 2,000 feet above sea level and from it the Anaktuvuk River flows north toward the tundra, and the John River south toward the forest. To east and west the Brooks Mountains run away into the blue distance, a disorderly mass with many spurs. The highest peaks are about 6,000 feet.

The lower-lying country to the north is a huge area extending toward the Arctic Ocean. At first it slopes rather unevenly from the mountains, where rivers from many valleys hurry down. Then the land flattens out into an endless plain where the rivers collect. The greatest mass of water is carried by the Colville River (*Kûkpik*), the old Nunamiut traffic route.

I once flew over this part of Alaska: an immense treeless

plain dotted with thousands of lakes and intersected by a multitude of watercourses, as if the rivers did not know how to reach
the sea, but died away in aimless zigzags; indeed, it sometimes
looked as if they were on the point of running back upon themselves. Here and there along the banks were bright patches of
willow; elsewhere was naked desolation, divided into sharply
defined polygons, formed by water and frost, red, brown, dark
green, or mauve, according as moss, heather, marsh plants, or
saxifrage grew upon them. The Brooks Mountains and the
Arctic plains lie for the most part north of the forest limit:
from Raven Lake in the Anaktuvuk Pass it is about thirty
miles to the forest.

A curious feature of the country is the sporadic occurrence
of willow along the large river channels. It is of many kinds,
some trees standing as high as 16 feet, and 16 inches thick.
They grow as far north as about fifty miles from the Arctic
Ocean; then the vegetation becomes low scrub. A little alder
and aspen occurs here and there as a modest but pretty orna-
mentation.

There are also, throughout the light summer, fields of low-
growing, gaily coloured flowers. In autumn the ground is
flecked with red patches of cranberry; there are plenty of bog
whortleberries, and in places the yellow cloudberries also are
seen. On the slopes of the valleys are carpets of bluish-white
caribou moss, and in the damp places the cotton grass sways
in the wind.

But on the whole the vegetation is sparse. The mighty Arctic
empire gives above all an impression of nakedness. There are
no woods to give protection against the winds.

It is a cold country. The temperature in the course of the
winter was regularly between —5° and —40° Fahrenheit; occasionally it fell to below —50° F. In summer there can be
fairly hot days, but there are sometimes chilly intervals with
snow. The rainfall is very slight.

It is a good deal colder among the mountains than farther
north in the Arctic. At Point Barrow, the nearest Eskimo set-
tlement on the coast, the average temperature is $+9.7°$ F.
The lowest temperature is $-55°$ F. and the highest $+75°$ F.
The average temperature in July and August is about 39° F.
The average rainfall in the course of the year is 5.7 inches.*

Mosquitoes and sandflies are the scourge of the country. The
mosquitoes usually begin in the middle of June, the midges
in August and September, and they are the worst. There are
times when the insects become such an intolerable plague that
the caribou grow quite desperate and run about like mad things.
Indeed, it can be so bad, the Eskimos say, that the cows run
away from their calves.

We have the wilds to ourselves. In this vast stretch of
mountains, which covers a distance as great as from New York
to the northern tip of Maine, there are practically no other
human beings. Occasionally Indian hunters in the east or
Noatak Eskimos in the west make trips into the mountains,
but these are few and far between and are a long way from
us. To the nearest coast Eskimos at Point Barrow it is about
255 miles as the crow flies, while our nearest neighbours to the
south, the Koyukuk Indians, are about 100 miles away. This
last distance signifies little, for the upper part of the John River
is difficult to navigate in summer, and because of the long
winter the snow in the woods is frequently so deep that it is as
tiring to walk a mile or two as fifteen or twenty miles in open
country.

At intervals there have been scientific expeditions to the
mountains and the Arctic plains, but the region is immense,
and the Eskimos maintain that there are parts where no white

* These figures are for the years 1881–1926 and are taken from "Geology
and Mineral Resources of North-western Alaska: Geological Survey Bulletin
815."

men have yet been—which are, indeed, strange even to themselves. The Brooks Mountains are a world of their own, almost
untouched. One may wander far and wide through valleys and
gorges, along rivers and lakes, and enjoy the fine flavour of the
land's virginity. One can meet mountain sheep or bears which
stand rooted to the ground at the sight of a man, because they
have never seen such a thing before. Giant trout swim in the
lakes, multiply, and die of old age. And in the heart of the
mountains is a little band of men.

The Nunamiuts in the Brooks Mountains are divided into
two groups, the Raven people (*Tulugarmiut*) and the Killik
people (*Killermiut*). These last have their regular hunting
grounds on the upper part of the Killik River, but in 1949
they moved eastward and joined the Raven people. There are
sixty-five souls in all, divided into thirteen families and twelve
tents. The Raven people consist of five families, the Killik group
of eight.

The people have little knowledge of the world outside. Only
a few of them have been farther south than the Koyukuk River.
The greater number of the many children have never even seen
the sea. The important event in the people's life was its stay in
the eastern coast regions between 1918 and 1938. In those days
there were fewer caribou in the home hunting grounds, and
the high prices for white fox were an additional inducement.
Most of the people settled on a desolate stretch of coast near
the Canadian frontier, trapped white foxes, and learned how to
hunt seal. Now and again they roamed southward to the inland regions and hunted caribou and mountain sheep; some
remained in the eastern part of the inland regions and had less
contact with the coast.

But the tribe's old hunting grounds in the mountains called,
and so the people came back, the Raven people to Chandler
Lake, the Killik people to the Killik River. Then, in 1947, the

Raven people moved to the Anaktuvuk Pass, and two years later, as I have said, the Killik people joined them there.

Of late the Nunamiuts have given up the annual spring journeys to the mouth of the Colville River, where they used to trade with the Barrow Eskimos. Now they live year after year quite by themselves in the mountains. Sometimes necessity compels them to make a sledge trip over the long and difficult route south through the forest to a trading station on the Kobuk or the Koyukuk, but this is not often. Few white men have visited these Eskimos, and then only for a short time. Neither clergyman, doctor, nor trader had (till 1949) found his way to this remote corner of the world.

Between the Nunamiuts and the outer world there is such a wide, tangled wilderness that communication has to be by plane. The main prop of their existence is, as I have said, the airman Sig Wien. Several times a year he or one of his men flies in with a quantity of simple things such as ammunition, tobacco, coffee, a little cotton material for the women, knives, saucepans, etc., and takes their wolfskins in exchange. What the Eskimos thus obtain from outside is very modest in quantity, for they are poor and transport is expensive.

There is thus a dash of civilization in the Eskimos' material culture, but in essentials their life takes the same shape as that of their ancestors. Caribou hunting is vital to them now as before; from it they obtain food, clothes, tents, sewing thread, rope, etc. Caribou meat is, generally speaking, served at all meals. They live a nomad life in the caribou's tracks. If luck is with them, and thousands of beasts stream over the countryside in the neighbourhood of the settlement, there are rejoicings and festivities among the mountain people. But it may happen that the barren country is empty, with not a living creature in sight. The last time the caribou failed, many Nunamiuts died of starvation.

CHAPTER 3

A Glimpse of the Old Times

After the last ice age, while the great glaciers were still melting, groups of Asiatics came via northeastern Siberia to Alaska, an intermittent trickle of people through thousands of years, much as when herds of animals migrate. They came to a good country. In contrast to the main part of North America, Alaska was not covered with inland ice, except for the larger mountain ranges. A wealth of animal life must have collected here.

Some tribes stayed in the north; others felt their way slowly southward. Centuries passed, the glaciers melted, and the forests, prairies, and mountains of North America spread themselves again. Much happened to the many racial groups in the course of time. Some grew strong, others went under or blended with neighbouring peoples. There were migrations, now in one, now in another, direction. Manners and thought adapted themselves to living conditions. New cultures took shape.

In historical times North America has been conspicuous as a patchwork of many peoples and races, some with features in common, although there might be thousands of miles between them, others profoundly different in spite of being neighbours. Most were what we call Indians, but another element in the picture was provided by the dwellers in the far north—the Eskimos. They live in scattered groups from regions a little south of the Yukon northward to the Bering Strait, eastward along the Arctic coast of Alaska and Canada and south to Labrador—in fact, as far as eastern Greenland. In this vast area they number about 43,500. In essentials they have a common culture. Their languages have the same root. A Greenland Eskimo can understand an Alaska Eskimo without much difficulty; only south of the Yukon and in the western regions is the difference in dialect too great.

Most Eskimos live by the sea. A few groups occupy a special position and dwell inland: west of Hudson Bay there are a number of caribou hunters on the tundra. On some of the Alaskan rivers are Eskimos who live mainly by fishing. Finally, there are the Nunamiuts, the hunters in the Brooks Mountains and on the tundra farthest north, the people about whom I am writing.

Different stages in Eskimo culture can be established; the oldest archaeological finds have been made near the Bering Strait and are estimated to be about two thousand years old. But where did the culture which specially characterizes the Eskimos arise? Or, to put it more correctly, from what area did it originate in a specialized form? Some say Siberia, some the interior of North America. Where do the Nunamiuts come into the picture? Are they coast Eskimos who have gradually found their way into the interior, or do they represent a rather more original race?

The men and women who support life today in the heart of the Brooks Mountains are the remains of a people which must have been fairly large, reckoned by primitive conditions. They have roamed over the vast inland area which stretches from Noatak in the west to near the delta of the Mackenzie River in

the east. At the beginning of this century their number was
diminishing and was about 800. The caribou was the vital factor
in their lives then as now, and hunting compelled the people
to live in scattered groups.*

Their neighbours to the north were the coast Eskimos, whose
life was different from that of the inland people. They hunted
whales first and foremost, also seal of different kinds, walrus,
beluga, etc. In the winter they usually remained permanently in
their huts, which were different from those of the caribou
hunters. The Nunamiuts' neighbours to the south were the
Kobuk Eskimos and the Koyukuk and Chandalar Indians.†

These neighbours wandered in over the Brooks Mountains
and the tundra hunting caribou. Some had settled there. Pro-
longed feuds followed. The Nunamiuts were in permanent
enmity with the coast Eskimos, and it is significant that their
women were forbidden to marry with them. The Chandalar
Indians too were their bitter enemies. These long ago suffered
a great defeat at the hands of the Kobuk Eskimos, and about a
hundred years ago the Nunamiuts accounted for a large number of redskins in a fight in the Anaktuvuk Pass, where the dead
lie buried. This caused the Indians gradually to withdraw.

Curiously enough there was a sort of friendship between the
Nunamiuts and the Koyukuk Indians. They often met for feast-
ing and hunting together in the mountains. It is also worth not-
ing that at the regular trading places there was always peace.

Long before the white men came to Alaska there were extensive trading relations between the primitive peoples of the
north. In the course of time regular trade routes had come to

* A few groups may be named, from east to west: the people on the Saga-
varnirktok River (*Sarwarniqtuormiut*), on the Itkillik River (*Itqilirmiut*), on
the Colville River (*Kûkpigmiut*), at the headwaters of the Colville River
(*Kangianirmiut*), on Raven Lake (*Tulugarmiut*), on Chandler Lake (*Najwar-
wagmiut*), on the Utukok River (*Utuqqarmiut*), and on the Noatak River
(*Napâqturmiut*).
    † Koyukuk Indians = *tagjarwikmiut*.
    Chandalar Indians = *uyarârmiut,* i.e. stone people.

exist, over lakes, mountains, and tundra, and the peoples went year in and year out to old meeting-places. The routes in northern Alaska, however, were only a part of a larger network of trade routes which spread out westward to Siberia and

Fight with bows and arrows.—Drawn by the Eskimo Paniaq.

eastward to Canada. It ran round a considerable part of the Arctic Circle and also had branches which ran far toward the south.

From Siberia goods were carried over the Bering Strait to Kotzebue in Alaska, one of the great trading places in former times. Eskimos streamed to it from many directions, and long before the white men came to America, things like tobacco, pipes, and iron could be obtained there by barter.

In summer, some of the westerly Nunamiuts made their way from the mountains to Kotzebue to trade. Other caribou hunters traded with the Kobuk Eskimos and the Indians. But most of all the Nunamiuts went to the northern coast. This was natural, since most of the rivers ran into the sea there, and not the least important factor was that the annual trade journey in spring coincided with the caribou's migration northward.

These long journeys to the north coast were always great events for the Nunamiuts, but now there are no more, though many of the Eskimos who live in the mountains have themselves taken part in them. Their eyes glow when they tell of the journey to the Tariurmiut, the salt-water people. For the long, weary winter was over. Spring sparkled over the Arctic lands. Migrating birds in thousands were making their way north, and the caribou were wandering slowly in the same direction. The various groups of hunters in the mountains became restless too: onto their sledges they loaded their tents, skins, dried meat, fat, etc., and set course for the great waterways of the tundra, among them the Colville and Utukok Rivers. There they made their way to various regular dwelling places which the people had used on these journeys for ages past, and where they left their skin boats every autumn, on a staging along with other things, well covered over. Then came a busy time, making the boats seaworthy, especially the large women's boats (*umiaq*), made of eight big sealskins and able to carry about a ton and a half. Some had brought ready-hewn spruce wood all the way from the forests in the south to repair the boats' frames.

Now and again from the ice-bound river came long complaining groans. And then, in the middle of May, the ice piled up and eventually collapsed. The mass of water pressed on and drove the ice before it with such force that it sometimes swept far in over the land. In a few days it was over, and the river, as yellow as mud, flowed through the tundra.

The skin boats were launched, the articles for barter and other urgent necessities were loaded, and the rest were packed away on the stagings. Hunters, women, and children went aboard, and the boats were pushed off. A number of kayaks started at the same time, slender, graceful craft with high bows, with caribou hide drawn over them. They passed the big boats and frolicked playfully down the river. The younger hunters wielded the paddles.

A delightful journey followed through the bright spring days and nights. The river wound its endless way, and the landscape was constantly changing. Sometimes caribou were sighted; the boats were then steered to land, and the hunters hurried off. They returned with heavy, blood-stained loads, and bonfires were lighted on the bank. At other times they fished. At this season masses of fish came racing up from the sea.

The delta spread out northward, and the sea lay blue on the horizon. Important ceremonies were now carried out, for they had come from the domain of the caribou to that of the seal. These ceremonies ensured that the caribou were not offended and that there would be good hunting later.

The different groups had various destinations. The Utukok people went down the Utukok River, the Killik people usually descended the Ipikpuk River and arrived at Point Barrow, while many, among them the Raven people, followed the Colville River to the ancient trading place Nerleq, on the western side of its mouth. As soon as the Nunamiuts reached Nerleq, they set up their pointed summer tents. Then they waited for the Barrow Eskimos. These had a difficult journey, for the sea ice was negotiable for only a short way. First they used the dog teams, with the skin boats lashed fast to the sledges; later they made their way up one of the rivers, and then over a string of lakes.

The peoples met; there were feasts, sporting contests, and trade. A swarm of birds twittered over the lake and the plains of the delta. The days and nights were light in a village of tents on a barren shore.

The inland people offered summer caribou skins for anoraks, wolf and wolverine skins for edging; mountain sheep and fox skins for socks and finery; caribou sinews for sewing thread; dried caribou meat and fat, flints, jade, and birchwood for snowshoes; tent posts, alder bark for colouring hides, large ladles made of wild sheep's horns, and sometimes green tobacco from Siberia, etc.

The coast people offered seal oil for the stone lamps, large soapstone cooking lamps which they have obtained from farther east, bearded sealskin for boat coverings and for the lower parts of waterproof footgear, walrus-hide ropes, seals' intestines for making windows, whalebones for use in trapping wolves and snaring duck, sledge runners made of whale jawbones, delicacies like the skin of the buluga, whale-blubber which has fermented in sealskin bags, etc.

But the inland people could not stay long. It was of the greatest importance that they should not miss the summer caribou hunting, as the hide is at its best for winter clothing between the end of July and the end of August. In the second half of July they struck camp and set course inland. If there was a fair wind from the northeast, they hoisted sails and might for a long time have an easy journey upstream. But more often than not they had to paddle hard. Sometimes dogs were harnessed to the skin boats.

Each group now made its way back to its regular autumn camp—i.e. the place where the boats were found and the winter equipment left behind. Here they pitched their tents and hunted caribou and fished. Then, when the ice was safe, they harnessed the dogs to the sledges and went on to their hunting grounds in the mountains.

The Nunamiuts who went to Nerleq in the summer did little seal hunting there; the harpoon did not even form part of their equipment. It was otherwise with the Utukok people, who had their hunting grounds nearer the sea. During their stay on the coast they hunted common seal, bearded seal, walrus, and beluga. Not until well into August did their group return to the interior.

Not all the Nunamiuts went on the trading expedition to the coast in summer. Some remained in the inland regions all the year round.

Today only a handful of caribou hunters are left in the mountains. What has happened to the rest? They have gradually moved to the coast, most of them presumably in the course of the last seventy-five years. After the introduction of firearms into northern Alaska the caribou were so severely harried in every region that a nomad people's chance of supporting life was seriously reduced.

Even in primitive times existence was difficult enough. When now and again the caribou failed, the inland people moved down to the coast. Many returned to their hunting grounds, but there are stories of people having migrated eastward. It is not improbable that parties of Nunamiuts, driven away by a catastrophe in their own country, were among the first Eskimos to reach the Arctic coast of Canada; indeed, their descendants may at length have passed on to Greenland.

After Bering's discoveries the Russians began to exploit Alaska about 1750. It was furs they were after more than anything. They concentrated on the western areas and a part of the interior. In 1867 the country was sold to the United States for $7,200,000. The most northerly area and the Eskimos in it were long unknown. Not till about 1850 did the Barrow and Point Hope people come into desultory contact with white men; these were whalers who, in the years that followed, hunted Greenland whale with great tenacity.

The Nunamiuts lived in such isolation that it was some time before they came into contact with the new culture. Gradually they obtained guns by barter, but as late as the turn of the century bows and arrows were used simultaneously with old-fashioned muskets. Our earliest information of any significance concerning them dates from the 1880's, when the first exploration of the interior of northern Alaska was begun. Stoney and Howard, in particular, give interesting details of their journeys to the country around the Kobuk, Noatak, and Colville Rivers. In 1908–9 Vilhjalmur Stefansson was with a party of Nunamiuts who were living not far from the mouth of the Colville

River, and to him we owe the most important information about this people. Later, Knud Rasmussen and Helge Larsen made valuable contributions.

But, when all is said and done, our knowledge of the caribou hunters in the interior of northern Alaska is scrappy and incomplete. The two groups which live in the heart of the mountain and form the subject of this book have not been studied till now.

CHAPTER 4

People

It was not long before I was at home in the Eskimo camp. During my life with these simple people, civilization and all that it meant gradually faded from my mind. The thousand things which before were so immeasurably important were lost in a distant haze. Caribou hunting became of greater significance than the political situation.

I constantly pay visits to the tents. The first thing to be done is to make one's way between the dogs which are tied up all over the place. There are nearly two hundred of them in camp— fifteen or twenty to each family, big strong beasts and tremendously aggressive. The Eskimos maintain that the dogs are of Siberian origin. A good deal of intermixture has certainly taken place in the course of time, but individual dogs are of the handsome, pure-bred type with pointed ears, sharp muzzle, and a stiff, comparatively short-haired, white coat. Some dogs have a strain of wolf in them. Large, strong beasts are needed, for they have not only to draw sledges but also to carry heavy packs.

When I push the bearskin door aside and enter, I no longer

meet with curiosity; the Eskimos just look up with a smile and
continue with their tasks. The woman, who has her regular
place by the stove, usually sets out some caribou meat or a raw
marrow-bone. The whole atmosphere is homely and everyday.
I am one of them.

It is pleasant inside these curious caribou-skin tents (*itsalik*),
where the wife sits working at skins or preparing meat, while
the man works at a snowshoe or something else, and the children
crawl about. The dome-shaped tents these nomad people use
are of an ancient type (photos following page 48). The frame
(*qalorwît*) consists of about twenty-three thin, bent willow
stakes 12 to 15 feet long. They are driven down into the soil
in a circle, and the diametrically opposed stakes are tied together. A large sheet of caribou skins sewn together, with
the hairs turned outward (*itsat*), is stretched round the walls.
Another is laid over the roof. Canvas (formerly caribou skin)
is stretched over the whole. The threshold is made of turf,
usually with a top cover of caribou skin, and is fairly high.
From a cross-pole hangs the door, a grizzly bear's skin, which
falls into place of itself and shuts tight. Several of the tents have
windows of bears' intestines. Round the tents are squares of
turf stood up on edge.

Inside the tent there is plenty of room; it is about 10 feet by
9 feet and about 5½ feet high in the centre. There is seating
room for fifteen or twenty people; if the posts are moved farther
out, the tent will hold up to sixty people at a pinch. Just to the
right of the door as you go in stands the stove, which the
Eskimos make of sheet iron brought in by plane. The floor
is covered with willow boughs laid side by side and packed
close. On the innermost third of the floor lies a carpet of caribou skins sewn together (*ikuwâq*) with the hairs underneath.
Here the family sit at ease with their backs against bundles of
skins, sleeping bags, etc., piled up against the wall.

It is a good warm home in bitter cold. The tent rides out the storms like a snow hut, and is also convenient to transport on a sledge, even if it is rather heavy when the frost has bitten deep into the skins. It is a firm, solid object in the landscape, like a dome-shaped granite rock.

In former times the tents were usually smaller and had two layers of caribou skin as covering, the outside one without hair. They were kept warm by stones which were heated outside. In winter it was quite usual to cover them with a fairly thick layer of snow. This froze solid, so that a snow hut remained when the tents were moved (*saquyyaq*). Neither the Nunamiuts nor the coast Eskimos north of them built dome-shaped snow huts, the so-called igloos which are used by the Eskimos on the Arctic coast of Canada. Instead, they occasionally made rectangular snow huts (*apuyyaq* or *aniguyyaq*) with roofs of caribou skins sewn together. Sometimes they built a snow house outside the tent, but this was usually in an emergency.

During their stay at the trading place on the coast in summer the Nunamiuts, as I have said, used a pointed tent. This was called a *nappaqtaq* and had sewn caribou skins (*tilaingît*) as covering. In the interior, turf huts were also used, of which I shall have more to say later.

The equipment in the Nunamiuts' homes is scanty; a few dented pots and pans, some cups, knives, and other oddments. Strangely, there are two radio sets in the camp. Jazz and that sort of thing does not interest the Eskimos; the girls say frankly that the white men's dance music is ugly. For that matter, only one or two of the Eskimos know any English. But sometimes there is an Eskimo broadcast from Aklavik on the Mackenzie River intended for the Canadian Eskimos. That interests them.

Of civilized food there is barely a trace. The Killik people, who were unlucky with their wolf hunting the year before, have practically nothing. One or two of the Raven people have some coffee, a scrap of sugar, and a little tobacco. The small quantity of bought food is just a dash of luxury to vary the caribou meat which is the universal food.

If things are occasionally not as in the old days, when the only resources were skins, stones, bone, wood, etc., this is overshadowed by the primitive atmosphere. Certainly the hunters have rifles, but the boys shoot small game with bows and arrows. The women's crescent-shaped knife (*ulu*) is still in use; the only difference is that the blade is now of steel, as with the skin scraper and axe also. For crushing bones a stone hammer with a willow handle is used, as formerly. The fishing implement is a spoon made of walrus or mammoth bone, with a nail let in as hook. The bow drill is still used, and the older hunters have flint, steel, and willow cotton in their hunting bags when they go into the mountains. With this they strike a light as quickly as we do with a match.

It is midday. There is an autumn chill in the air, and it is so clear that distant hills and moraines seem quite close. A comfortable peace prevails in the camp. A party of boys are long-jumping; a few little girls are sitting on a patch of sand playing with stones and sticks. Raven Lake is like a mirror; now and again the shining surface is broken by a trout swimming close beneath it.

I pay a few visits, first of all to the Raven people. I lift up the bearskin door of the tent next to mine and slip in. There lies Paniaq at full length, asleep with his nose in the skins. Suddenly he wakes, sits up, runs his hand through his thick black hair and says, smiling: "I'm an awfully lazy fellow."

It is his habit to say so, but he is on safe ground with his self-depreciation, for everyone knows what a dashing hunter he is. The fact is that he takes his work rather by fits and starts, but sticks to it like a leech when he has once got going and never slackens. He sleeps when he feels inclined. He is a free man.

Paniaq is the kind of man one cannot help noticing. His eyes are brown, with a humorous gleam; his mouth is wide and sensitive. The forehead is well arched, the nose high-bridged and straight. The black-browed temples project a little; the chin bone too is clearly marked, but not strikingly so. His complexion is rather dark. He is about fifty, but his hair has no tinge of grey. He is a tall, splendidly built man, broad-chested, narrow at the hips, with sinewy limbs. His height is 5 feet 9 inches. He weighs about 175 pounds. His hands are small and well shaped. He seems as well trained as a long-distance runner and has the easy walk of the mountain dwellers.

We start talking about all kinds of things, mostly of animals, nature, and the Eskimos' life in days gone by. He is a born storyteller with a remarkable gift for bringing a scene to life with flashes of picturesque detail. From time to time there is a touch of humour, and he bursts into a roar of laughter. He also has a very good memory. He tells me his genealogy back to his great-great-great-grandfather, and not only remembers all the names, but gives fairly detailed character sketches of several of his family who lived a hundred years ago. Indeed, he still knows the names of his great-great-grandfather's dogs.

"My good memory comes from my mother," he says. "She remembered everything, and when I was little she told me no end of things about the old times." His mother's name was Kiktureaq, and I hear from the other Eskimos that she was a well-known medicine woman. She came from Point Hope. Otherwise his family has its roots in the mountains, and as far as he can trace his ancestors they have been caribou hunters. They must have been a sturdy race, with many notable personalities. The best known was his great-grandfather Suwlo, the great medicine man who led the Eskimos in the battle against the Indians in the Anaktuvuk Pass.

When I ask Paniaq a question, there is usually a long silence, sometimes so long that I think he does not mean to answer. He is thinking. It is characteristic that he does not approach a problem direct, but first takes time to consider the matter. Indeed, there is an almost scientific thoroughness about him. If he is asked about something of which he is not quite sure, he always expresses himself with great caution, a thing which is of special value to me in evaluating the ethnological information he gives me. We consider questions of many kinds, and I always find a response in this man who has never seen a town.

He has an admirable mental balance, a capacity for taking reverses calmly. But it is also part of his nature to try to keep up his own and other people's spirits; he seems to be constantly on the lookout for what is diverting in life. If spirits are at all low in the tent, he may suddenly say: "Let's be happy," and then begin to sing.

People like being with Paniaq, and visitors are continually arriving. His tent is usually the hunters' assembly place of an evening. He offers the best he has with matchless generosity, and in a twinkling he has no tobacco left, or anything else. By virtue of his personality, Paniaq has much influence in the community, and his advice is gladly sought. I seldom saw Paniaq morally below par; I never saw a base characteristic in him. I cannot remember his ever speaking evil of anyone.

Time slips by unnoticed when one sits in a tent talking. And there is plenty of time so long as there is still meat enough on the stagings outside. At last Paniaq's wife, Umialâq, sets before us some cooked and some raw meat, and we eat it.

Umialâq is about twenty-nine—twenty years younger than her husband. She is pretty, small, and slight, but as tough as a willow. Her hair is done in two plaits which meet on her neck. It falls a little way down over her cheeks and is like a blue-black frame to her copper-brown face. The youngest boy, Wirâq, crawls about the floor of willow boughs, almost naked. He is only a year old, but has already begun to suck meat.

Over there on a caribou skin sits the three-year-old boy Ayaqiujaq, seriously occupied in whittling a willow twig.

Suddenly two boys come rushing into the tent. They delve
among the caribou skins for a moment, heaving things this
way and that. Then they find what they have been looking for
and are off in a twinkling. These are the elder sons, Kanigjaq,
aged twelve, and Kanayuq, aged seven. But quite alone under
the window sits the daughter of the house, the six-year-old
Sikiârjuk, lost in thought. She is not really pretty, but there is
something soulful about her. She sits with her hair in tousled
strips down over her face and her mouth half open, staring into
a childish world of her own.

Paniaq's father-in-law Kakinnâq, aged fifty, lives nearby. He
has another name, too, Ula. Kakinnâq is an individual type, a
thick-set little fellow with a black moustache, as quick as a
weasel and bubbling over with life. He always seems full of
good humour, which sometimes boils over into shouts of laughter. But he has his serious side, too; for example, he is a man
with a profound knowledge of family traditions.

Kakinnâq is the *umialik* (rich man) of the tribe. According
to our ideas he does not own much, but the Eskimos tell one
with profound respect that Kakinnâq has more dried fat than he
can use himself and both wolf and wolverine skins from previous
years. *Umialik* actually means a man who owns a skin boat, and
since long before the white men came to the country it has
been the designation of a well-to-do Eskimo. It is used, for
example, in a large number of their old stories, and it is clear
that the rich Eskimo has had a strong position in the community. That is noticeable here, too. It is not that Kakinnâq is
at all domineering, but he has an air of importance and he likes
to be the man to whom people come in an emergency. His
prosperity is due not to luck, but to efficiency and vigilance.
Paniaq can take a day or two off when it suits him, but a
great deal is required to make Kakinnâq spend a day doing

nothing. While Paniaq is almost recklessly liberal with all he has, Kakinnâq observes strict economy without it being possible to say that he is mean.

His wife Unalîna has such lovely eyes that the plainness of her face is hardly noticed. She has much understanding and a warm heart. Her great sorrow is that she cannot have children. To make up for this, other Eskimos have given her some of theirs, and she cares for these with great affection. She has a half-grown boy called Anga and little Tullaq and the girl Alasuq —the one with the smile.

Aguk is about seventy. A more vigorous old fellow I have never seen, active from early morning till late in the evening. He runs over the hills like a wolf. It is a sight to see him out hunting, getting over the ground in a very pronounced forward crouch of his own. And when he fires he never misses; ten or fifteen caribou in one hunt is nothing out of the ordinary for him. He has a bright face covered with laugh wrinkles. He is a thoroughly good fellow, of the type which is always eager to help others. And he helps himself where most get stuck. All the Eskimos are clever with their hands, but Aguk is in a class of his own. He is the owner of a great heirloom, an old watch. One day the spring broke and this disaster was talked of with sorrow all over the camp. Then Aguk took the whole watch to pieces. He made holes in the spring with his bow-drill and riveted it neatly together. Then he replaced all the parts, and the watch is now going as well as ever.

Aguk is the most travelled of all the Eskimos. In his young days he went east all the way to the Eskimos on the Coppermine River in Canada and lived there for a time. He was restless, but he always returned to the mountains of his fathers. His wife is called Iyaq and they have a great number of children. One of them is Kimmaq, one of the prettiest girls in the camp, and much sought after.

Then there is Agmâlik, a capable hunter of about fifty. He is tall and thin, with a rather curved nose and protruding lips, and seems generally rather different from the others. Most of his family are Kobuk Eskimos. His wife Kaliksuna is a big woman, an energetic worker, always friendly and helpful. There are a number of children in their tent.

Finally there is the young hunter Aguâq and his attractive wife Qutuk. They have a crowd of delightful children, among them the little girl Puya, as trustful as a puppy.

The most distinguished among the Killik people is Maptirâq, about seventy-five years old, a tall, upright gentleman of the old school, with a quiet manner and a warm gleam in his eye. His whole personality bears the stamp of the culture which has been created in the course of the years by a distinguished hunting people. When he was young, there were still people who hunted the caribou with bow and arrows. He has experienced a good deal that to other Eskimos is history. In spite of his age he still hunts the caribou and wolf and cuts a good figure. Maptirâq is a widower; he lives with his young daughter Tatqawina and his son Tautuq.

Inualûjaq is another veteran; he may well be about sixty-five. He is reputed to have been one of the best runners in the mountains in his younger days. He is a quiet, pleasant man and an energetic hunter. He, too, is a widower and lives with his daughters Paniulaq, who is a widow, and the unmarried girls Aqarwik, Nukâluk, and others. He has had no fewer than eleven children in all, most of whom are living. He still has an eye for feminine attractions.

Mikiâna is the only coast Eskimo in the community, and the difference is quite striking. He is comparatively short and more thick-set, and the shape of his face is rounder. He is a good enough hunter, but he does not cover the ground with the agility and grace of the mountain people. He is married to Maptirâq's daughter, and according to custom he has moved to where his wife's parents live.

He is a very good fellow, and readily gives me help of many kinds in collecting materials. He too has a large family, including three unusually attractive girls, Kunnâna (fat), Nauyaq (gull), and Sisualik.

Then come the younger Killik hunters: Angâq, with the wild eyes, of whom some of the Eskimos are a little afraid; he has a quiet wife called Tugli. Arnarniaq, Qawwik, and Piliala are other young hunters. The last-named is a handsome, strong fellow who is considered the best runner in the tribe. Piliala is newly married; his charming wife is called Sigluk, and they have a small child. It is always a pleasure to pay them a visit; one feels that it is a happy tent.

"The Eskimos on the coast are different people from us," the Nunamiuts say, "and they do not look like us." The difference is quite striking. The inland people are consistently taller, their faces seem longer, and their noses have higher bridges. Whether this is due to adaptation to a particular milieu, or whether there are two different racial types with definite hereditary traits, is not clear. Fifteen of the Nunamiut hunters have an average weight of 150 pounds and an average height of 5 feet 6 inches. It may be stated by way of comparison that the average height of a Greenland Eskimo is 5 feet 3½ inches, and with other Eskimos it varies between 5 feet 2 inches and 5 feet 4 inches. The material available in those regions, however, is much more abundant and the result consequently more reliable.

There is no fundamental difference between the Nunamiuts' language and that of the north-coast Eskimos, but the dialect varies. The speech of the Barrow and Point Hope Eskimos is more sing-song, while that of the inland people has an even rhythm. The dialect of the Kobuk Eskimos too is different. The Nunamiuts say: "We speak the same language as the Eskimos on the Noatak (*napâqtormiut*) and those who used to live on the Utukok River (*utuqqarmiut*). We are the same people, and from ancient times those who have spoken this language have ruled over the tundra and the mountains." It is worth mentioning that the Nunamiuts have a number of words which are not used on the coast.

They maintain that they have no admixture of white blood, and this is probably true, as they have lived for many generations in such an out-of-the-way region. Maptirâq's family certainly has rather fair skin, but as we know from primitive Eskimo groups this is no proof of a white admixture. It is probable, on the other hand, that there is some Indian blood in these peoples. This can hardly be due to association with the Indians themselves, but has come by way of the Kobuk Eskimos, who occupy a special position in several respects.

Searchlight on a Community

It is curious to find a community so utterly primitive in its structure. There is no social organization, no chief or other head, no criminal law. The one stable feature is the family. Here there is a feeling of unity based on blood relationship, traditional culture and milieu, and the security against starvation and enemies which comes of many standing together.

This society is not communistic, for as a rule every man hunts on his own account, and his bag is his own. Sometimes the hunters work together when shooting or fishing, and the bag is divided according to established rules, but this is rather a business arrangement. Great store is set upon individual freedom, and on personal initiative. There is nothing to prevent a good hunter being richer than others in hides, meat, fat, etc.

But at the same time a sense of social responsibility runs through the community; there are unwritten laws for the common good. Among the most important are those which decree that all must take part in the fight for existence, and that fortunate hunters must help those who are in need.

Aguk is about seventy, but runs over the mountains like a wolf. A splendid fellow, always ready to help others

The Nunamiuts use a peculiar dome-shaped tent (*itsalik*). After the snow has been swept aside, long bent willow stakes are placed in a circle and bound together

When the framework of the tent has been set up, a long series of caribou skins sewn together is stretched round the walls and another over the roof

Canvas is stretched over the caribou-skin covering of the tent. A series of caribou skins, without hair, sewn together, was formerly used for this purpose

Turf is placed round the bottom of the tent. The door is a grizzly bear's skin, which usually hangs down and falls into place of itself. The window is generally smaller than that shown and made of bear's intestines

Bosom friends Uyarâq and Alasuq enjoying themselves

Paniaq with a big ram shot high up in the mountains near the "Giants' Valley"

It takes a great deal to make an Eskimo react when someone has committed an offence. If the offence is great, or if it is repeated, the perpetrator usually receives a warning. In former times the neglect of a warning might lead to a killing. Lampoons were also employed, and it was customary to brand a man by giving him a name corresponding to the crime he had committed. But the most serious deterrent is that a criminal comes to feel that he stands alone against the others, on the outside edge of the community. This leads him to fear complete expulsion.

In earlier days the blood feud was generally recognized, and the duty of carrying it on was laid upon quite distant relations. Sometimes a whole settlement might take the part of the dead man's relations. The blood feud was undoubtedly one of the main causes of the Nunamiuts' endless quarrels with the coast Eskimos and the Indians.

The Indians have their chiefs, but when the Nunamiuts have a decision to make, no one has the last word, although, as always in human affairs, the opinions of people of wisdom and experience carry weight. In former times it sometimes happened that the shaman or the "rich man" became the leader *de facto,* and there were cases of power being abused. Such a case was Atangaujaq, the notorious shaman at Point Hope, who set himself up as a tyrant and killed people when the fancy took him. Finally he himself was murdered. He was Paniaq's uncle.

The Nunamiuts' ancient belief was that there was a spirit in every stone, in every flower, in everything on earth, and that both men and animals had a soul which lived on after death. Moreover, the earth was populated by a multitude of spirits of a dangerous kind, against which men had to protect themselves in different ways. Their most effective defence was the shaman.

The Eskimos' religion has found expression in a mass of legends and myths which have been handed down from the Stone Age. A great number of them are still told among the

Nunamiuts, who fully and firmly believe in them, even if they
no longer have shamans.

On the other hand, Christian teaching has found its way into
the mountains. It came to the Nunamiuts later than to any
other native group in Alaska; it began to trickle in, I suppose,
about the turn of the century. It was not very difficult for the
Nunamiuts to accept it. Material advantage undoubtedly played
a part, at any rate to begin with. Here was a god who could
make good hunting certain, protect against misfortune, and
ensure a good life after death.

Whether Christianity has gradually acquired a deeper significance is not very easy to say. From time to time the people
gather in one of the tents or in the open air and sing their
hymns in Eskimo, no doubt with naïve sincerity. But the same
evening the hunters may tell tales of fantastic spirits and of the
medicine man's strange powers. Thus two spiritual currents
collide, and at the back of men's minds the old ideas live on.

As I go about among these people and gradually become
accustomed to the conditions, I come to realize strongly what
the home means to them. It stands out as a firmly welded unit,
a real force. When I push the bearskin door aside and see husband, wife, and children seated on the willow-bough floor, I
feel myself in the presence of something utterly secure, something as old as the hills. I feel rather than understand that
marriage is virtually the only real foundation on which this community is based.

There are several pretty marriageable girls in the camp—
buxom Tatqawina, piquant Kimmaq, the fresh, rosy-cheeked
sisters Kunnâna, Nauyaq, and Sisualik, who remind me of Norwegian peasant girls, and Aqarwik; nor should the good-looking
widow Paniulaq be forgotten. There is an old ban on marriage
between even quite distant relations, so that it is getting rather
difficult to find enough husbands in the little community. In the

previous generation matters were simple, for the mountain people were far more numerous then than now.

When a man and woman have agreed to live together, they move into a newly made tent. A recent development is that couples like to have their marriage registered by the white men, and when possible the young people make a sledge trip to the trading station on the Kobuk River to arrange matters.

Families merge into one another through marriage, which involves connections and obligations of various kinds. The newly married couple pitch their tent close to the wife's nearest relations, and it is their duty to help their parents with meat, fat, and hides when things are short. The parents, therefore, have a strong interest in whom their children marry, and like to have a say in the matter.

A wife's capabilities are an important factor when a man is deciding on a wife. In a community like this so many exacting tasks fall to the woman's lot that if she fails to do her bit the whole economy collapses. She has to dress and sew skins, fetch, cut up, and skin caribou, provide meals, get fuel and water, look after the children and dogs, drive the sledge on long journeys, help to pitch camp, and much else. Most of them are admirably skilful and quick, and carry on cheerfully however much they have to do.

But practical considerations are by no means all that influences a hunter in his choice of a wife. He has as much sense for feminine charm as we have; love is not a privilege of the white race.

In former times a hunter had several wives. That could be good, and it could be bad, one of the Eskimos said, and he went on to tell me about an oldish man called Alûjaq. Alûjaq had two wives. He said it was like sleeping between two mad caribou. At last he left them both.

Divorce is a simple matter, now as in the past. Husband and wife separate and the wife usually goes to her parents. "My

Uncle Ayaquijaq was divorced almost every spring, he was,"
said Paniaq smiling. "He was a tough nut, and so was his wife,
Kumigana. They had only an adopted child. Once he hit her
across the face with a caribou-skin boot, but it did no good.
Every year when spring came near Kumigana had had enough;
she took her workbag and went and stayed with relations. But
after a time she got tired of it, and one day she came wandering
back. This happened year after year. Kumigana took her workbag and went."

There is, on the whole, a good relationship between man and
wife, but there is no doubt who is master in the tent. Now and
then a man strikes his wife, but it is not often. She never inter-
feres in anything which has to do with hunting, and the hunter
leaves all decisions regarding meat, skin, and so on, to her.

Exchange of wives was once fairly common. It often had the
practical object of establishing a community between two families. The children became stepbrothers and -sisters, and the hunters had an obligation to help one another. Exchange of wives
is one thing, but it is quite another that a wife herself should
think fit to have dealings with another man. What wives feel
about being exchanged I do not know, but I have a vivid impression of the violence with which a husband reacts when a wife
is unfaithful.

The Nunamiuts now only have one wife, and exchanging
wives is no longer done, as far as I could learn. And infidelity—
well, that is about the same as before. "But we have a good
remedy for that," Paniaq says. "If the wife is seduced, it is an
old custom for the man to avenge himself at once by seducing
the seducer's wife. That usually does the trick."

I go into Piliala's tent, and there he is lying on his back,
holding the little girl Napigaq up in the air, talking to her and
singing snatches of song to her. Most Nunamiut parents are
very fond of their children. The children are hardly ever struck,

seldom corrected, and are allowed to do practically what they like. They may burst in, clamouring for this and that, disturbing the grown-ups at their work, but they are always met with inexhaustible patience. In this connection it should be noted that the children's freedom is combined with responsibility. They are expected to help with various kinds of work, and they do.

The many children are like a fresh breeze blowing through this little community among the mountains. And these children are something out of the common. Here is a pack of noisy boys aged from three upward. And here is a swarm of little girls who are fully their equals—wild little creatures in long caribouskin cloaks and with bristling wolfskin edging round their laughing faces, each with its own indescribable charm—like mountain blossoms of varied colours.

They very soon realized their power and tyrannized over me mercilessly. My tent is continually full of them, ten or twelve at once. And there is no end to their monkey tricks. If they get too wild, I sometimes get angry and turn the whole pack out. They slip out smiling, not in the least overawed. But if, by any chance, a day passes without a child's face appearing in the door, the place feels dreary and empty. When they pour in again brightness comes into the tent with them.

They are mountain children, these—with deep, wide chests and powerful limbs and aglow with vitality. At three years old they dash up the hillsides like goats, at seven they can run for a long time without getting tired. They are like animals in their sensitive alertness and swift reactions. And they are sharp. They play with stones, sand, sticks, and bones and have tremendous fun with them. They form teams and play old Eskimo games, rush about trying to catch one another, and nearly pull the tents down. They are never bored, but are fully occupied all day long till they drop down to sleep among the caribou skins in the evening.

Children are regarded as wealth. One thing is that they make a home and that their parents are fond of them, but what is just as important is that children secure their parents' future by giving them help while growing up and in later life.

To be childless is counted as a misfortune, and it is a common thing for relations or friends with a large tribe of children to give one or two of them to a childless married couple. As I said above, Kakinnâq has received three. I also hear of children being bought and sold.

The Nunamiuts do not practise any kind of birth control, and many families have a great number of children. It is often hard to feed them all, caribou being such an uncertain quantity. With conditions of life in the mountains so hard, one can understand that in old times mothers could put their newly born children out in the snow and let them freeze to death.

It is something of a marvel to find an Eskimo community in Alaska so sound and vital as this one. This is due in the first place to the people having had so little contact with civilization. While the coast Eskimos have felt the full blast of modern culture—brandy, civilized food, diseases, and a view of life based on dollars—the Nunamiuts have, on the whole, escaped it. They have their mountain world to themselves.

Venereal diseases do not exist, and I know of only one case of tuberculosis. It is also worth mentioning that there is no alcohol. Their greatest danger is the aircraft, which can introduce sicknesses which the Eskimos have little power to resist. Last year, after a plane had landed at the camp for a short time, the whole population was struck down by severe influenza. Three children and one adult died, and others only just pulled through.

There is something so good-humoured and cordial about these people that one cannot help liking them. They have an infectious humour which makes life brighter, a broad humanity with few reservations. Yet it is easy enough to put one's finger on things that jar. And there are dark spaces in their souls. Suddenly, and at times when one least expects it, some utterly primitive feeling will flash out, savage and incomprehensible. Sometimes the situation becomes such that it is better for a white man to exercise patience than to prove himself right.

But one can say unreservedly that they are easy to live with. It is a solace to be with people who are absolutely themselves, who make no effort to assert themselves, who make it their object in life not to elbow forward, but to get some brightness out of the days as they pass.

C H A P T E R   6

Caribou

We are sixty-five human beings
who have to eat our fill every day,
and nearly two hundred dogs. Whether we shall depends on
hunting. I brought a quantity of provisions with me, but obviously I, the only white man, cannot sit brooding over my
possessions. Some went to the children, some to other people,
and in an incredibly short time it was all gone. It was a relief
in a way, for now we are all in the same boat.

Everything depends on the caribou. The caribou are always
in our thoughts. When we come together they are the main
subject of our conversation, and if we are doing one thing or another outside the tent, we cannot help searching the valleys
and hills with our eyes.

From Raven Lake two long lines of cairns (*inuksuit*) have
been set up, one running up the hillside, the other along the
valley. The cairns are made of turf, and are about forty yards
apart, and serve to lead the caribou down to the lake.

Peace prevails in the settlement. An old woman is sitting in
front of the tents peering out with eagle eyes across the flat
valley. She has been sitting like this for several hours, almost
motionless. Suddenly she jumps up crying, *"Tuttu! tuttu!"*

(Caribou! caribou!) And the children immediately take up the same cry.

The camp is transformed. People tumble out of their tents and stand staring, while the hunters drop whatever they have in their hands, seize their guns, and dash off at full speed across the valley.

There they are, a herd of about fifty caribou. Their grey-brown fur blends almost perfectly with the moss and marsh grass. They are going northeast at a good pace. The animals move forward lightly and gracefully over boulders and tussocks. The leader is a cow, then come several bulls with mighty antlers, and after them the rest.

Here and there out in the flat valley and up the slopes toward the mountains I catch a glimpse of the Eskimo hunters. They are still running at full speed in different directions. Then they throw themselves to the ground and wait.

Suddenly the caribou herd stops as at a word of command; the animals stand dead still and gaze. The long row of cairns across their path rises out of the landscape as dark threatening objects. The beasts give a frightened start and run nervously now in one direction, now in another. Shots ring out, caribou fall. The herd is seized with panic and dashes off like the wind in the direction from which it came. More shots. Again the animals approach the caribou fence, but swing off sharply and hurry along it; not a single animal dares to pass between the cairns. At last the herd finds its way right out into the valley and continues northward at a high speed.

It is not uncommon for herds to come so close to the camp; now and then the beasts start to swim across Raven Lake and are an easy prey. But what we shoot in the neighbourhood of the camp is quite insufficient. Sometimes we have to go a long way into the wide pass or in among the mountains.

Meat and hides are brought home by the dogs; each dog has its pack, made of short-haired, untanned caribou skin. It is impressive to see what heavy loads these beasts can carry for hours on end over difficult ground.

The Eskimos are masterly hunters. They train from boyhood and are still young when they bring down their first beast. To their own experience is added all the knowledge accumulated by generations: a comprehensive instinct for animal psychology. There are a multitude of things which they are so accustomed to observe and work upon that they know what ought to be done without reasoning further. The hunters know how the caribou will react in given conditions, which route it will choose in accordance with the nature of the ground, where it will graze, and much else. Thus, they are able to place themselves so favourably that they often get to close quarters with the herds.

More often a man goes out hunting alone and can be away from early morning till late evening. He takes his time, relaxes completely, and makes his way through the wilds at a gentle saunter, not from laziness, but because to take in all the details of the landscape is an essential part of hunting. He will sit down on a heap of stones and examine the country with the greatest care. If he then sights caribou, he is transformed: bent half double, he flies like the wind to the most favourable cover, thence perhaps to worm his way forward inch by inch to a place where he has the beautiful living meat close before his eyes.

In many places the caribou have left hard trampled tracks behind them, and from time to time new herds come along them. Sometimes the hunting consists simply in a hunter placing himself in ambush along one of these tracks. At other times, and especially in the bitterly cold winter days, the caribou are very shy and it is almost impossible to stalk them. Then the hunter may have to follow his quarry for a long time. It may look hopeless, but a good hunter with sufficient endurance gets his chance sooner or later, when the beasts stop for a short time or begin to zigzag.

It is not very often that men hunt together by arrangement.

On the other hand, it quite frequently happens that several men set out against the same herd and so quite accidentally become dependent on one another. Sometimes they post themselves according to plan, but at other times individuals attack the herd without any special regard to the others. The rules for the division of the bag are fairly elastic. Most often each man has a right to the beasts he himself has shot. Much can depend, however, on whether there is a shortage of meat in the camp, and on the fortunate hunters' liberality. I have taken part in joint hunts after which the bag has been divided equally or in proportion to each family's requirements. A man who has wounded a caribou must pursue it at once to maintain his right to it, or make it known that he is going to continue the pursuit next day.

The Nunamiuts have unusually sharp eyes and are also good shots. It may be mentioned as a curiosity that there are stories of Eskimos who have been able to pick up the scent of caribou rather like dogs. Hitherto I have had little belief in powers of that kind in primitive people, but the detailed information I get here about Eskimos with a finely developed sense of smell seems to me quite credible. Paniaq tells me of a hunter named Arniaq who could not only pick up scent from an animal's tracks, but also scent game directly.

As I wandered into this endless mountain world, I often stumbled upon old signs of caribou hunting—traces of vanished times. Along the slopes of the valley where the caribou have their tracks, I quite often came upon rows of little stone cairns. These were to lead the caribou to the spot where the marksman lay in wait with bow and arrows. At some places the hunters had built themselves stone screens, sometimes in a square like a small house without a roof.

On one beach a mass of caribou bones, half overgrown, lay strewn around. Here the beasts must have been driven into the water and then slaughtered from kayaks, being stabbed with a

spear (*pana*) behind the last rib, close to the spine. The Eskimos have many stories of this kind of hunting, which was
formerly of great importance. Sometimes hundreds of animals

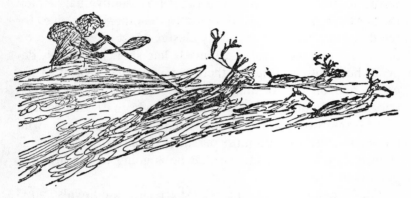

Caribou hunting from kayak. The hunter paddles up to the swimming
beasts and kills them with his spear. Sometimes a great quantity of caribou are killed. This was one of the Nunamiuts' principal methods of
hunting.—Drawn by the Eskimo Paniaq.

were killed, and were usually divided equally between the
families which took part in the drive.

At another place I found the remains of a *kangiraq,* i.e. a
large enclosure into which caribou were driven. These were
usually set up on a height near a river and might be a hundred
yards or more in diameter, consisting of a number of tall willow
rods driven into the earth or snow. Along the inside of this
enclosure snares made of animals' skins were placed at suitable
intervals and fastened to a stone or stick. There were usually
several enclosures, one inside another; the maximum number
was four, and then the contrivance was called a *sisamailik.*
There were snares along each line totalling several hundreds.

The caribou found their way to the gate by following two
lines of cairns which began several miles out in the open country, and which led across the river up the slope to the enclosure.

Close to it there might be two snow walls. Thus a "street" was formed outside which the animals did not venture; far from the enclosure it was broad, and then gradually became narrower.

A herd of caribou had to be driven into this "street" often from a long way off; there are stories of drives which took several days. The drivers worked together, running continually. This was child's play to them, thoroughly trained as they were.

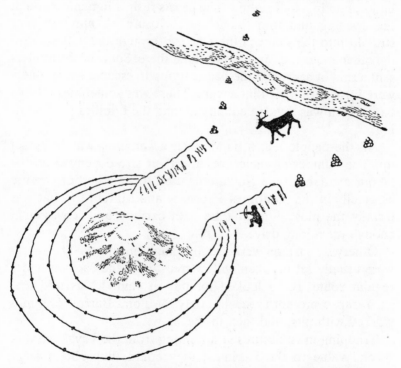

Sketch of a *kangiraq,* an enclosure for catching caribou. This is a *sisamailik,* i.e. there are four circular fences, one inside the other. From the enclosure two snow walls run forward and two lines of cairns run farther out into the country. The herd of caribou is driven in between the cairns and farther into the enclosure, where a number of snares are set.—
From a drawing by the Eskimo Paniaq.

Indeed, they sometimes amused themselves by arranging a kind of relay race in combination with the drive. They divided themselves into two sides and posted reliefs along the valley where sooner or later the herd of caribou would pass. The side which had its runner nearest the herd at the end was the winner.

When the caribou had at last been driven up the slope towards the enclosure, people ran up from both sides, clapping their hands, hooting, and yelling. The beasts rushed in panic through the opening and into the inner enclosure. A number went straight into the snares; others broke through the willows into the other enclosures and were snared there. Some of the hunters sent a rain of arrows at the beasts trying to escape, while others were busy with their flint spears. There was sometimes a large bag, which was divided equally among the families participating.

All the people lent a hand when a *kangiraq* was to be set up. The number of enclosures and their size depended on the labour available. The Nunamiuts used this method of capture especially in the months of February and March, for that was usually the most difficult time with caribou and it was light enough for a long drive.

Otherwise caribou were usually caught in snares. The snares were usually set between willow trees; here the caribou had a regular route. But I looked for pits in vain. I was told that such traps were not used, that only the Point Barrow Eskimos worked with pits, and then in the snow.

Trapping in enclosures and hunting from the kayak were of special value to the Eskimos; they could thus obtain large quantities of meat at one stroke and provide for the future. Hunting with bows and arrows was also important, but to a lesser degree. The bow was straight, made of spruce and bound with thin strips of sinew to strengthen it. The length of the arrow was the distance from the clenched fist of an outstretched left hand to the throat. The tip was made of flint, or preferably of caribou horn, and was then fairly long—from the tip of an outstretched middle finger to the hindermost depression in the back of the hand.

There are at least a million caribou in northern Alaska, according to Sig Wien, and he ought to know better than most, for he has been flying over the country for years and has always had his eyes open for animal life. A large part of the stock belongs to areas which lie south of the Brooks Mountains— to forest regions, in which there are, among others, Grant's caribou and the big Osborn's caribou.

The caribou which lives in the Brooks Mountains and on the plateau to the north of them is the tundra caribou, *Rangifer arcticus stonei*. It is identical with the north Canadian and rather larger than the reindeer, its European cousin. The number is not easy to determine, but I should guess that a couple of hundred thousand head roam over the Nunamiuts' old hunting grounds. The tundra caribou is like a migratory bird; every spring it makes its way toward the sea, every autumn it withdraws in the direction of the forest limit. It follows the ancient migratory routes with an extraordinary instinct. It is the same in Siberia, northern Alaska, northern Canada, and it also applied to the caribou in Norway in old times.

To understand the typical caribou hunter's existence—either among the Nunamiuts, the Indians of the north Canadian tundra, the inland Eskimos west of Hudson Bay, or the people who lived several thousand years ago in the shadow of the inland ice—a closer acquaintance with the caribou is a preliminary condition. The study of the caribou hunter must begin with the study of the animal.

Natural conditions in the different Arctic countries can lead to many variations in the migratory habits of the caribou, even if the essential feature is common to all: the move toward the sea in the spring and toward the forests in autumn. In northern

Canada, for example, the matter is not so complicated, for the country undulates gently from the tundra in the north far into the forest lands to the south, so the animals naturally keep to a regular migration route for a considerable time. But in northern Alaska the country through which the caribou moves is extremely varied: the huge wall of the Brooks Mountains in the south, and the wide lowlands of the tundra in the north. This leads to a number of peculiar features in the migration picture, a fact which has a very great influence on the Nunamiuts' way of life.

It is March. There is dazzling sunshine over the Brooks Mountains, a glitter of snow against a blue sky. Thousands of caribou are grazing in the Anaktuvuk Pass, some in the valley, others up the slopes. The herds are seen far away as black spots on the snow. The creatures look peaceful enough as they wander about, scrape in the snow, and munch the caribou moss. They have their thick, grey-brown winter coats; the bulls' antlers have just begun to grow.

Suddenly they become restless and stop grazing. They draw together and then move off northward in a long procession. The leader of each group is most often a cow. There is something purposeful about their movements. Month after month the caribou stream through the valley and out of the pass northward. Then they descend the slope toward the wide Arctic plains, moving more slowly as they begin to graze. There are now great patches of gadfly grubs under their skins.

At the beginning of June the tundra is full of life—there are thousands of animals. It is early summer. The rivers have thawed and are thick with mud. A carpet of moss and heather, patched with snow, is spread far and wide. The cows have just shed their antlers, and then comes the great event: the calves are born. Woolly heaps in the moss, a little blood—and graceful calves rise on long legs. For a little while they stand there in perplexity, gazing out into the world; then of a sudden they are alive and as swift as the wind.

Most of the caribou move up to the country round the Colville River; some scattered herds move farther north, while some remain on the lower mountain slopes. It is well into June now; it is becoming quite hot and the mosquitoes are intolerable. It is moulting time, and tufts of the hairy winter coat whiten in the moss and heather. At the end of June moulting is over. A brownish fur has grown, but it is still so thin and short that the Eskimos can only use the skins for such articles as gun cases and dogs' packs.

The mosquitoes get worse and worse—but in the south the cool mountains, rising into the sky, beckon. After a few weeks on the tundra the caribou masses take another of their quick decisions; the needs of thousands of beasts lead instinctively to common action. They crowd anxiously together; then the greater number set off toward the mountains in the southwest, the rest remaining on the Arctic plain as though they belonged to it. In the mountains, the caribou keep to the cool glaciers by day, descending into the valleys at night to graze.

At the end of July great masses of caribou are on the move again; in scattered herds the beasts descend from the mountains and make their way north. In the Anaktuvuk Pass this migration begins almost every year in the week of July 20–27. It is welcome, for the Eskimos have then been out of touch with the larger herds for about six weeks. A steady stream of caribou passes—first the cows with their calves, then the young bulls, and lastly the full-grown bulls, which move at great speed. These now have fully developed antlers covered with a greenish hairy skin which does not begin to peel off until the beginning of September.

This migration is of special importance to the Eskimos, who

now obtain the skins needed for winter clothes. From the end of July till the end of August the skins are at their best, the hair being suitably short and thick. During September the hair is so long that the skins are most suitable for stockings and breeches.

At the beginning of October the last herds of bulls disappear northward, and the valley is for a time empty. The animals have reached the tundra again. The bulls are a magnificent sight; their antlers are huge, they are fat, and their coats are bright and shining. Their necks swell and they become fierce—the mating season is at hand. There are fights, with clashing antlers, and round the victors a herd of cows collects.

At the end of October, sometimes rather earlier, the caribou move south again toward the mountains, mating as they go. This time the journey through the Anaktuvuk Pass is rapid; the great masses of beasts are through in a fortnight. Then they spread over the mountains, or south through the woods, in herds of varying size. In some years many find their way as far as the Koyukuk or the Kobuk.

The bulls, which before the mating season had several inches of fat on their backs, are now as thin as rakes. They shed their antlers. At last they have rid themselves of the gadfly grubs under their skins, and the holes have healed. The skins are admirably suited for making soles for the Eskimos' kamiks, and are at their thickest from the beginning of September till the end of October.

The long winter follows, in which nothing certain is known of the caribou's movements. Many factors contribute to this: wind, cold, snow, changes of the moon, and the wolves which are continually after the herds. In some years the caribou are peaceful; thousands of them can graze in the same region for months on end—sometimes near the forest, sometimes in the heart of the mountains, at other times on the slopes down to the

Arctic plains. In other years they can do nothing but roam about restlessly. In some winters they seem to have been blown clean away—and the Eskimos starve.

What happens to the caribou when they disappear completely? The Nunamiuts tell me that they have occasionally found a sick animal, or one which has been frozen to death, but these are sporadic occurrences. In Spitzbergen surface ice has a considerable influence on the numbers of reindeer; they cannot cut their way down to the moss, and so they die. In 1938–39 many musk oxen perished in eastern Greenland from the same cause. In northern Alaska, on the other hand, surface ice is uncommon and most often local. All things considered, it is reasonable to suppose that the caribou, in the years when they are absent from the Brooks Mountains, migrate eastward into Canada. There seems to be close connection between the numbers of caribou there and in northern Alaska.

In what I have written above about the migration of the caribou I have had the Anaktuvuk Pass especially in mind. The beasts use routes through a number of other valleys in the great Brooks Mountains, and according to the Eskimos their migrations there follow a similar course. But it seems that east of the Endicott Mountains and over toward the Canadian frontier special conditions come into play. The Eskimos say that in these areas the spring migration takes a northeasterly and the autumn migration a southwesterly direction, in old times right down to the country round Allakaket.

Even if the caribou population is considerable in the Brooks Mountains and neighbouring regions, there is no doubt that formerly it was much larger. It is peculiar that only isolated herds now make their way to the coast lands in spite of the good grazing there, and although we know from a number of other Arctic countries that it is the caribou's nature to make for the sea in summer. A number of circumstances indicate that in the past, the spring migration continued to the coast. It is probable that intensive hunting by the coastal Eskimos on the most important migration routes caused the caribou even in primitive times to avoid the coast region to some extent. It grew worse when firearms came into use.

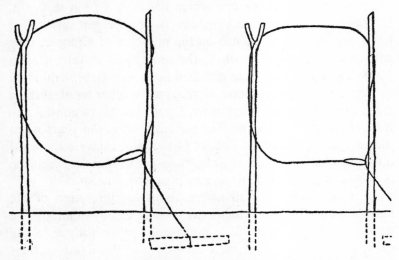

Where caribou and mountain sheep had their regular routes between willow trees, the Nunamiuts used to set skin snares. The left-hand snare is for caribou; the other, squarer, is for mountain sheep. The string was made fast to a stick which was trodden down into the snow, where it was frozen in.—Drawn by the Eskimo Paniaq.

In the long run one instinct prevailed; the caribou kept away from the areas where it was dangerous to calve. Something similar has happened in northwestern Canada and elsewhere. This is an important factor in our understanding of the life both of the Nunamiuts and of the coast Eskimos in former times.

The musk ox, that queer shaggy creature of prehistoric appearance, is not found in Alaska. Like the Eskimo and the caribou, it has migrated eastward for thousands of miles along the coast of northern Canada, via the Arctic islands and northern Greenland to northeast Greenland. There is today a small group on the mainland of northern Canada, a good stock on the islands north of it, and in northeastern Greenland there may well be 20,000 head.

Some musk-ox horns have been found on the tundra north of the Brooks Mountains, and the Nunamiuts, among other things, have come upon several. A very old Eskimo at Point Barrow told me that there were no musk ox in his time nor in his father's, but that there were in his grandfather's. He told me also that he had found musk-ox hides in a ruin north of Wainwright. Charles Brower tells of the discovery of carved horns in the ruins of a house near Point Barrow; Frank Russell writes that the musk ox was formerly common between the Mackenzie River and Bering Strait, and that old Eskimos at Point Barrow say the beasts were common in their parents' time.

Against this background what the Nunamiuts have to tell is of interest. Paniaq says that in the past the people lived mainly on musk oxen. He also tells an old story which confirms this. He adds: "The musk oxen disappeared eastward because they were hunted so much. Old people say that when this animal has been hunted one way it continues to go in that direction."

Thus it seems that the musk ox was exterminated in Alaska about a hundred years ago. It is presumably a long time since there was a large stock there; most of the bones are now overgrown or decomposed. When the beasts disappeared, it was probably because this was an area which right back in the oldest times was fairly vigorously exploited by primitive tribes, in part by the coast people, but not least by the roaming Nunamiuts, who were everywhere.

Nor were there, as in northern Canada and Greenland, extensive areas more or less out of range of the Eskimos and Indians, where the animals could recuperate in peace. When the

Eskimos came upon a herd, it was doomed. The musk ox is helpless against men; it often stands still and lets itself be slaughtered. Thus it is quite reasonable to suppose that in northern Alaska the species was wiped out in quite early times.

CHAPTER 7

Hunting with Paniaq

On these sunny autumn days it is an experience to wander through the endless mountain world with your gun on your back. It puts a man on his mettle and gives a pleasant feeling of coping with difficulties. Sight, hearing, and general sensibility are sharpened, small details of nature are grasped. I wake in the tent of a morning, fresh and keen and with a little thrill of excitement: what will the mountains offer today? As I wander into the torn, jagged country, the black ravines, the caribou moss, the yellow moraines, and the rivers losing themselves in the dim distance, are pleasant to the eye. At any moment caribou, wolf, or bear may bring the landscape to life and make my blood run quicker.

I am out after food in an almost virgin country. My only companions are a small band of Eskimos. I feel my thoughts slipping into the same grooves as theirs, conforming to the simple ideas which are of importance here. And I miss hardly anything, for their world is full of brightness; indeed, I am among people who feel a joy in life denied to those who are condemned to wear out shoe leather in a city street.

Most often I wander about alone, and enjoy it. At other times I join one of the Eskimos, and that is always delightful. For these primitive people the wilds are their whole world. They are as familiar with every little thing here as we are with what surrounds us in civilization. On the march, or when we rest by a fire, it often happens that what we see or hear starts a new train of thought in the Eskimo, and he begins to tell stories. Now he tells me about quite practical things connected with nature and animals, now of strange old-time events in which a kernel of truth is spun up in a web of fantasy and superstition. And when we travel deep into the wilds, strange stories do not seem so altogether unreal. I tell myself that no medicine man can pass straight through a mountain, that no one lies in the northern lights, that no woman can turn herself into a grizzly bear, and yet it all blends so perfectly with the atmosphere of the blue mountains, the strangely weathered masses of rock and the black ravines.

The first sunbeams were playing over the camp where the smoke rose into the air; the dogs were lying in the heather, their coats covered with rime. I went into Paniaq's tent. The family was seated, breakfasting upon a huge dish of caribou meat. The children smiled at me from behind large joints, into the raw meat of which they were digging their teeth.

Paniaq got ready and we set off through the mountains. There had been rather a shortage of caribou in the last few days; he was bothered about meat and wanted to try his luck with the mountain sheep (*ovis dalli dalli*), which the Eskimos hunt only occasionally. The stock is fairly large; farther east the Eskimos have seen flocks of over a hundred head. There are probably more mountain sheep in the Brooks Mountains than anywhere else in North America.

He moved uphill with his swift, rather swaying gait; like the moose, he gets along quickly without giving the impression of speed. On his back was his hunting bag; its hide strap goes round his arms just below the shoulder. His rifle was slung in the same way. The case is of undressed caribou skin with the hairs removed; it can be opened by a single pull on a hide string. The Eskimos never use sacks with straps over the shoulders; my Bergans rucksack has not even exchange value in their eyes.

He held in his hand a peeled willow stick to help him in climbing, for if one is after wild sheep one has to climb high and among loose boulders and over ice-covered slopes. He was clad in a caribou-skin anorak with the hair turned inward; he never wears a hat either in winter or in summer. On his legs he had kamiks which reached up to below his knees. The lower part was of bearded sealskin, the leg part of common sealskin. This is the summer footwear and is called *qarlik;* it is waterproof and airy and immeasurably superior to clammy rubber boots. Since the trading expeditions to the coast Eskimos have stopped, skins of these kinds have been brought in by aircraft. They are expensive and are constantly in short supply. Sometimes the Nunamiuts have to make do with summer footwear of caribou skin; it is well greased every other day.

In the hunting bag the Eskimo keeps cartridges, needles and sinews to repair his kamiks, a small kettle, a whetstone, and a coiled-up skin rope. This is used when skins or meat have to be carried or carcasses hauled down from the mountains. There are also flint and steel for lighting fires and some willow cotton for kindling. At our heels we had the dogs Kiglu and Sigjik, two big fellows each carrying an empty pack of undressed, short-haired caribou skin.

Chit! chit!—we heard this sound continually as we ascended the moraines. It was the ground squirrel sitting on his haunches outside his hole, enjoying the morning sunshine or picking a little breakfast on the grassy hillocks. There are quantities of these animals about, to the joy of the grizzly bear, who finds them a particularly delicious mouthful.

Now and again a lemming darted away from us. The Eskimos

call this creature *qilangmiutaq,* which means "from heaven," a
name which probably derives from the fact that suddenly and
inexplicably the country may be flooded with millions of them,
just as if they had fallen from the sky.

We followed the bank of a little river with a scattered growth
of willow. A flock of ptarmigan started up, swerved away over
the moraines, and was gone. There were both mountain and
valley ptarmigan among them, but more of the latter. In the
spring the great majority of them go to the coast, where they
hatch their young in the low willow scrub; in the middle of
September they make their way back to the mountains.

Suddenly Paniaq stopped and pointed to a heap of willow
leaves neatly piled up under a bush. *"Ikautit,"* he said, smiling.

This is a little mouse which dries its winter supplies in this
manner. Paniaq has an eye for all kinds of animals; none is so
small as to be without interest.

In the last scanty willow scrub on the river bank a robin sat
singing in the morning sun; its breast gleamed like a tiny
flame among the twigs. After that we had only naked land as
we ascended. But it was easy walking, for the ground was
dry; it rains so seldom.

Here the vegetation is very much as on the mountains of
Norway: caribou moss, heather, grasses, saxifrage, mountain
flowers, little ferns, cotton grass, and mosses proper of many
kinds. Flowering time is long past and the slopes are clothed
in the rust-red tints of autumn.

Paniaq pointed in the direction of the Big Arsehole River
(*Iteqmalukpak*) where an oval sandhill rose above the sur-
rounding country, and said: "Once there were such huge swarms
of mosquitoes that the caribou went quite mad. A crowd of
them climbed up onto that hill and ran round and round there.
They ran close-packed at a great pace, and there was a strange
noise which could be heard a long way off. Many calves were

trampled to death. It's not often caribou do that kind of thing; only a few Eskimos have seen it. We call it *katimmijaqtut*."

We sat on a stone up on the hillside and surveyed the landscape. Below us spread the wide pass with gleaming rivers and lakes; we could just see the cluster of tents by Raven Lake. Mountains on all sides. Here they are of the so-called Lisburne limestone, which is one of the oldest formations in northwest Alaska. In the valleys the moraines stand out sharply, witnesses to the last ice age.

A little willow scrub showed up here and there along the river beds. This is of importance not only to the Nunamiuts, but also to many kinds of animals, which otherwise would have difficulty in maintaining existence in the mountains. Valley ptarmigan, small birds, and sometimes a number of snowshoe hares make their way to it. The fairly numerous red foxes in the mountains find a good deal of their food in the willow beds, even if they also live on lemmings, birds, and the remains of what wolves have killed in the open country. Curiously enough the red fox occurs right up to the Arctic Ocean. The moose goes nearly as far—to nearly sixty miles from the mouth of the Colville River. Finally it may be mentioned that the great Arctic hare, which is white all the year round, is, curiously enough, a rarity in the whole of northern Alaska.

We went on into the mountains, keeping a sharp watch. The land became more torn and bare; in places only black mountains and huge moraines met the eye. Paniaq *knows* these mountains. In the course of years he has roamed over them far and wide, but there are regions where he himself has never been. Now and again he let fall words which threw swift light on the wilderness around us. The Nunamiuts know the main part of the Brooks Mountains and the geography of the tundra, and several of the hunters can draw a surprisingly good map of the country.

I am learning a great many of the Eskimos' place names.

Most of the higher hills, valleys, lakes, and rivers have their
names, a fact which shows that the people have been roaming
through this wilderness for many generations. Every name has
significance. Some give a vivid description of the landscape,
such as Giants' Valley (*Inukpasugjuk*), where there is a group
of hills resembling giants. Others tell of practical things, like
Big Haul of Fish (*Imaerneqpak*), Place Where the Red Dye Is
Found (*Iwisâq*), Place Where There Is Flint (*Agmâlik*). Then
there are names connected with the people's history in peace
and war, such as Meeting Place with the Indians (*Kanngûmawik*), Place for Wrestling Matches (*Sororwik*), etc. There are
also names derived from the people's mythology; for example
Umiat, or Place Where the Skin Boats Were Drawn Ashore
(during the Great Flood).

We arrived at a high, rather steep hill. A golden eagle was
hovering just below the summit, sailing round in wide circles,
hunting. Paniaq suddenly stopped, peered upward, and said
abruptly: "There are four." I then caught sight of the chalk-
white sheep high up on the steep slope just below the weather-
worn terraces: a big ram, two full-grown sheep, and one lamb.
These were no doubt what the eagle was watching.

The steep slopes offered next to no cover, the ram was on
guard, and these animals have even sharper eyes than a caribou.
As soon as he saw us, the beasts would flee to the top of the hill.
Our only chance was if the sheep suddenly decided to move
downhill, across a deep ravine, and then up the rugged hill beyond it, where it was easy for us to find cover behind boulders
and hummocks.

Paniaq stared upward for a moment and then, without a
word, lay down on the ground. In a few minutes he was asleep
and snoring gently. I have never met anyone with such power to
relax altogether when it suits him. In this respect he has an animal's capacity; he can go to sleep quickly at any time and any-

where, even in snow. The soggy hillside was certainly far from being an inviting couch, and it was cold, too, but this did not seem to worry him at all.

I surveyed the situation for a few minutes and then began to pick cowberries and whortleberries along the side of the hillock, keeping an eye on the sheep all the time. Suddenly the ram, who had stood still for a long time, began to move. And, upon my word! he moved off on a slanting course downhill toward the ravine! The rest followed.

I did not need to wake Paniaq; the snoring stopped and he sat up wide awake. It was as if he had been keeping an eye on the game in his sleep.

We tied the dogs to a boulder and set off to climb up the other hill, where the sheep could be expected when they had crossed the ravine. Then the grind began, the pitiless grind which is always part of sheep stalking. On and on, up steep hillsides till one's muscles ached and one's lungs worked like bellows. Paniaq at fifty was like a goat, he never seemed to tire.

The ram fell. We rolled him down the steepest part, then used the hide rope and hauled him down to the foot of the hill. "He's nine years old," Paniaq said, after counting the rings on the horns. The beast probably weighed about 200 lb. A full-grown ram is as heavy as a caribou cow and a good deal stronger. We flayed the animal, which had an uncommonly thick, warm skin. The skin is rather heavy and at this time of year is used only for socks, mittens, and tent matting. In July it is finer and the hair is shorter, and then it is sometimes used for children's anoraks; the hunters prefer the lighter caribou skins.

The first thing Paniaq did after he had skinned the animal was to cut out a small sebaceous gland between the hooves (*akunnerun*) and a rather larger one on the back of the neck (*kauksik*), which the Eskimos consider a great delicacy. He gave me half, and we ate them raw. They had a pleasant taste which was quite new to me. The dogs flung themselves upon the entrails like wolves.

Before we had finished the skinning, a pair of ravens came along. The birds flew over us, reconnoitring the position, and circled round the hill with hoarse cries, as much as to tell us, angrily and impatiently, that it was time for us to clear off. It is remarkable how these birds are on the spot immediately after an animal has been shot. They are sometimes troublesome to the hunter; they may fly over him when he is in ambush waiting for a wolf or caribou, so that the quarry suspects danger. At other times they can be useful; as the gulls show where the herrings go, the raven may sometimes lead the hunter to the herds of caribou. Kakinnâq once saw two ravens hunting a large herd; they were flying low over the beasts shrieking, and apparently thinking it a most amusing sport.

Paniaq talked about ravens a little as he cut up the sheep. There is always a quaint mixture of seriousness and humour about him when he talks about the *tulugaq,* the chief character in their mythology and the scapegoat in so many amusing fables.

Now we made a fire, grilled the fat ribs, kidneys, etc., on a spit, and were as well off as men can be. The flesh of wild sheep is tender and tastes good; indeed, I know nothing better.

We remained sitting by the fire for some time and were very comfortable. It was a long way back, but we had done what we set out to do, and it mattered little whether we got home in the evening or late at night. Our time was our own; we were not responsible to anyone.

The sun was low, and it was quiet in the heart of the mountains. Far away a wolf's howl rose and died away in a faint streak of sound. Close by us the stream trickled over some curious black stones. The dogs lay in the heather resting comfortably after an enormous meal. Pipes were produced. Paniaq's is of willow wood, as is customary with the Eskimos. The stem is a piece of twig which has been split in two, scraped clean of pith, and bound together again with sinews. A pipe like this lasts for five or six days; then it gets a burnt taste and is flung aside. A new one is made in no time.

"It is not good for a hunter to live without tobacco," said Paniaq, puffing away. "Our people used tobacco in old times, too, long before the white men found this country. It came from Siberia, was green, and was packed in mottled reindeer skins. But it was very dear. Only a few pinches for one cross fox. . . . Pipes were finer in the old times. The heads might be of polished stone, copper, or alder wood. Once I made a fine pipe of alder wood for my father; I put a lot of work into it."

"There can't have been very much smoking in the old times, when the price was so high," said I.

"The hunters smoked differently in those days. They drew the smoke down into their lungs, and then they sat holding their breath for a long time, till they almost fainted. They liked it that way. Once there was an Eskimo who wanted to kill another. First, he gave the man a little tobacco. Then, when he had smoked a little and was quite stupid, he stuck his knife into him."

The eagle, which till now had been hovering high up in the blue, sailed down a little lower, and began to circle over a large heap of stones at the foot of a sheer rock. "He's looking for marmots (*sigjipak*); he loves them," said Paniaq. He told me that there are a good many marmots in the mountains. They hibernate in the winter and come out in the middle of May, a bit later than the ground squirrel.

"When the marmot's scared, it's a devil for whistling," says Paniaq. He told me an old story of a mighty eagle which had carried away a woman to its house high up on a mountain. When the husband pursued it to get her back, he had trouble with the eagle's "watchman," a marmot which whistled every time he came near. So the man lighted a fire, and then the marmot was so busy sniffing the smoke that it stopped whistling. Finally, it went to sleep. The man went into the eagle's house and cunningly got his wife out, and many other women who had been made prisoners along with her, and they ran home to their settlements.

Then we talked of wild sheep. Paniaq had seen numbers of them in different parts of the mountains. Far east, by the Jago River, he had seen herds of several hundred. But there was an enormous quantity of other game there, too, for there was "evil medicine" over those mountains for many years, and no Eskimo but a medicine man dared to go hunting there.

"The sheep are a good thing for men," said Paniaq. "When the caribou have failed, many have saved themselves from starvation by hunting sheep. Often they are snared. In the old days the Nunamiuts sometimes set the dogs to hunt the sheep up into the steep places. Then they shot them with bow and arrow. I have snared sheep myself. The ram's an awkward customer; he's as strong as a caribou bull."

We sat in silence for a moment, and then he continued reflectively: "Sheep are queer things in a lot of ways. When I was young there were several parts of the body which a woman might not eat."

On my asking the reason, he told me an old story of a chief of the sheep who was as big as a moose, had huge horns, and lived high up on a mountain. He had the power of making sheep die and come to life, or of turning the number of sheep into a multitude. When the chief was angry, he licked his upper lip; when all was well, he kept his mouth closed. He knew about all the hunters, too, and could bring misfortune on them if they broke the laws. And there were laws which laid down that a woman must never eat the inner meat of the ribs or the front part of the legs, nor might she drink the gravy when a sheep's

Sikiarjuk carrying her little brother Wirâq

Mikiâna and his daughter Kunnâna cutting "ropes" from a caribou skin

Unalîna, Kakinnâq's wife and a warm-hearted woman. When food was short she gave th
Author a dainty marrow-bone

head was boiled. If she did, her husband would have severe pains in the chest, legs, or head.

"There were many laws of this kind," Paniaq continued. "It was none too easy for the people. It was like being a fish when the water is full of nets. If a hunter had killed a wolf or a bear, there were so many regulations to be observed that if I told you all about them now I should never be finished." He looked up toward the mountaintop where the eagle was still circling round, and said: "Bear and eagle must never be brought into the same settlement. That happened once at Raven Lake, and many people died a short time afterward."

The sun lay low over the mountains when we set out on our return journey. Kiglu and Sigjik came swaying along behind us, each with a full load of meat in his pack. It was wonderful how they kept up a steady pace hour after hour on difficult scree, up and down steep slopes. Now and again one of them tumbled down one of the steepest slopes and rolled some distance. But it scrambled onto its legs unwearyingly and went on with its curly tail waving proudly in the air as if nothing had happened.

In one of the passes they suddenly got busy and began sniffing eagerly round. "Bear," said Paniaq, pointing to a fresh clawmark here and there among the stones. We took a breather in the gap in the mountains and surveyed the country in the silent hope of perhaps sighting the animal somewhere near by. It was too late to start a long pursuit.

It is the Arctic grizzly (*Ursus Richardsoni*) which lives in these parts, a big fellow who goes right up to the Arctic coast, even to Barter Island, the Eskimos say. He is brownish, sometimes almost black, about 6 feet long and weighing 350–700 lb. The claws are up to 3 inches long.

There is a good stock of them in the Brooks Mountains, where they live practically undisturbed, eating berries and roots, hunting ground squirrels, and devouring the wolves' kills which are scattered about the countryside. The grizzly is too slow to hunt caribou itself. It hibernates in the winter and comes out in the middle of April.

The black bear, which is smaller and of which there are great numbers in Alaska, is seen only on the southern slopes of the mountains. Nor does the brown bear have its home so far north; it lives for the most part in the coastal regions from the Alaska peninsula inclusive southward, and lives to a large extent on salmon. It is the largest beast of prey in the world, an incredible brute. The hide of a record animal killed in 1949 measured 12 feet 4 inches by 10 feet 4 inches. The creature weighed 1,800 lb. Its height at the shoulders can be as much as 6 feet.*

Paniaq pointed to a group of hummocks to the northeast and said, "I shot a thumper there last spring. One has to let the bear come to close quarters, and then put a bullet through his head, or sometimes through his shoulder, for then he's helpless. The grizzly isn't as fast as the polar bear; I've raced them both. They're left-handed, did you know that? I've often seen that with the grizzly bear. If I throw a stone he always strikes with his left paw."

He went on talking about some of his bear hunts. He shot his first bear at fourteen. Once or twice he had pretty narrow escapes. The grizzly bear is a terrifying beast when irritated. But Paniaq is as cool as a cucumber. He has the worst possible firearm for bear hunting, an old 22 Hornet which is a saloon rifle with reinforced ammunition. It shoots crooked, too, but he knows exactly how crooked. As I finger the rusty little weapon, I cannot help thinking of the doughty white bear hunters who come to Alaska with ultra-modern large-calibre rifles and are tremendous fellows.

Then we proceeded at a steady pace toward the camp. The sun had gone down; there was a lovely light-red afterglow in

---

* There are an astonishing number of bears in Alaska—about 20,000 brown and grizzly bears and about 75,000 black bears.

the sky, and the mountains stood out jet-black in sharp outline. The last light died away, the stars came out, and streamers of northern lights (*kigoruyaq*) shot up in the east. Their colours were still pale, as though they were just rehearsing for the winter. Paniaq looked up at the shimmering veil of light and said: "Now the people of the air are playing football with men's heads." This is told of the northern lights in one of the old legends. And there must be something in this that makes a strong appeal, for a similar legend exists among many Eskimo peoples, even among the Greenlanders.

Suddenly a ferocious barking was heard through the darkness; the camp dogs had got wind of us. And it was not long before the children, as usual, came pelting out. They found out the result of the hunt in a second, and were off again. Before we reached the tents the whole people knew about the ram we had shot. And a good many of the hunters tacitly decided to look into Paniaq's tent at a suitable time—so as to be on the spot when Umialâq placed the great dish of fat mutton on the willow-bough floor.

CHAPTER 8

Big Fish and Mad Wolves

A short way from the camp a spring rises and forms a rippling green stream which runs out into Raven Lake. Here many kinds of minerals in solution must be brought up from the depths of the earth, for the spring is rich in vegetation. The stones downstream are clothed in deep-green moss, waterweeds cover its bottom, along its banks rushes and grasses grow more abundantly and more vividly than elsewhere. It is a favourite place for lively little snipe and flocks of duck. The glittering river with its bird life and lush greenery is like a little picture set in a field of stone-grey.

This influx of fertility has great influence on the stock of fish in Raven Lake. There is a wealth of them. The great trout, fat and red-fleshed, lies with his nose to the river mouth. He is an extremely ignorant creature who has never seen a fisherman's fly. At the beginning of July the herrings come in large schools to spawn, stay till the beginning of September, and then go out into deep water. Then there are whitefish, grayling, sucker, Dolly Varden, pike, and the long, slimy ling cod. This last can weigh over 30 lb. and has a liver by which the Eskimos set great store. Finally there is a queer little reddish fish which the Alaska people call "old man" and the Eskimos *angayuqagjaq*.

I do not often see the Eskimos fishing. If they had had nets no doubt it would have been otherwise, but they are too poor. People still remember the old art of making nets from sinews, but that involves so much work that they cannot bother.

When they do occasionally fish, they use, in the old fashion, a spoon bait made of walrus or mammoth's tooth with a bent nail as hook. Sometimes pieces of whalebone are let into the bait as "eyes." They do ice fishing with a similar bait. Traps made of plaited willow boughs are occasionally used, being placed in front of a narrow opening in a close-set barrier of sticks, driven into the bottom across a river. Then the Eskimos scare the fish toward the barrier and into the trap. The catch is shared equally among those who have taken part.

The small catch of fish which the Eskimos make in autumn they hang up without removing the entrails. The air is so cold that the fish has only a suggestion of rottenness. It is served throughout the winter as a delicacy, eaten frozen and raw. The flavour is rather high.

I have a net which I set near the mouth of the river. I saunter down to Raven Lake, where the loons are swimming about in the morning mist, untie the boat, and row out to the net. And then great trout and other glittering fish slip over the bulwarks, while the children and dogs on shore follow my proceedings eagerly. And when I take a turn up the slope among the tents, the women peep out and smilingly accept the regular morning gift.

I get a trout which weighs 11 lb., which I consider a lot, but the Eskimos say he is small compared with the thumpers that are found in the bigger lakes in the heart of the mountains. In Chandler Lake (*Najwarwak*) they have caught a trout 4 feet long and so heavy that it could not be pulled up into the kayak.

In this lake, which is about ten miles long and very deep, there
are also some strange giant fish, the Eskimos say. Aguk, Kakinnâq, and Paniaq give objective and detailed information about
them. Once or twice several of them at the same time have seen
one of these giant fish swimming on the surface. Another time
Kakinnâq saw two. His wife caught sight of one under the boat
and says that it was dark above and had a reddish tinge along
its belly and very black eyes. Those who have seen the fish on
the surface maintain that about 10 feet of it was visible and
think that it must have been larger. A similar creature is said to
occur in a lake which the Eskimos call Nasaujaq, near the
upper part of the Colville River.

This is the evidence of men who are particularly observant
and unusually sober in their accounts of what they have seen in
nature. They add that once, a long time ago, a caribou which
was swimming across Chandler Lake suddenly disappeared;
the giant fish must have taken it. Here they are in the world of
fairy tale, but this does not mean that the accounts of their own
observations are fantasy. Moreover, the Eskimos' old legends
usually contain a kernel of fact.

Probably these "giant fish" are unusually large trout. Sig
Wien, who now and then flew supplies to the Eskimos when
they lived by Chandler Lake, says they had once caught a trout
weighing about 30 lb. and said that this was "half-size," meaning that a trout should weigh about 60 lb. Such a fish can be an
imposing sight when it rolls on the surface of the water—and
perhaps there are still bigger ones in that lake.

From the Anaktuvuk Pass southward, along the upper
course of the John River, the Eskimos say there are not many
fish. It is otherwise north of the watershed; all over the tundra
country, as far as the Arctic, there are a great many both in
rivers and in lakes.

The little-known fish population of the mighty Colville River is of particular interest. In the months of April–June the trout come up the Colville, but not very far. From mid-June till mid-July comes a rush of big whitefish, which weigh from 4 lb. to 15 lb. These go far inland, almost to the sources of the river, up the Chandler River, the Killik River, and others, but the Anak-tuvuk River is too swift. The latter part of July is the time for a fish the Eskimos call *pikuktûq;* it weighs 3 or 4 lb. and has a hump on its neck. Then there is a smaller kind of whitefish which makes its way up the Colville twice a year, in September–October and in January. Shoals of inland herring stream into the lower part of the watercourse just before the ice forms. The different kinds of fish return to the sea at slightly different times during the autumn and early winter. In addition to those named there are also ling cod, Dolly Varden, sucker, grayling, pike, etc.

Alaska's five kinds of salmon also occur in the Colville, but in small numbers. The red salmon behaves rather irregularly; farther south millions of them go up the big rivers and far inland. They become miserably thin on the way, while the silver colour gradually changes to fiery red. Finally the fish ascends small shallow river channels to spawn. Its mission in life is now ended. The whole mass of salmon die, and rotting corpses drift down the river or float about in backwaters. The red salmon in the Colville also assumes a fiery red colour on its journey up the river, but the Eskimos say that it does not grow thin and does not die; on the contrary it comes down again, shining and fat, and without spawn. It has also received a name which expresses surprise—*ayatqik:* the meaning of the word is "he who comes again." This fish may possibly be the Arctic red char which sometimes has a red hue over its belly (*Salvelinus alpinus?*).

The ice forms on the Colville at the end of September and the beginning of October. After that time fishing was carried out through the ice, partly with tin bait, partly with nets.

Finally, I might mention as a curiosity that a fjord seal, the spotted seal, sometimes goes a little way up the river. It has no great practical importance for the inland people, but occurs in many of their old legends.

I hauled up a long slimy fish, a ling cod. Paniaq looked at it and said: "That fellow has an easy job. He just holds his mouth open, attracts small fish with his feeler, and they swim straight in. It's easy to see that this happens, for they always lie head downward in the ling cod's stomach.

"The ling cod (*tittâleq*) is the queerest of all fishes," he continued, "for it is made of almost everything on earth. We know that from an old story. First it had no body, but was something like a puff of smoke. There were too many fish in the lakes, and the ling cod wanted to have a body so that it could catch some of those fish." He went on to tell how it made itself a body from the most different things. It took a roll of skin from an old Indian woman and made a forehead; a *beluga* was used to make ears, and it put walrus whiskers in the ears; it made a backbone of whalebone and fastened to it behind one or two spruce with many branches; it made gills from a swallow and a mouth from the handle of a bucket, and a little woman who was carrying water in a skin bag was used as a chin-bone. The story goes on thus with infinite variation. At last the ling cod got a complete body. There was only one thing it could not manage properly, and that was to provide itself with such wide bowels that the food would go through comfortably. It was obliged to keep the fish in its stomach so long that it was rotten, and then it threw up the bones.

"It's easy to see that this story is true," Paniaq concluded. "If you examine the fish closely, you will recognize all the parts I have mentioned and see that the creature is made of almost everything on earth."

The craft the Nunamiuts generally use when fishing and for spearing swimming caribou is the kayak. A few years ago they had many, but one winter, when there was difficulty in finding wood, they used the frames as fuel. They have not yet managed to make new ones, but they still possess the old art of making these slender craft with a caribou-skin covering. The inland people's kayaks are rather different from those of the coast Eskimos. The bow is curved higher, and the deck forward is rounded higher. They think, too, that they have a narrower and longer kayak than, for example, the Barrow people. In the mountains it is about three and a half Eskimo units of measurement long, i.e., something over sixteen feet. The ribs and the ring round the hole are of willow, all the rest of spruce. Three (bull) caribou hides are required for one kayak. An elaborate technique is used in sewing them together; there are two seams, and in one of them the needle must go only halfway through the skin, never right through. The threads are two twisted fibres from the caribou's leg sinews. The skins are sewn together and stretched over the frame while still wet.

When a hunter is going to make a kayak, the rule is for the men and women of the settlement to help him without any kind of pay. A craft like this is eloquent of ancient tradition. Every little detail seems to be calculated exactly, and all these details are blended into a beautiful whole.

Nunamiut kayak drawn by Paniaq, who has made many himself.

A plane is approaching—a visitor. It is Dr. Robert Rausch, a young parasitologist from the Government Research Institute at Anchorage. He and his colleague, the ornithologist Laurence Irving, make occasional trips up to the Nunamiuts, who collect animals for them. Apart from Sig Wien, these are the only people who have any close contact with the Nunamiuts. During

his short stay we discuss the various kinds of parasite which influence the lives of human beings and animals in the north.
Quite a number of Alaskan Eskimos and Indians get tapeworm
from eating raw fish.

Then there is another small parasite whose effects are far
more serious and which attacks caribou, moose, sheep, and
man. This is *Echinococcus granulosus*. The eggs are carried
from the excrement of dogs, foxes, and wolves. When the grub
has completed its development in the intestines, it eats its way
out into the blood system and establishes itself in the liver, lungs
or brain. I have now and again seen the liver of caribou infected
by this parasite, but it is then in the larval state and human
beings are not affected if they eat the liver.

In Alaska trichinae have been identified in a number of animals, such as the polar bear, grizzly bear, the great brown bear,
dog, wolf, and fox. Of particular interest is the fact that trichinosis has also been found in the beluga. Scandinavian scientists
have hitherto made no corresponding discoveries, but have
been very suspicious of this member of the whale family. There
is reason to believe that the beluga has been the cause of a good
many cases of trichinosis among Eskimos, for example, in 1947
at Disko Bay in West Greenland, when three hundred Eskimos
were attacked and thirty-three died. Fortunately the risk of
trichinosis disappears if the meat is well boiled or roasted.

When our guest had gone, the Eskimos smiled a little at his
interest in intestinal worms and other parasites, and seemed to
think white men are queer people. I replied that perhaps they
were not so utterly useless. I mentioned hydrophobia, which
also is due to quite minute creatures, and said that by studying
these the white men had discovered a medicine which effects a
cure. Maptirâq replied that formerly the medicine men could
cope with this illness, and that no one needed root about in the
stomachs and bowels of all kinds of animals. The others nodded
approvingly.

I learned that from time to time there was a good deal of hydrophobia among the wolves in the Brooks Mountains. Paniaq said that in the previous winter he was awakened in the middle of the night by a tremendous disturbance among the dogs. He seized his gun and dashed out of the tent. Furious fighting was going on and there was an appalling noise. Suddenly a large animal detached itself from the rest and came straight for him. He only just managed to fire at a few yards' range—the beast fell. It was a mad wolf. Two of the dogs died the next day.

Another time he saw a large pack of wolves rushing along pursued by a single wolf. He shot the pursuer. It showed clear signs of hydrophobia.

"They're afraid of nothing then," Kakinnâq said. "But people aren't *always* ill if they've been bitten by a mad wolf. Once my father, Avik, was sitting on a hillock looking out for caribou. Suddenly a wolf came at him from behind, bit him, and tore his anorak. He jumped up and laid about him with his hunting stick. It was a regular scrap. At last the wolf ran away. When my father reached the settlement his anorak was in rags, and he had been bitten in many places, including his face. But the wounds healed, and he didn't get ill although the beast had foam on its jaw as mad wolves usually have."

CHAPTER 9

The Herds Thin Out

The northward migration of the caribou toward the tundra is beginning to slacken. There is no longer the steady trickle of animals through the Anaktuvuk Pass; the herds are coming more sporadically. They may be fairly large, but often they come at such a speed that it is hopeless to try to reach them in time. Although we are out hunting almost every day, meat is beginning to run short.

Kakinnâq and Agmâlik are better off for meat than the rest. When they have shot a few caribou near some willow bushes, they do not carry the kill home, but bring the wife to the kill. Then she cuts the whole carcass into pieces, which are hung on the nearest bushes to dry. When the snow comes, it is brought home by dog sledge. Ravens and other predatory creatures seldom take meat like this. Indeed, even caribou carcasses on the ground can lie for quite a long time before wolves and foxes dare to touch them.

One day we caught sight of a tame reindeer in one of the

herds. It is smaller than the caribou, has shorter legs and a straighter head, and is rather lighter in colour. The animal had come a long way, presumably from a small herd near Point Barrow, 260 miles as the crow flies.

The story of the domesticated reindeer along the coast of northern and northwestern Alaska is a depressing one. In the years from 1892 to 1902, 1,280 animals were imported from Siberia and distributed among the coast Eskimos. A number of Lapps came over from Norway with their dogs to help. As the caribou had disappeared from the coastal regions and the white men had made severe inroads into the stocks of whale and walrus, there was a prospect that the new industry would give the Eskimos a better life.

For a time things went well. The herds grew. Then white businessmen joined in. In 1930 stocks were about half a million head. Later they were catastrophically reduced, owing to politics and failure to understand what the keeping of domesticated reindeer required. The Government bought the beasts that remained, and a new attempt to help the Eskimos is now being made. There are now not more than about 40,000 tame reindeer in Alaska.

On the coast there are undoubtedly great possibilities for domesticated reindeer. Wolves are certainly a pest, and there is danger of the animals joining up with the caribou herds, but similar difficulties exist in other places also. If the tame reindeer in northern Alaska are kept like those in Norway, and care is taken in the first place that the animals are herded efficiently all the year round, an important industry will develop to the advantage of the coast Eskimos.

Early one morning word was passed round that caribou were in sight. We stood in a bunch in front of the tents peering across toward the other side of the valley. Far away to the southwest the beasts could just be seen as black dots on the slopes under the mountains. They were making northward, but surprisingly slowly, and seemed to be grazing from time to time. There was a chance for us if we could get across the valley at top speed and find cover in time.

Old Inualûjaq, Kakinnâq, Agmâlik, and I set off. We took the little boat across the river and lakes, and dragged it across country where necessary. We hurried till the sweat poured down our faces, now and then throwing a glance at the herd of caribou, which drew steadily nearer. The valley was disgustingly broad.

At last we reached the moraines on the other side. We rushed up them as fast as we could, for the caribou were to be expected close under the steep drop; it was one of their regular routes.

The Eskimos sped in every direction to take good cover; I myself followed Kakinnâq. No plan had been worked out for the hunt, nobody had given any directions; but it was clear that the Eskimos immediately understood what each man should do.

The advance guard of the herd came in sight a little farther on. By Kakinnâq's side I wriggled forward on my stomach toward a little hummock. There we were, excellently placed, looking toward a depression. The Eskimos' plan was now clear; the caribou were to be caught in a "sack." On the outer side of the sack lay Kakinnâq, Agmâlik, and I. The inner side of the sack was the steep drop, and at the bottom of the sack Inualûjaq lay, some way from us.

There they came, a living brown-grey mass among stones and bluish-white caribou moss. There were a number of bulls, some with mighty antlers and majestic bearing; here and there one or two calves frisked about on long lanky legs. They passed into the gully just below us. I heard gentle snufflings and felt as if the bright eyes were looking straight at me.

I nudged Kakinnâq. He lay cool and watchful with his gun resting on his arm. We could have brought down several beasts with the greatest ease, but that would have ruined the whole plan. The caribou streamed past, and soon only a few stragglers were to be seen.

Suddenly a shot rang out. Inualûjaq at the end of the "sack" had got the mass of caribou opposite to him, and now he blazed away at them. The animals swung round, dashed back terrified for a short distance, and were in front of us again. The whole thing seemed to be a shock for them; here was danger, but where did it come from and in what direction was it safe to flee? Some stood staring, others milled around in confusion. It was an easy matter to bring down the beasts we needed.

Here was food for a long time ahead. Yet it was sad to see these beasts, a moment ago such a lively and charming feature of the landscape, lying dead on the ground. The Nunamiuts, for that matter, do not indulge in reckless slaughter. What they shoot is used, and if they have plenty of meat, it often happens that they let herds pass without troubling to hunt them.

We set about skinning and cutting up the beasts. It is interesting to see how their technique differs in many respects from that of the Indian caribou hunters in northern Canada. I refer, in particular, to a group which bears the name of "the caribou eaters." * They live on the fringe of the tundra northeast of the Great Slave Lake, where also there are multitudes of these beasts. The Indians first cut off the caribou's head. They make a cut on the inside of the forelegs and treat the skin of the leg carelessly. Elsewhere they frequently use the knife to get the skin off the body. In cutting up the deer they certainly followed a system, but it was a rough one.

The Nunamiuts leave the head on for the time being, make a cut on the outside of the forelegs, and take extraordinary care that the skin of the legs comes off uninjured right down to the hoofs. In flaying the body they scarcely use the knife at all except for the cut on the belly; they push and pull the skin off so

* The author lived with these Indians in the years 1926–30, and recounted his experiences in *Land of Feast and Famine*, Knopf, New York, 1933, p. 112.

that it is completely undamaged. In cutting up they go to work quickly but meticulously, and according to regular methods.

Not only as regards flaying and cutting up, but also in utilizing the meat and skin, the Eskimos' technique is ahead of the Indians'. This shows up when the caribou-skin clothes are seen. The Eskimos wear anoraks which bear the stamp of smart tailoring, and excellent footwear made from the skin of the legs, while the Indians usually have a draughty caribou-skin coat, open in front, and chilly moose-skin moccasins. Taken all round, the Nunamiuts' treatment of the caribou and its products is far more advanced. This is because the Indians were originally a forest people.

A fact which points to an ancient "caribou culture" is that the Nunamiuts have a name for every part of the caribou; I noted over a hundred. It is probable that these names are among the oldest words in their language.

The work was done and we sat down by a little stream. There we lit a fire and on spits we roasted a number of tidbits from the fattest beast. Kakinnâq took charge. He was a splendid cook, managing the fire carefully and adroitly; the meat was roasted just right, finely flavoured and oozing. For dessert we crunched a few stout bones and ate the marrow raw. Then I passed tobacco all round, and the willow pipes were produced.

Very pleasant it was, sitting there among the mountains. On one side of me I had Kakinnâq, short and sturdy and sparkling with humour as ever. On the other side I had Agmâlik, tall and bony; he, too, has a sense of humour. Opposite sat old Inualûjaq, friendly and quiet: a thoroughly genuine fellow, one of the old school.

We were in the best of moods after good hunting and good food, and talk flowed freely on one subject and another. When I was flaying the last deer, I found some pieces of black flint on a hillock, and Kakinnâq said that a hunter must have been sit-

Kakinnâq, one of the best hunters—always overflowing with high spirits

Mikiâna has made new snowshoes for the winter. They are of much the same type as those of the Indians

A charming robber-band encamped outside my tent

From an encampment in the Anaktuvuk Pass

Umialâq, Paniaq's wife, with their youngest boy Wirâq on her back under her caribou-skin cloak. She is small and slim, and as tough as a willow-stem. She is wearing over her cloak a flowered cotton coat brought by air

ting there with bow and arrows waiting for caribou. They often filled up an interval of waiting in making arrowheads. "There are masses of flint in this country, both in the mountains and in the rivers," he added, and told me the places from which the Nunamiuts used to get the best flint in times past. One of them was a tributary of the Killik River.

On the subject of caribou, I told them about a calf with two heads. A trapper brought the hide into Fairbanks; it was stuffed and is now at the Alaska University.

Inualûjaq said: "When I was young, there was a hunter who said he had seen a caribou with two heads. But he was a shaman, so we thought he had seen something supernatural."

Kakinnâq said: "A long time ago, when I was with my father, Avik, in the mountains, far away to the east, he saw a track of which the forelegs were like a reindeer's and the hind legs like a mountain sheep's. Mikiâna's father was in those parts, too, and saw the same track once when he was out by himself."

"Do you think there can be calf if a caribou mates with a sheep?"

"I don't know, but Avik was an old hand who never made a mistake over a track."

Then I mentioned something Paniaq had told me—that in the last generation there was a hunter who saw a caribou with five legs. Kakinnâq said: "The caribou's a queer beast—there are many things about him one can't understand at all." He was silent for a moment or two; then he said: "Our people have a story about the caribou. I heard it from Qasuneq, who is dead. It's a story that has played an important part in my life."

He told us about a newly married couple who went to a good place and built themselves a turf hut. The husband was a great hunter who shot many caribou, and there was always plenty of meat on the stagings. But then the wife began to have difficult moods, and grew careless in handling meat. Every time this happened the husband was unlucky in hunting. Finally, everything went wrong; the caribou always made off when he tried to stalk them. The couple were then living only on dried meat and were threatened with starvation.

Then one day when he was out hunting he caught sight of a man with big horns on his head. When he came nearer, he saw the man's heart hanging in the air close to his body.

The hunter said that he could no longer get any caribou. The man with the horns replied: "That is because your wife is careless with the meat; she throws the caribou heads on the ground so that they get dirt into their eyes. I am the chief of the caribou. My heart hangs in the air, so that I shall never die. All my relations, the caribou, have their hearts hanging in the air, too."

"What shall I do, then, to get caribou?" the hunter asked.

"Tell your wife what I have said and ask her to handle the meat properly. Then the deer will come. Look back now."

The hunter did so, and suddenly there was a multitude of caribou where previously there had not been a single beast.

"Go home now and shoot some of those deer," said the man with the horns. "You will never see me again."

The hunter went back, and not far from the turf hut he shot all the caribou he needed with ease.

Kakinnâq sat reflecting for a few moments, and then said: "If the man's wife had gone on being difficult and careless with the meat, no more caribou would have been left in this country. But as she changed her ways, we've had masses of caribou till now."

Kakinnâq had spoken with energy and concentration, while his eyes had been far away in a distant world. He had spoken as if he was expounding something of great significance.

As we sat round the fire in the peculiar mood induced by the story, a herd of caribou emerged from a gully under the mountain. The deer slipped quietly past in a long procession among the moraines. Suddenly a big bull appeared on the top of a hillock. It stood there for a few moments with raised antlers—outlined against the sky. Then it joined the herd. Not a man took up his gun. The Eskimos just looked up at the beast and became curiously quiet. Did they feel a connection between Kakinnâq's story and the caribou bull which had appeared up there so suddenly?

We carried a lot of meat down to the boat and moved off toward the settlement. It began to grow light. We made our way forward as before from stream to stream, dragging the boat across country and carrying the meat.

Our spirits were high, as always when we were returning from good hunting. We chatted about one thing and another; Kakinnâq sang a few snatches. Then he and Agmâlik exchanged a few words and laughed heartily. Then I was told about one of the older Eskimos and a difficult love affair of his —which, in fact, was to lead to complications later on. His loved one was a pretty girl of about nineteen. He himself was getting on in years: as tough as nails and a vigorous hunter, but on the downward slope all the same. This incongruous difference in age appealed strongly to the Eskimos' sense of humour. They let themselves go in mischievous jesting.

So we approached the camp in fine fettle. The tents were just ahead of us, and soon everyone would know of our successful hunt. Each of us would be asked how many deer he had shot, and we would give the number quite casually, as if it were nothing to make a fuss about. Then the meat of the fattest beasts would be cooked, the marrowbone would be served, and a crowd would assemble. A good lively meal was to be expected.

The children came racing toward us as usual. But they were not laughing and smiling as usual. When the little ones swarmed round us their faces were breathlessly anxious. The little girl Alasuq cried: "Tullaq's ill, terribly ill."

Tullaq was Kakinnâq's adopted son, a boy of three, of whom he was very fond. A splendid little fellow with a bold carriage, finely shaped features and the brightest smile. He was one of my special friends. The day before, I had been playing with him and a mob of little girls. We were playing with a caribou-skin ball, throwing it from one to another. He was a man and would not be beaten by any of the girls, even if they were twice his size, but eagerly snatched the ball from them time after time. And when he threw it was always to me, for we were two men together.

We ran toward the tent headed by Kakinnâq, pushed the bearskin door aside, and went in. It was full of silent people. His wife Unalîna was sitting over by the stove, and in her lap lay Tullaq, wrapped in caribou skins. He was staring blankly in front of him; his jaws were pressed tightly together and from time to time his little body was twisted with convulsions.

CHAPTER 10

A Wake and a Burial

It was midnight, and little Tullaq was fighting for his life. He had had only three years in the wilds, and now it did not look as if there would be more. But we still hoped.

The tent was full of people all the time, sitting close-packed on the floor of willow boughs. A boy had perched himself on the cold stove, and two girls were sitting on the threshold. Now and again the bearskin door was pushed aside, a face appeared for a moment or two and then vanished.

Unalîna sat in silent grief with the sick boy in her arms, staring in front of her with half-open mouth. She is in her forties; her face is too lined to be pretty, but her eyes have warmth. Beside her sat Kakinnâq, the father. He is a strong man, but who is strong when his child is dying?

The convulsions grew worse. We had been watching the left arm for a long time as if fascinated; at short intervals it had been agitated by the most violent spasms. Now it lay still, as though the nerves and everything in it were worn out. Then the convulsions started in the right arm. The jaws were all the time pressed

101

tightly together. Several times the father tried to open the child's mouth, but only just succeeded. The child's face streamed with sweat; the eyes were wide open and seemed to be staring into another world.

The night advanced, while the child's life slowly ebbed away. There is something very pathetic about these simple people who are so utterly helpless when sickness descends on them. I felt that they were looking to me, the white man, in the hope of help. But what was to be done? By all indications it was a case of lockjaw and nothing would be of any use.

Everyone was serious, but the atmosphere was not so gloomy as with white people in similar circumstances. Now and then the silence was broken by someone saying a few words about everyday things, and from time to time someone smiled. They are such vital people and so occupied with the hard struggle for existence that in the midst of disaster they cannot stop thinking about ordinary matters. But that does not mean that they feel any the less keenly.

Time after time Unalîna's dog, Mamaraq, was over by the tent, trying to thrust his muzzle in under the bearskin door, but was pushed back. He was Tullaq's constant playmate. Not that he could do very much, but he trotted about the settlement with the boy and let himself be pulled about without growling. Mamaraq is very old, thin, and mangy, good for nothing at all, but he has toiled for Unalîna and Kakinnâq for many years, and so they let him live.

Outside there was moonlight, and a fine arch of northern lights in violet and green was stretched over the valley. The dogs began to howl; two hundred dogs struck up a discordant lament like a huge orchestra. It stopped suddenly, as if the sound had been cut off.

Paniaq's sensible wife, Umialâq, came in with a quantity of dried meat laid on a board. Aguk made a cut in the largest slice, and it was seen to be full of white maggots. They crawled out in a mass. Most of the Eskimos had a good laugh at that. The rest of the meat was good; we swept the maggots aside and ate.

Hours passed, and we still sat there. Ayauneq's baby, which she had on her back under the caribou-skin cloak, began to scream. She began to rock her body, a long way forward and then back again, quite endlessly. She has a peculiar way of doing it, abrupt and rather irritating, quite different from the gentle rocking of the other women.

A grey streak fell into the tent through the window of bears' intestines. Day was breaking. The light in the tent was put out, and the people's faces changed.

The boy's spasms were no longer so violent, but we all perceived that it was not that the convulsions had relaxed their hold, but that his vitality could no longer offer much resistance. Kakinnâq put his hand in under the caribou skin which covered the boy, then turned to us and said, with his lips drawn back in a kind of smile: "His legs are beginning to grow cold. Soon I shall have no son."

Just before sunrise, Tullaq died.

The women at once set to work, sewing a white garment and white footwear for the dead child. Two of the hunters made a coffin which also was covered with white material; they did it sitting on the ground outside the tent. The sun was up by now, a flood of light over the valley and the mountains.

It was such a little coffin.

A short service was held in Kakinnâq's tent, and a few hymns were sung in Eskimo, as the older people had learnt to do on the coast. I was not there, but the singing could be heard faintly through the wall of the tent.

After a time Paniaq came over to me and said: "He's to be buried on the tundra out in the valley; you can come to the feast."

"Feast?"

"Yes, it's our custom to have a feast when a dead person is to be buried."

When we were about to start, he pointed to the staging on which my film camera lay under a caribou skin and said: "You can take the picture-box with you." He always has a kindly thought like this for me; he knows very well how keen I am on filming anything out of the ordinary.

I replied that I would not think of taking photographs on such an occasion. But Paniaq continued energetically: "You take them, none of us will mind." I followed his advice and filmed this remarkable burial and feast.

We marched out over the tundra in a body. The hunters had their rifles and hunting bags over their shoulders; some of the women carried bags containing meat and other things. We sat down near the middle of the valley where it was quite flat, a brownish-yellow plain of autumnal heather and grasses with patches of sand here and there.

Piliala, as strong as a bear, began digging the grave. It was a long and tiring task, for it had to be five feet deep, and beneath the surface the ground was frozen hard. He dug so hard that the earth flew up; he hardly paused for breath. When he was tired he would be relieved by someone else. They would have to work in shifts if the grave was to be finished before evening.

The young girls ran down to a lake with a patchy growth of willows and came back in a smiling procession with great armfuls of wood.

Soon two fires were blazing, and cooking-pots brimful of caribou meat were hung over them. The people sat scattered about on the ground in their caribou-skin cloaks. The hunters had gathered in small groups; they had now taken off their rifles and hunting bags, which lay close to hand. The women were gathered a short way off. They had drawn the caribou-skin hoods over their heads, and all those faces framed in the bristling wolf-skin edgings were a remarkable sight. The tiniest babies were there, too, either under the cloaks on their mothers' backs, or sitting with bare bottoms on the cold earth. The rest of the children were all over the place.

Kakinnâq was everywhere; it was his son who was to be buried and he was responsible for the feast. His face had re-covered its former strength; no one could see any longer what he felt. Prompt and businesslike, he was now ordering wood to be brought, now giving an eye to the fires and cooking-pots or saying a word to the man who was working in the grave. His wife Unalîna helped him. Her eyes told me that her thoughts were far away—but she forgot nothing. After the meat was cooked, they took great care that everyone got plenty. They produced a bag of their best dried meat and fat and laid the stuff in a heap so that everyone could help himself. All in honour of their dead son. There was a cheerful atmosphere, with joking and laughter, as we sat on the ground eating caribou meat by the fires.

Two men came across the tundra from the camp; we saw them as small objects in the distance. They came nearer; they were Tautuq and Iluppak, with the little white coffin on two poles, which rested on their shoulders. They put it down care-fully a little way from the fires. Everyone looked that way, but went on eating and the talk continued as before.

Then the children began to play. They divided themselves into two sides, each of which had its "house" marked with a circle of stones. The players had to run for a certain distance, and each side had to catch the other side's runners before they got back to the "house." Anyone who was caught had to remain in a particular place, but could be freed by one of his own side if the latter was quick enough. The children were wild with excite-ment over this game, flying about, dodging and turning sharply, as swift as animals. Laughter and shrieks rang out over the plain.

And all the time the men dug deeper and deeper into the frozen earth.

Suddenly the hunters began to peer eagerly across toward the other side of the valley. A large herd of caribou was moving along there; the beasts were passing in a long line under the steep mountainside. Without a word Agmâlik slung his rifle over his shoulders and left the funeral to try his luck as a hunter.

At last the grave was finished. It ran from north to south and was so deep that a man standing in it only just had his head above ground. A few cross-sticks were now laid a little way from the bottom, resting on edges cut for the purpose, and were covered with boughs. Thus the coffin had a floor of its own.

Then the people assembled round the grave. The father and mother stood at the northern end, the others as they liked. The little white coffin was lowered into the grave so that the head pointed north. Earth was shovelled onto it, and a cross placed on the grave.

Evening was now approaching. The sun was sinking behind jagged mountains, and the sky was fiery red over the wide valley and the little mound in it.

We returned to the camp in groups, and there was talk and jesting, for it was a feast, and a feast it should be. But the mother walked by herself along the edge of Raven Lake, which rippled gently, with the red of the sunset reflected in its dark surface. She walked with a stooping gait, her arms pressed against her breast.

CHAPTER 11

Dancing and Racing

Two evenings later there was dancing in the great tent which was pitched in the middle of the camp. Dancing has been customary from ancient times when a death has occurred among the Nunamiuts.

People drifted into the tent and sat down on the ground along the walls. On one side the women, the married ones with the youngest child on their backs, on the other side the hunters, while children of all ages filled the empty spaces. A little in front of the rest the drummers and singers sat by drums made of caribou skin drawn over round frames. Jokes and smiles ran round the festive circle of cheerful, expectant people.

Suddenly the music began; the singers struck up strange, wild melodies at the top of their lungs. Then all began to sing, some moving their bodies in time with the rhythm or stamping their feet. I felt myself being drawn into it.

Two of the older women rose, drew on white gloves, went out onto the floor, and began to dance. They stood almost still, and twisted their bodies and moved their hands now to one side, now to the other, with gentle movements of their arms.

Then Mikiâna, also wearing gloves, sprang forward onto the floor and did the Hunters' Dance. This was something quite different: a lightning tempo, a supple agility, and an endurance which were quite impressive. He danced almost on the same spot all the time, while his body, arms, and legs were in the closest rhythmical harmony. Now he squatted, now he sprang up. What caught the eye more than anything was the stiff, grotesque movement of his arms and hands.

Spirits rose. One dancer after another came forward. Now two women or girls, now a hunter. There were smiles on every face. If women were dancing, the young girls sat and made the same motions of their hands and arms. They showed easy naturalness and spontaneous enjoyment.

Kunnâna, one of the girls, was a sight to see when dancing: her heated face framed by her blue-black hair—her supple body swaying in time with the drumming and singing—graceful movements of her arms with her head thrown back a little—and above all her hands.

The quite small children were in action too. Here was the little boy Kûpak, dancing the difficult *sayûn* like a full-blown hunter! But most delightful of all were two tiny little girls dancing away, all smiles without a trace of shyness; they looked like dolls in their long caribou-skin cloaks.

The night was far advanced, and people were dancing as hard as ever. The Eskimos never seemed to grow tired—except the very smallest children, who had fallen asleep in the corners of the tent. I went out for a walk. A muffled sound of drumming and singing came from the tent; all round me was a wilderness of black mountains under the stars. Not till early morning did the dancing stop.

Dancing occupies a central position in the Nunamiuts' existence, but apart from funerals a dance is no longer connected with any particular occasion. People assemble when the fancy takes them, to feel the inspiration of the drum and the old songs.

But in the mountains there is not often time for merrymaking; the conditions of life are too hard. Among the coast Eskimos, on the whole, it is otherwise; there whales are caught in the light season, while in winter the people live to a great extent on accumulated stores and have a good deal of fun. The Nunamiuts, on the contrary, have to be always moving after the caribou throughout the winter. It is mainly in the autumn, when caribou are sometimes in abundance, that there is time for dancing.

The dances are of four types, named in accordance with their speed: *atûtiqpak, atûtipiaq, sayûn,* and *atûgaujaq.*

The *sayûn* is strictly formal, and I have never seen it danced by women. In the others the dancer is allowed to move as he will, but always within the rules which hold good for Eskimo dancing and give it character. Each dance is always accompanied by drumming and singing. There are a number of dance songs which are named after one of the four types of dance. I will deal with singing generally in rather more detail later on.

In old times the slow dances, the *atûtiqpak* and the *atûtipiaq,* were the most popular, and they are still danced in the mountains. But people's taste changes with the times, and this has always been true of the Nunamiuts: they are undoubtedly conservative, and the basic rules are not broken, but within the framework of the old there is ample possibility of variation. Now they want quick dances. Just as the rumba, samba, etc., have with us largely replaced the slow waltz and tango, the swift, exciting *sayûn* has become popular with the Eskimos.

The Nunamiut dances are related to the dances of the coast Eskimos who inhabit the Kotzebue–Point Barrow region. Paniaq asserts further that they resemble the dances of the Eskimos in Siberia and on the Diomede Islands, in the Bering Strait. On the other hand they are very different from the dances of the Eskimos south of Nome and on Herschel Island, in Canada. Curiously enough the neighbouring Kobuk people have a dance which is quite different from those of the Nunamiuts. It bears the stamp of Indian influence and is called *kugwagmiutaq* or *itqiliarjun*. It should be added that Paniaq, when he lived on the coast, occasionally met Eskimos from Herschel Island, Nome, the Diomede Islands, Siberia, etc., and has had an opportunity of making comparisons.

The Nunamiut dancing does not seem to have been noticeably influenced by their closest neighbours, the Koyukuk Indians in the forest to the south, although the mountain people have been on friendly terms with them for a long time. The two forms seem to be essentially different. For instance, the Eskimos' funeral dance is lively and realistic, as though to keep their spirits up and help them in their struggle for existence; but the Indian dance on such an occasion often takes a mourning form and is performed to sad music.

A curious part of the Nunamiut dance is that the hands are covered with white gloves, an ancient feature which has parallels among other primitive peoples, as well as the Persians, Greeks, Romans, early Christians, and others. Norway still has a survival of the custom in Hordaland, where the bride has her hands covered with a white "handcloth" when she approaches the altar.

There have been several different reasons for this. The belief that on certain ceremonial occasions one should cover the body or parts of it as a protection against spirits has been widespread among primitive peoples. The train of thought, more or less clear in different cases, seems to be that the hands, which are in daily life used for all kinds of work, are unclean and must not touch what is holy, nor be displayed at a meeting with higher powers.

The last remnants of the Nunamiuts now live as isolated in
the mountains as on a desert island, and the time when the inland people and other tribes assembled for a grand feast with
dancing, games, races, and ceremonies of many kinds, is past.
They now hold their feasts alone. But the older hunters who
took part in the spring journeys to Nerleq, at the mouth of the
Colville River, remember the feasts of those days in detail as
great events in their lives.

The grandest of all feasts was the invitation feast (*kiwgiq-
soat*). The first consideration was that there should be enough
game for the guests to have plenty to eat. Then messengers were
sent off to the people who were to be invited; they took with
them small pegs marked in a particular way. The marks indi-
cated which persons were to come to the feast.

The guests set off in a band. In winter dog-sledges were used,
in summer they came on foot or by skin boat, according to local
conditions. When they were about half a day's journey from
their hosts, they stopped and sent off messengers to the settlement challenging the people to race them. The hosts sent their
best runners to the place where their guests had halted. There
the race for the settlement started. The prize was a skin tent.

Old Maptirâq, who is famous as the winner of one of the
great races with the Barrow Eskimos at Nerleq, told me:

"The runners stripped till they had nothing on but short
breeches and skin shoes. Crosswise strips were sewn over the
soles to prevent us from slipping.

"Then the Nunamiuts' runners rose and went back a little,
while all the time we sang an old song. Finally, we cried 'Kra!
kra! kra!' and hid behind a mound.

"Suddenly our leader, old Apayaujaq, cried, giving a side-
ways jump: 'Now you must look alive, it'll be hard to beat the
Barrow men, they've started.' This was the sign for us to start.
The others had got a bit ahead, imitating the noise of geese."

Maptirâq described the race itself in detail—how the lead

changed hands and how at the end there was only one Barrow runner in the foremost group. Then, thinking: "I shall win the tent," he put on a spurt and was first in through the tent door, where Makpiri held the bearskin aside for him.

Then he described the actual feast: "It was a large tent, crammed full of people, and there were twenty drummers. First, food was served to the Barrow people. While they ate, the drums beat, and the inland people sang, while the women made slow dance movements with their arms. The Nunamiuts sang a very old song:

> Why is this festal tent not built of timber?
> Why has this festal tent not posts of mammoth's teeth?
> Why has this festal tent not a door made from the giant mouse's skin?
> Why is there not a door-string made of the giant mouse's back sinews?

"After the Barrow people had feasted, they drove the inland people out of the tent. The drums beat all the time. Then the coast Eskimos struck up a song they called *anaisaisaq,* and danced. The inland people came in again, bringing presents for the guests: fox, wolverine, wolf, and other animals' skins. Then they danced the gift dance. Songs were also sung about many things which the guests would *not* receive.

"The feast went on for a long time, and there were many dances. Next day things were exchanged, and there were contests between the inland people and the coast people. We wrestled, jumped, paddled, and competed in other forms of sport.

"That was a feast one can't forget," concluded Maptirâq. "A lot of coast Eskimos were there, and almost all the people from the mountains, from Raven Lake, the Killik River, the Colville

River, and other places. When the drums were beating and all these people singing and dancing, it was grand."

The feasts which the Nunamiuts held in the mountains must have been equally fascinating. There are many strange stories about them. Sometimes the Kobuk Eskimos were their guests, at other times the Noatak Eskimos made the long journey by dog-sledge to Raven Lake. But most curious of all must have been the Nunamiuts' feasts with the alien people—the Indians.

Marriage Troubles and Meat Diet

One morning Kayuq suddenly got busy, fitting the packs to the dogs and stowing away in them not only what it is usual to take on a long hunting expedition in autumn but old winter clothes, snow-shoes, a quantity of caribou skin, and other things. He was glum and curt of speech as he did all this. Then he threw his hunting bag and rifle over his shoulders and went off across the valley with a string of heavily loaded dogs swaying at his heels. Later, from a height, I saw his hunting tent on the other side of the river, a grey speck among scanty willows.

He had left his wife. "It was bound to come," Paniaq said laconically, and the few words signified a great deal.

Kayuq was about twenty-five, a skilful hunter and a rather good-looking fellow. Most noticeable were his eyes: strikingly large, with a dark gleam in their depths. He smiled often, but the dark gleam somehow blunted the impression of the smile. He had a violent temper. He had made trouble in the past, and one or two of the Eskimos were afraid of what he might do in a bad mood. His wife was called Sailaq and was about the same

HARRISON COUNTY
PUBLIC LIBRARY
105 North Capitol Ave.
Corydon, IN 47112

age. She was not very pretty, but there was something warm and winning about her. They had a little girl of ten. Sailaq was pregnant, and the child was expected during the winter.

A week passed, and Kayuq began to have second thoughts. Getting rid of his wife and living alone was not quite what he had imagined it would be. Apart from the hunting, a lot of odd jobs cropped up with which he had not troubled himself before. Wood had to be fetched, food cooked, and footwear mended, and there was a lot of other women's work. When he lay of an evening staring at the tent cloth, everything was dead still; there was no chattering girl, not a soul to talk to or abuse. And he thought of the child his wife was to bear, which was suddenly lost to him. It might be a boy.

But crawl to his wife on his knees—oh no! There was, however, another way of arranging the matter; he went to one or two of the older hunters and said something of this kind: "My wife has made it impossible for me to live in my own tent. It would be best to hold a council and clear things up."

The evening of the council came; all the older men were to assemble in one of the tents. A couple of hunters came and asked me to take part in the council. I said that my presence might not be very advisable when a private matter of this kind was to be dealt with. The Eskimos replied that it would help greatly if I were there, for I must certainly have had plenty of experience of difficult married people.

We slipped into the tent one by one and sat down in a large circle on the willow-bough floor. The newly separated wife and the daughter of the house, the young widow Paniulaq, were the only women. The latter has a little boy of four, who had gone to sleep under a pile of reindeer hides.

First we sat for a long time talking and laughing as if we had just met to enjoy ourselves. Then Kayuq spoke. He was no fool, and began by saying that it was all the same to him whether his wife would have him back or not. All he wanted was to make a definite agreement for the future, so that he would know where he stood. Then followed a long account of the matrimonial tangles, which were certainly not his fault. His wife was more in her father's tent than in her own home, and that had annoyed him. It would annoy any man.

He spoke shrewdly and confidently, with a temperamental passage now and then. A speech to the gallery. Not once did he allow it to appear that he was eager to have his wife back. But his eyes told another story.

Then it was Sailaq's turn. She sat with her arm round her daughter, looked straight in front of her as if no one else was present, and talked in a quiet, melodious voice. She had a broad, little face and a pleasant smile—there was something resigned in her expression, as if she had been through a great deal. There was no sting in her voice. Reflectively and with many pauses she told the story of her marriage. It could be seen how intensely she felt the misfortune of the whole thing, not least on account of the child yet unborn. Every time she found it difficult to express herself, a little wrinkle formed at the top of her nose.

She made it clear that her husband had been harsh with her. But she did not make this into an accusation; she simply stated a fact. She said it was he who was seldom at home. He was always sitting in his father's tent with other men, and she was alone nearly every evening. She felt that if they resumed their life together, it would soon all be the same again.

When she had finished, one or two of the older men put some questions to the couple—and then came a long series of speakers, one after another. They all made speeches; no one cut it short. The members of the council were married, and like most married men, they were fairly convinced of their unfailing insight into the problems of marriage.

I sat listening to the vigorous Eskimo language and was astonished to find how easy it is to manage. One would think there would at times be some hesitation in view of the great many different terminations which have to be tacked onto the root words, but no. Speech flows in a level stream; the speakers never came to a halt or fumbled for an exact expression.

It was far into the night. The stove had been cold for a long time, and there were several degrees of frost in the tent. But no one seemed to notice it but myself. I froze where I sat on the willow-bough floor. The daughter of the house, the widow Paniulaq, had carried on with her work all the time without taking very much notice of what was going on. Then her four-year-old son woke up, threw the hides on one side, and sat up, with caribou hairs among his own dark locks. He suddenly became aware of his mother and caught hold of her. She bared her breast, and the sturdy boy began sucking, while the flow of words continued undisturbed.

At last the fathers of the couple spoke again. They emphasized this point: If the marriage had taken a wrong turn because the husband and his wife had clung too much to their respective parents, both could now be sure that *they*, the fathers, would do their best to see that it did not happen in future. They advised a reconciliation.

It was clear that Kayuq was willing, but Sailaq did not reply; she clasped her small daughter, who had now fallen asleep in her arms, a little tighter.

As all these oratorical efforts had not led to any result, the hunters were somewhat at a loss. Then Paniaq asked me for my opinion. I was in grave doubt as to how this affair should be handled. It was a delicate matter. I approached this responsible piece of arbitration with mixed feelings. With linguistic help from Paniaq, I talked on, noticing to my surprise that the arguments marshalled themselves quite nicely. Matrimonial problems appear astonishingly easy to overcome where other people's marriages are concerned.

I began by saying that all who were present in the tent

certainly had had matrimonial differences (the men sniggered at this). But they and their wives had not at once separated because of them. Much could be arranged and must be arranged for the children's sake. Then I set clearly before the couple the future that awaited them if they parted company. How would he be able to dress skins, make clothes, fetch wood, and do much else when he had no woman to help him? And how would she and the children manage to get on without a man? Their fathers and others would no doubt give them a helping hand, but there was little pleasure in being a continual burden to others. I advised them to give their marriage another chance. If it then proved quite impossible to live together, well, they could separate.

This speech certainly contained nothing original, but I could see that some of it hit the mark. It was followed by a few moments of silence, and then by an eager discussion. When they had finished, Sailaq looked across at me with the faintest smile. We broke up and went out into the night, each of us to his own place.

Next day the couple began to live together again, and the marriage continued for as long as I was in the mountains. Gradually a number of Eskimos began coming to me with their problems. I valued their confidence and did my best. They talked of the most private matters quite openly and without the least shyness. In many respects these people had soft natures and were easily impressed, if treated in the right way. It was not only my personality that counted, but also what I stood for—the insight which they attributed to the white man in certain fields. The more I had to do with them, the better I understood the dominating position the shaman had held among these simple people, so easily swayed.

Thus I obtained an insight into many of the most intimate aspects of their attitude toward life. Only in two cases had I to deal with really deep-rooted matrimonial difficulties. In these cases the situation was that if an unsuccessful marriage was bad, a separation was worse. Collaboration between husband and wife was the very foundation of this nomad people's existence. If a married couple with children separated, they suffered, it is true, no direct hardship, but the whole affair became a complication, a burden for the nearest relations and harmful to the children. In former times husband and wife could each join other hunting groups where there was a chance of re-marriage. But now there is only this group left in the mountains; the separated persons must stay in the same camp, and no man or woman will marry anyone who has his or her partner of an earlier marriage hanging about the camp. In short, the prospects after a separation are pretty dismal.

Most of the marriages are firmly based. The skin tent with its bearskin door and windows of bear's intestines, where man and wife sit on the willow-bough floor with their children round them, is a home in the best sense of the word. Each of the partners undertakes his or her share of the work good-humouredly. If the wife is positively overburdened with work, the husband may give her a hand at scraping skins; indeed, he may even mend his own footwear. There is a spirit of give and take which might give cause for some reflection on matrimonial conditions in the communities which we call civilized.

I am writing at the beginning of October. Now the women are going for trips up the hillsides in small parties and enjoying themselves picking berries and gossiping. They find a fair number of cranberries and whortleberries, but no great quantities. Cloudberries are scarce in the Anaktuvuk Pass; there are said to be more farther north, on the tundra.

The berries are stored raw, sometimes in a washed-out caribou's stomach, and mixed with melted fat or lard. This dish is called *asiun* and is considered a special delicacy.

They also dig up some roots. The most sought after are

maso,* *qunguliq* (mountain sorrel),† and *airaq*.‡ What is collected is consumed before winter sets in. No new green food is
to be had till May; then roots and the fresh shoots and inner
bark of the willow are eaten. Thus, for about seven months the
Nunamiuts live on an exclusively meat diet, and for the rest of
the year their vegetable nourishment is very scanty.

The caribou is dealt with traditionally. Every single part of
the animal is eaten except the bones and hooves. The coarse
meat, which in civilization is used for joints and steaks, is the
least popular. In autumn and spring it is used to a certain extent
for dried meat; otherwise it is given to the dogs. The heart, liver,
kidneys, stomach and its contents, small intestines with contents (if they are fat), the fat round the bowels, marrow fat
from the back, the meat which is near the legs, etc., are eaten.
Both adults and children are very fond of the large white tendons on the caribou's legbones; they maintain that food of this
kind gives one good digestion. The head is regarded as a special
delicacy; the meat, the fat behind the eyes, nerves, muzzle,
palate, etc., are eaten. Finally, there are the spring delicacies—
the soft, newly grown horns and the large yellowish-white grubs
on the inside of the hide (those of the gadfly) and in the nostrils. The grubs are eaten alive.

The meat is often cooked, but to a large extent it is also eaten
raw. The children often sit on a freshly killed caribou, cut off
pieces of meat, and make a good meal. It is also common practice to serve a dish of large bones to which the innermost raw
meat adheres. Dried meat and fat are always eaten raw.

The Nunamiuts' cuisine also offers several choice delicacies.
First and foremost is *akutuq*. To prepare this dish, fat and marrow are melted in a cooking-pot, which must not get too warm,
meat cut fine is dropped in on the top, and then the woman uses

---

* Belongs to genus *Polygonum*.
† *Oxyria digyna*.
‡ Belongs to genus *Oxytropis*.

In summer and autumn dogs are used as pack animals and give invaluable aid when a caribou is shot a long way out of camp. It is incredible what heavy loads they can carry for hours on end in difficult country

Kakinnâq with part of his kill on a lucky day when we shot a large number of deer. They are skinned and quartered with care by the Nunamiuts' old method

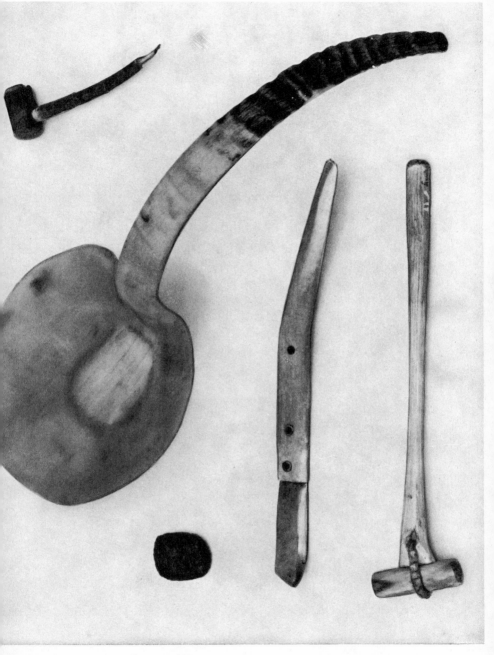

From left to right: Willow-wood pipe; scoop made from a ram's horn; flint skin-scraper found in an old ruin; curved knife with shaft of caribou horn; hammer with willow-wood shaft and head of caribou horn, formerly used in cutting flint tools

Nukâluk

her fist and arm as a ladle to stir it about. The result is strong and tastes very good. *Akutuq* has since ancient times been used on journeys as an easily made and nourishing food and is fairly often mentioned in the old legends.

Then there is *qaqisalik*, caribou's brains stirred up with melted fat. A favourite dish is *nirupkaq*, a caribou's stomach with its contents which is left in the animal for a night and then has melted fat added to it. It has a sweetish taste which reminds one of apples. Finally, there is knuckle fat. The knuckles are crushed with a stone hammer to which a willow handle has been lashed. Then the mass is boiled till the fat flies up. The Eskimos attach great importance to the boiling's not being too hard; they regulate it by throwing in snow. This fat has a peculiar delicate taste. Sometimes it is mixed with blood, and then becomes a special dish called *urjutilik*.

The Nunamiuts like chewing boiled resin and a kind of white clay which is found in certain rivers. Salt is hardly used at all. If an Eskimo family has acquired a little, it is used very occasionally, with roast meat. The small amount of sugar, flour, etc., which is flown in in autumn is of little significance and has, generally speaking, disappeared before the winter comes. Some Eskimos do not like sugar.

For a while coffee or tea is drunk, but these are quickly finished. Then the Eskimos fall back on their old drink, the gravy of the cooked meat.

The Nunamiuts thrive on this almost exclusively meat diet; scurvy or other diseases due to shortages of vitamins do not exist. They are, in fact, thoroughly healthy and full of vitality, so long as sicknesses are not imported by aircraft. They live to be quite old, and it is remarkable how young and active men and women remain at a considerable age. Hunters of fifty have hardly a trace of grey hair, and no one is bald. All have shining white teeth with not a single cavity. The mothers nurse their children for two or three years.

It is an interesting question whether cancer occurs among the Nunamiuts or among primitive peoples at all. On this point I dare not as a layman express an opinion, but I heard little of stomach troubles. During my stay among the Apache Indians in Arizona (1936) a doctor in the reservation told me that cancer had not been observed among that people. According to a Danish doctor, Dr. Aage Gilberg,* cancer is never seen among the Thule Eskimos in northwestern Greenland. The matter deserves more detailed investigation; it may possibly give certain results of assistance to cancer research.

The Indian caribou hunters I once lived with in Arctic Canada had a similar meat diet and good health. As for myself, my fare was the same as the Indians' and the Eskimos'—practically speaking, I lived only on meat for nearly five years. I felt well and in good spirits, provided I got enough fat. My digestion was good and my teeth in an excellent state. After my stay with the Nunamiuts I had not a single hole in my teeth and no tartar.

No doubt the hunters of the Ice Age, in Norway and elsewhere, lived in a similar way many thousand years ago. We are probably in the presence of what is most ancient among the traditions of primitive peoples. Taught by experience, they have arrived at a manner of living which, despite its onesidedness, fully satisfies the body's requirements. The principle is to transfer almost everything that is found in the caribou to the human organism.

It is interesting to note that the stomach and liver of animals are regular features in the diet of primitive peoples, whereas modern science has only quite recently established that these contain elements of special value to human beings. The remedy for the previously deadly pernicious anaemia is obtained from them. The contents of the caribou's stomach and the newly grown horns merit a closer examination by modern methods. It is a question, for example, whether the cellulose of the moss is

* *Eskimo Doctor,* George Allen and Unwin Ltd., London, 1948.

decomposed in the caribou's stomach and thereby becomes available to the human organism. With regard to the horns, it is of interest that certain deer's horns from northeastern Manchuria have from time immemorial been a regular article of commerce in China, where they have been used as a cure for impaired virility.

The Eskimos usually have two meals a day, one in the morning and one when the man comes home from hunting in the afternoon or evening. When we sit down on the willow-bough floor and the dish of steaming caribou meat is set before us, the procedure is scarcely that of a smart dinner party in our own world, but it is civilized after a fashion. The common idea that primitive peoples fling themselves upon their food and gulp it down like wolves is wrong. Certainly the hands are used, and it is permissible to pick about in the dish to find a tidbit, but eating is controlled and follows definite rules. Eating has its technique; there is an art in tearing the flesh away from the bones in the most effective manner. Sometimes the eaters dig their teeth into one end of a piece of meat while holding on to the other, and then cut off piece after piece close to the mouth. At other times the knife is used while the bone is held in the hand. Every scrap of meat, sinews, and fat is cut off and eaten. Finally, they attack the raw bones and cleave them with a few blows of a stone or axe, so skilfully that the marrow is disclosed undamaged. When the meal is over a heap of bare bones is left.

When the time for the evening meal approaches, a regular gang of children gets busy. The question is: In which tent is the best meat being cooked? There is a great difference between lean and fat caribou meat, not to speak of fat mutton, which stands in a class by itself. First the children fly from one tent to another, apparently on an errand of some sort, but with the definite intention of finding out where supper should be taken. When that question is settled they vanish into the open air, to

plunge into the chosen tent with incredible punctuality ten sec-
onds after the dish of meat has been placed upon the willow-
bough floor. They usually remain standing just inside the door,
staring fixedly at the food. At length someone beckons to them
to come and sit down in front, and they lose no time in doing so.

It is the established custom that all who are in the tent when
the food is served shall take part in the meal. Thus there is unlimited hospitality. This can be pretty hard on the few families
whose tents are usually the fixed place of assembly. But the host
takes it very calmly, even if he is eaten out of house and home
and has to hunt more energetically than the rest to keep things
going.

Fifteen or tweny years ago the system was different. Then
there was an assembly house, or *qajgi,* which was not only the
place where feasts were held, but the regular resort of men who
were not out hunting. The Nunamiuts' wandering life in the
mountains often made it difficult to erect an assembly house,
and then one of the inhabited tents was used.

Thus the men had their own world in the daytime and in the
evening. The woman had no business there except at feasts and
when food had to be brought in. Each wife came with her portion of cooked meat as a contribution to the hunters' common
meal. It sometimes happened that one of them was stingy and
brought a meagre portion or bad meat. She acquired a bad
reputation. The hunters still talk of certain women of that type
and have a special name for them (*aquwirinaqtuk*).

A common tent of this kind had been of great social importance for generations. There the hunters sat, repaired or made
their implements, talked, sang, or told stories. For the boys this
was a school. The older men taught them how to make their
gear according to tribal tradition, and when the old songs were
sung or stories of the tribe were told, the young ones sat round-
eyed, drinking it all in.

"There was always life and plenty of laughter in the assembly house," said Paniaq, "and I wish we would go back to the old system." I myself notice, too, that the tone becomes merrier and freer whenever the hunters find themselves sitting together in a tent with no women about. Then one of them will say, as though with relief: "Now we're only men here, just as if we were in a *qajgi.*"

CHAPTER 13

Eskimos and Indians

It is no easy matter to find fuel in the neighbourhood of the camp by Raven Lake, for in the course of time the Nunamiuts have cleaned the place up thoroughly. The Eskimos make shift with the low-branching willow scrub, which is burnt green after the women have tied together small bundles of the shoots suitable for putting into the stove.

One day when I was looking for fuel among the tall willow bushes, I became aware of a party of children approaching across the open ground. They bustled along, laughing and chattering. Then I whistled, standing concealed behind the bushes. The crowd of children stopped short, and their laughter died away. I whistled again. Then they turned quickly and raced back toward the camp like frightened hares.

I spoke of this later to the Eskimos. They were not in the least surprised; they told me that something similar had happened a week before, a little farther south. Two of the younger hunters were on their way toward a river when they heard whistling among some willow bushes. They fired a shot and ran straight back to the camp. It must have been Indians.

I am told that the Indians have from old times been accustomed to signal to one another by whistling or by imitating the calls of birds. No, the Nunamiuts have no doubt at all that redskins have been about, although the foundation for the belief is so slender. They tell me that something of the kind happens every year or so, not only here but also with the Noatak Eskimos. Maptirâq says: "One can never feel safe, for the Indians have much to avenge up here in the mountains."

So firmly rooted is the ancient enmity. And, perhaps, the fear of the redskins is not so imaginary. The Nunamiuts say that as late as 1946 a Noatak Eskimo killed two Indians in the mountains between the Noatak River and the Kobuk River. They believe that the blood shed will be avenged as soon as opportunity offers.

The Eskimos' relations with the Indians are a curious chapter, much of which is obscure. Over a great part of the huge Arctic and sub-Arctic areas in which the Eskimos live—from Alaska in the west to Labrador in the east—the Indians are their neighbours. Sometimes there may be a kind of no man's land between them, at other times their hunting areas are contiguous; sometimes, indeed, they use the same hunting grounds. There have often been hostilities between the two peoples, but there is friendly intercourse also at times.

Comparing the Eskimos and Indians, it is the differences that first strike one. The Indians are forest people, while the Eskimos with few exceptions are adapted to life in the open polar country and by the sea. The language is basically different, likewise the songs and dances. There are also psychological features which seem different; that, anyway, is my experience after having lived among both peoples for several years.

Alaska is one of the areas where Eskimos come into close contact with the Indians, and this applies not least to the Nunamiut country. The Atabask Indians are their neighbours to the south. One group is the peaceful Koyukuk Indians (*tagjarwik-*

miut) with whom the Eskimos have almost always been on good terms and have often associated for hunting, feasts, and trade gatherings. Another group is the Chandalar Indians (*uyarârmiut*), or stone people, with whom they were always at war. These last seem to have been a queer-tempered people. Old-timers in Alaska tell me that right up to quite recent times prospectors have thought it risky to penetrate into their country.

In the Brooks Mountains there are many signs of the times when the Indians roamed through them. Sometimes one comes upon ruins of small stone huts which, according to the Nunamiuts, date from earliest Indian days.

Round about in the mountains there are also tent rings left by the Indians. There are other more puzzling signs which, the Nunamiuts think, also date from the forest people.

The Eskimos have a wealth of traditions concerning Indians. To hear one of the old people telling of them in his vivid, detailed manner is to see with one's own eyes the Eskimos and the sons of the forest in peaceful intercourse and fierce fighting.

Most fascinating are the accounts of the feasts held in common with the Koyukuk Indians in the mountains or in the forest country near the old Indian capital, Tagjarwik,* on the Koyukuk River. These, too, were invitation feasts. The procedure was much the same as between Eskimos. Messengers were sent out with invitations, there were races to the settlement, and so on. There were differences, however, for here were two peoples with different languages, songs, dances, etc.—a strange meeting.

But it was a wary friendship. Indians were Indians, and the Eskimos never felt themselves quite safe. Paniaq says drily: "When the Nunamiuts held the feast in the mountains, our runners always beat the Indians. When the Indians held the

* It is believed to have been on the north bank of the river a short way east of Allakaket.

The time of darkness approaches: the sun just floodlights the mountain-tops

Aguâq, composer of a new song for the baby girl Ayapana, who was born in the time of darkness and had a tuft of black hair in the middle of her head

Maptirâq, the best composer among the Nunamiuts, about seventy-five—a gentleman of the old school. He is still vigorous and hunts caribou and wolves

feast in the forests, we always let them win, for one could never know what people like that might do if they turned nasty."

I have elsewhere given a few outstanding features of the protracted fighting with the Chandalar Indians. It was not war as we understand it, but sporadic guerrilla fighting. There were seldom any large-scale combats. To kill a sleeping enemy was accounted a smart piece of work; broadly speaking, neither Eskimos nor Indians were troubled by conceptions of honour where fighting was concerned. The thing was to win, no matter how.

The Indians did no scalping, but they sometimes mutilated corpses. They once attacked an Eskimo camp when only women and children were at home and killed them all except one young girl. The women's breasts were cut off and hung up. Vengeance was not slow in coming, and the whole party of Indians was slaughtered. I have never heard of the Eskimos on their side mutilating corpses, but they might plunder them for articles of value, such as crystal beads.

Stories are sometimes told of famous Eskimo warriors who killed a large number of Indians. Iglugalûjaq, the great archer, is said once to have disposed of twenty. They tried to storm his turf hut, but he stood coolly at the door and brought them down one after another.

The blood feud continued, and life in the mountains was always insecure. The Nunamiuts had not only to face the hard struggle for material existence but also to be constantly on guard against their enemies, the Indians and the coast Eskimos. They took to pitching their tents on heights which afforded a good field of vision, or on the side of a river away from the country of their most dangerous enemies. These were often inconvenient dwelling places. One often sees tent rings on heights from which it is a long way to any wood for fuel, but which have a good field of vision—and this in a region where it is easy to find an excellent camping ground with good shelter and fuel in abundance. It was also a common practice of the Nunamiuts to build palisades of willows (*saigut*) round their settlements. Sometimes they posted a couple of watchers outside. It was in this way that the Indian chief Staka was outwitted. He was shot down from behind when stealthily approaching a settlement. He had a great quantity of crystal beads on him and is said to have been the richest of all Indians.

Their weapons were bows and arrows, spears, flint knives, and clubs. Old legends mention also a small axe with a flint head. Certain Eskimo tribes in Alaska used a cuirass made of bone, but the Nunamiuts had nothing of the kind.

Fight with flint knives.—Drawn by the Eskimo Paniaq.

It appears that they very seldom took prisoners to use as slaves. I have heard of only two cases of marriage between Nunamiuts and abducted Indian girls. There have presumably been children, but no doubt these were exposed immediately after birth. It is also interesting to note that both the Kobuk Eskimos and the Barrow Eskimos have typical legends which indicate an admixture of Indian blood, whereas the Nunamiuts deny that they have any.

The contact between Eskimos and Indians has led to the exercise of a mutual cultural influence. With the Eskimos it has varied in the different regions. The influence is most clearly seen where they have had a strong Indian culture at close quarters

and where the two peoples have lived under the same conditions. A typical example is that of the Kobuk Eskimos, the nearest neighbours of the mountain people. The Nunamiuts tell me
that their customs, songs, dances, etc., are much the same as
those of the Indians. Indeed, they call the Kobuk Eskimos *it-
qileârjuits,* which means "almost Indians."

Among the Nunamiuts, too, Indian influence can be traced,
but it does not appear to go deep. The old caribou-hunter culture has been strong enough to assert itself.

We were coming down from the mountains and making our
way through the moraines along the side of the valley. It had
been a good day in beautiful, wild country, and two caribou
had been shot.

We were about three miles from the settlement when Paniaq
stopped by a high sandhill and said: "It was here that the Indians buried their dead after the last great fight with the Nunamiuts. My great-grandfather, the great shaman Suwlo, was
in it."

We went up to the top of the sandhill and rested there. The
formation showed that digging must have been done there at
some time. Close by me lay a piece of caribou horn which
looked as if it had been used as a spade. There was also a wolverine trap made of stone and overgrown with moss.

Evening was coming on. Over the mountains to the west
drifted a mass of dark clouds, and through them a red sunset
showed only in stray gleams. Paniaq sat in silence for a little
while, looking out over the country. Then he began to tell of the
fight which had taken place about a hundred years before. It
was the traditional tribal narrative, concise and detailed.

It was in spring. Both the Nunamiuts and a party of Chandalar Indians had pitched camp in the Anaktuvuk Pass. For
once they tolerated one another, but relations gradually became
rather strained. One day some of the Eskimos carried off two

Indian girls who had been out collecting wood. The girls got back to their own camp, but the bitterness between the two peoples increased. The Nunamiuts no doubt thought it was an advantage to strike first, and this is what happened:

First they enticed four of the leading Indians out on some pretext. They killed them and then stormed the Indian camp, giving no quarter. An old Indian called on them to stop fighting; the Eskimos should have all the crystal beads in the camp if they would leave the Indians in peace. But the Eskimos thought it was more dangerous to stop half-way than to go on, and did not heed him. Then the old Indian shouted to the women: "Smash up all the crystal beads of our dead so that the Eskimos shall not get them." This was done, and Paniaq said that anyone who digs in the sandhill will find no crystal beads there, only bones.

From forty to sixty Indians were killed; a few escaped, and two women were made prisoners. The Nunamiuts lost only a few men. The prisoners married Eskimo husbands; one, whose name was Hirshi, was first Ula's wife, and after his death was taken over by Suwlo.

Paniaq's story was much fuller than what I have recorded here, with descriptions of episodes in the fight and portraits of a number of Eskimos who took part in it. There were, for example, Aguaqutsit, a queer fellow with an impediment in his speech, and Aqsiataujaq, who stumbled over a sleeping dog as he ran forward to shoot. Then, when an Indian aimed his bow at him, he covered his face with his hand. The arrow struck him in the armpit. Then came a long story about Aqsiataujaq's wife, who later rose from the dead twice. Paniaq, without hesitating, gave me the names of a number of the Eskimos who were in this affair—Makkalik, Angukak, Kiatsaun, Amoqîq, Ilawgâluk, Aguaqutsit, Kaunulak, Ula, Ularjuaq, the great singer Tatpâna, and many others. Of the Indians he named Qawâtik, Tâjûtsik, and Tûllik. Thus a detailed, living picture was formed of the whole event, although so long had passed since it happened.

But perhaps what emerged most strongly from the narrative was the portrait of the great medicine man Suwlo. He must have been a considerable and singular personality.

"He was dangerous to the enemy, but good to his own people," Paniaq said. "No one had such strong medicine. Through it he saw where the enemy was, and he had the power to kill people who were far off. His eyes were slanting like a hawk's, and he could also change himself into a hawk.

"Many people tried to shoot Suwlo, but he was so quick that he dodged the arrows. Many tried to seize hold of him, but he always slipped away. The coast Eskimos often tried to kill him with their medicine, but it was too weak against his. Once he and his son were pursued by Indians right down to the Colville River, and there they were driven out onto a point. Then Suwlo shouted: 'If anyone dares, come and fight!' But no one dared, although they were much stronger.

"Suwlo had such powers that he could go right through rock. Many Eskimos saw that once on the Colville River. They had pitched camp by a high projecting cliff. Suwlo and another great medicine man, Arnigasaujaq, set out to test which had the strongest medicine and could go right through the cliff. Suwlo tried first and soon came out on the other side. Arnigasaujaq only got a little way through the rock the first time he tried, but the second time he, too, succeeded."

Paniaq told this in his whimsical manner, not for a moment making any effort to convince me. Why should he? That a great medicine man could go through a rock was nothing remarkable in itself; everyone knew he could. It was the competition between the two that made the thing a story worth telling.

We were quiet for a while. Paniaq sat slightly bent forward, looking toward the mountains. There was a calm over his face and his head and shoulders—he seemed to be a part of the landscape. And it struck me as a matter of course that this shrewd descendant of Suwlo, this keen hunter, who had a greater feeling for nature than any of the others and such strong faith, would have been the people's great medicine man if times had not changed.

After a time he said thoughtfully: "A little way west, over toward the Killik River, there is a cave. Suwlo sometimes went into it. He stayed there quite by himself and got strength for his medicine."

"What happened to him in the end?" I asked.

"His enemies were always after his life, but no one could catch him. Suwlo could fend for himself like a wolf. He became old. At the end he lived by the Killik River. Then he went into the mountains one day and never came back."

This struck me as a bold way of meeting death for a man who had lived such a strong, independent life. I said something to this effect. But Paniaq shook his head and said: "He didn't die. I may tell you that he once had a strange experience. It was after a long hunt. He lay down to sleep on the ground under a high cliff. In his sleep he came to a settlement of strange people who received him hospitably. When he woke up, he found one white and one black feather on his anorak, and then he realized that he had been with mountain ptarmigan."

Paniaq gazed reflectively over the darkening wilds; then he said: "No, Suwlo didn't die. He went away to live with the mountain ptarmigan."

CHAPTER 1 4

Snow

When I looked out of the tent one morning, my eyes met a changed world; a soft layer of snow covered valley and mountain; only the precipice stared me in the face as black as ever. Snow! All the women suddenly got busy dressing skins and making winter clothes. Every single person must be fitted out anew from head to foot. Much of the work would not be done before the really cold days came, so it would have been expedient to start sooner. That this was not done was presumably due to an old superstition: The women must not start to make winter clothes till snow lies on the ground.

The men were each to have an outer anorak, with the hair outside, preferably of calf or heifer skin. Two white, wedge-shaped strips from the caribou's belly are let in over the chest. A white strip also runs round the sleeves and along the lower edge of the anorak. The anorak is trimmed with wolverine skin everywhere, the thickest being on the hood, which falls down closely over the face. Then comes an inner anorak, with the hair inside. The breeches also are of caribou skin.

The women wear a long, closely fastened caribou-skin coat, with the hair inside, edged with wolfskin. It is so wide at the back that there is room under the cloak for the baby, who is supported by the belt. The child's head projects from under the hood.

Kamiks, the footwear, reach almost to the knee. The soles are of thick skin from a bull caribou, with the hair clipped short and turned inward. The rest is made from the skin of the caribou's legs and hocks, and the hair can be either outside or inside. Socks and mittens also are of caribou skin and have the hair on the inside. Sometimes the skin of the mountain sheep is used.

For the anorak the skins of caribou which have been killed between the end of July and the end of August are used, those from the middle of August being considered best; for breeches and socks, the skins are from caribou killed between the end of August and the middle of September. Bulls' skins for the soles of shoes are thickest and toughest from the beginning of September to the end of October.

The caribou's cerebral matter or liver is used in dressing the skins; the technique is much the same as that of the Atabask Indians, but the skin is not smoked. Sometimes the footwear is saturated with the brown stain of alder bark. It is characteristic that the Nunamiuts do not use urine either for tanning or for washing their bodies, as was the custom of the coast Eskimos in the north. They speak with a certain contempt of the Barrow Eskimos, who used to do that kind of thing. One of the older hunters tells of a pretty "salt-water girl" he met at the great trade gathering at the mouth of the Colville River. "I should have seriously considered marrying her," he said, "but she smelt so strong of piss that I was quite put off."

The Nunamiut women are expert at tanning; the skins become so soft and white that it is a pleasure to see them. They are equally good at cutting out and sewing. They have a sure eye for an exact fit, and the cut of anoraks and cloaks is as good as a Paris dressmaker could make it. The threads used are strips from the caribou's dorsal sinews, and the sewing is done with very small, close stitches which are only just visible to the eye.

For me, too, a complete suit of winter clothes was to be made. The main part of the task I entrusted to Angayiq. She is a spinster just over forty, rather shy and old-maidish, but always pleasant and helpful. I went down to my tailor's tent with the necessary skins, and we talked over a few details concerning the clothes. When I had gone, I realized that we had forgotten to take any measurements, but I supposed that it was just that she did not think there was any hurry before the skins were dressed.

Time passed. Then I noticed that now and again Angayiq was glancing at me long and covertly. Oh well, old maids are like that, I thought, and plumed myself a little at the idea of having made an impression. The fact that some of the Eskimos were beginning to tease me about her suggested that this view of the case was correct. They thought it a tremendous joke.

Then one day I was called down to one of the tents. There, with others, Angayiq was sitting. I'm to be measured now, I thought; but no, she produced anorak, breeches, etc., all ready made. I tried the things on, and they all fitted perfectly. I then realized that she had been taking my measurements all this time in the capacity not of spinster, but of tailor.

Umialâq had something of a problem in making anoraks for her two rebellious sons, Kanigjaq and Kanayuq, respectively nine and seven years old. Each of them insisted that his anorak should not be finished later than the other's. So their mother had to work now on one anorak, now on the other, with the boys watching closely. Finally, she gave one last emphatic stitch to each anorak and handed the garments to her sons, who put them on immediately. They were an amusing sight, for the beasts' ears had been left on top of the hoods. The boys looked like two little caribou calves.

The Eskimos undergo a transformation when they put on

their new winter clothes of thick-haired, shining skin, which fall
so comfortably and easily about the body and are so splendidly
trimmed with wolf and wolverine skins. They seem to be in festive attire. Clothes like this enable them to overcome the
winter; the Eskimos look forward to it without the slightest fear
of the cold. If snowstorms come on suddenly, they sometimes
lie down in the snow and go to sleep. I myself have never had
warmer and more practical clothes in the polar regions. No
modern polar equipment is equal to them; the only disadvan-
tage is that the soft footwear is not suited to skis, for which hard
soles are necessary. The upper part can be of skin or felt.

The hunters have for some time dallied with their preparations for the winter, but now the work is progressing quickly.
Large bulls' skins, first laid in water and scraped clean of hair,
are cut up into long strips and hung up to dry along the willows.
They are to serve as ropes for lashing things onto sledges, and
many other purposes. The first cut is made in the middle of the
skin, and the cutting goes on in larger and larger circles so that
one skin makes one long strip. The Indian method is different
and less effective; they cut skins lengthwise into a number of
strips.

For the plaited work on snowshoes thinner strips are cut, and
the skin of the mountain sheep is considered to last about twice
as long as caribou skin. The snowshoes are round or pointed in
front and turned up sharply, on the whole very like those of the
Atabask Indians. They are made of birch and are about 4 feet
long and 9 inches wide at the broadest point. Their manufac-
ture is a fine art. The Nunamiuts use a curved knife with a shaft
of caribou horn (see the photograph following page 120); it is
used with the hand turned upward toward the body. Holes are
made with the bow drill, which is most effective. The "needle"
used in the plaiting is a small bone of the mountain sheep.

The snowshoe is a necessity in the mountains, where the
snow is frequently troublesome despite the wind. Skis have

great advantages, but are alien to Nunamiut culture; I myself have used them and have been delighted with them when hunting caribou and wolf in the valleys and on the long downward slopes of the mountainsides.

The largest sledges are about 11 feet long by 1 foot 9 inches wide, are made of fir-wood, and have high, solid runners, uprights at the rear, a handle for steering, and a roughly constructed iron brake. There are only two of the typical Alaska sledges (basket sledges) here. They have thin runners and a slanting lattice-work from the uprights back to the point of the sledge, so that the cargo lies as if it were in a basket. Many of the sledges are coloured red with a dye which the Eskimos find in the mountains.

The Nunamiut sledges were formerly of a different type, rather small (*napulgit*). In those days the people had few dogs, and it was customary for women and men to help draw the sledges. Dogs' food was a much greater problem in those somewhat primitive times.

The Nunamiuts' old type of sledge, *napulgit,* which is no longer in use. It was usually about 10 feet long.—Drawn by the Eskimo Paniaq.

What a commotion when the dogs are harnessed for the first time! Excited and frolicsome, they set off at full gallop, and one has to hold on tight and steer skilfully as the heavy sledge sways and skids behind them. The dogs are harnessed in pairs along a common central trace, the leader in front. They are directed by voice: *hâ* means left, *dsji* right, and *who* stop. The Nunamiuts

are good dog-drivers, and unlike many Indians they treat their
animals well; most of them do not even carry a whip. This good
treatment is reflected in the dogs; their bushy tails stand up
straight and there is an air of cheerful self-confidence about
them.

Paniaq has about twenty dogs, and I am allowed to use any I
like. They are a lively band of good-humoured rascals, some of
them big beasts of incredible strength. We soon became excellent friends. The best leader is called Inugwik; he is chalk-
white and an unusually beautiful animal. Then there is the
greyish-brown Alâsin, named after one of the dogs which belonged to Paniaq's great-grandfather, the great medicine man
Suwlo: a dignified, somewhat reserved dog. Sigjik (ground
squirrel) is coal-black with kindly brown eyes, always playful
and lively though no longer young. Qunngiq (tame reindeer)
is also black all over, a splendid dog but rather more temperamental. Sulukpak (large wing-feather) is half wolf, a long
brownish animal with a hanging tail, an excellent draught dog,
and no harder to manage than the others except when hunting
caribou, when he becomes completely wild. Running loose over
the countryside he looks like a wolf; he runs fully extended
close to the ground, and his action is peculiarly supple and
graceful. All the two hundred dogs are tied up near our tents,
and when they set up a howling concert ours make a respectable
contribution.

The snow melts, then more snow falls. Sometimes there are
raw, soaking-wet days, with sleet and slush. But the very nastiest
weather does not seem to trouble the Eskimos much. Paniaq
and Agmâlik's experience on a wolf hunt lasting several days is
an example of this. They heard the howling of wolves far off
among the mountains and set off precipitately without giving
themselves time to put on their full skin clothing. After a time
they caught sight of the animals out on a plain, a mother and

five cubs eating a dead caribou. The ground offered no cover of any kind, so it was out of the question to creep up on them unnoticed. It then occurred to them to pretend to be bears, for beasts of prey are not usually very shy of one another. They crawled on all fours toward the wolves, which glanced up at them now and again, but went on feeding. At last they were within range and brought down the mother and one cub. The rest fled.

Paniaq and Agmâlik followed the trail for several hours. Suddenly the weather grew thick and a blinding blizzard came on. Some beasts rose just in front of them; they fired at random into the murk and brought down two. They proved to be caribou. Evening came on and the awful weather continued. The Eskimos built a wall of stones and sat down for the night under the lee of it, wet through and cold. They made themselves breeches of a sort from the caribou skins with the needles and thread they always carried. Then they ate some raw meat, and Paniaq fell asleep. Agmâlik, who is not quite so hardened, sat up shivering all night.

When morning came, they continued the wolf hunt, followed the trail far into the mountains, came within range again, and brought down two beasts. Then at last they set off homeward. After a time they came upon the fresh tracks of a grizzly bear, turned away at once, and began to hunt it. But they were short of food, and set a course for the settlement again. When they reached it they had been away five days. They spent the night there and in the morning set off again to continue the bear hunt; this animal, too, they succeeded in shooting.

In the evenings the hunters often sit together in one of the tents and talk of old times. I hear many curious tales of hunting, fighting, and adventures generally. The Eskimos do not tell these stories only in answer to my questions; they themselves delight in recalling bygone days. Indeed, the various events

which took place long ago, and the persons connected with
them, are more than just ancient history; they are described
with as much wealth of detail and clarity as if they had happened only the other day. Many dead hunters have their portraits painted so vividly that I seem to know them.

One evening Paniaq told us of the occasion when the Nuña-
miuts saw the first flintlock musket. It was during the trade
gathering at the mouth of the Colville River. An Eskimo from
Point Barrow brought it in; he had obtained it from some people
on board a Russian ship. Then the inland people's great shaman
Alunirjûjaq put his medicine on the gun. The Barrow man was
unable to fire a single shot. He had to beg the shaman to take
away the medicine. Alunirjûjaq did so, but not till he had made
the other promise not to endanger people's lives brandishing the
gun about.

"Alunirjûjaq was Maptirâq's grandfather," Paniaq added.
"He was bought as a boy from some Eskimos in the south.
Many children were bought and sold in the old times. My father
was offered a gun for me, but he wouldn't sell. Alunirjûjaq came
to a bad end, by the way. He had a quarrel with a great woman
shaman. They fought each other with medicine. First they crippled each other, and then they killed each other's children."

Then I hear detailed accounts of the fighting which took
place between the Nunamiuts and the Barrow people (called
utquearvingmiut or *qakmalit*) and with other Eskimo tribes
along the coast.

"Why all this fighting with the coast Eskimos?" I enquire.

"They are different," Kakinnâq replies.

"From where do the Nunamiuts come?"

"We have always lived inland, even before the great flood."

I have been given a new name. "You shall be called Ikâksaq,"
Kakinnâq said with a smile, "for your face is almost exactly like
his." Ikâksaq was a well-known hunter who died some years

ago, a relative of Maptirâq. He was obviously a capable fellow; a good many stories are told about him. The Eskimos emphasize that he had a strikingly long face and fair skin.

All the children are vastly amused at this rechristening. "Ikâksaq! Ikâksaq!" they shout in joyful chorus.

I have seldom heard the Eskimos use the term "white man" (*tannik*) in speaking to or of me. From the very first they endeavoured to pronounce my real name correctly; it required some effort at first. In giving me another they are acting in accordance with Nunamiut tradition; most of them have several names, the first being given at birth, the others later.

From ancient times the name has had its own soul, which goes on living when it is transferred to another person, or, indeed, to a mountain or other object. How far the Nunamiuts thought that some element of the dead Ikâksaq lived on in me, I cannot say. In any case I felt myself in good company with the old hunter's "name-soul."

The children carry on with their games, a number of which are ancient and traditional. Here, as in the civilized world, they change with the seasons. Indoors, the game with willow sticks is now very popular. A number of small sticks are laid on the back of the hand and thrown up in the air, and only one stick at a time must be caught. The player who catches the most wins.

Equally popular is the game which is called *ayarayagaqtut* (string-figure or cat's-cradle). A sinew with the ends tied together is placed round both hands, which are held a little way apart. Then, by different kinds of finger-grip, the most varied figures are made with this double string. It is incredible what they can do; the figures represent now human beings, now a caribou, bear, or wolf, a crystal bead, or a lip-plate (*labret*). And that is not all, they make the figures move along; two polar bears chase a fleeing man, overtake him, and kill him; a hunter dashes off in pursuit of a caribou, and so on. Each living picture is accompanied by a running commentary, and the whole thing becomes a kind of marionette theatre. Some of the grown-ups play this game, too, and are always greatly amused by the performance.

But one must be very careful not to play games of this kind in summer, for if one does, the little devil Erâq may come and kill everyone in the tent. The Eskimos say that a family had a narrow escape once at Raven Lake. A little boy was sitting in the tent playing with sinews, although his parents had said that he must never do so in the light time. Suddenly they heard a rushing noise, and there was Erâq coming through the air. He went round the tent once and then stood in the doorway. In a moment they would all have been lost, but luckily the boy had the presence of mind to make with the strings the figure of a crystal bead and then that of a labret, affording protection against evil. The little devil felt his power diminishing, slipped out of the tent, and rose again into the air.

The children are not so standardized as in the civilized world, where from an early age the mind is forced into definite channels. In the wilderness the infant mind is allowed to develop freely in its own way, like the wild flowers in the soil. There is no formal upbringing, and yet perhaps more real formation of character than in a civilized community. These children are wild creatures indeed, but full of fresh unfolding life and without a trace of malice.

From the time I got to know them, I have had continual visits. These youngsters are continually invading my tent, where they have by now established their rule. For that matter, they teach me a good deal about the language, games, and customs. They also try, with great patience and much laughter, to teach me some of their songs, but they do not find me a very good pupil. I try again and again, but find it impossible to master the peculiar Eskimo pitch properly.

After I have failed dismally the children often insist on my singing something from my own country. I am no singer, but there is no getting out of it. So I give them some Norwegian folk-songs. These are most successful, and one or two of them the children learn fairly quickly. There is one which they like particularly, and it has become a real hit. Now they sing it in chorus, in Norwegian, till it rings across the mountains.

CHAPTER 1 5

The Caribou Trail

The last flight of geese is disappearing southward. It is becoming chillier. The river and lakes are acquiring a fringe of ice; little pools and trickling becks are freezing over. The snow has its wintry dryness and has now decided to remain. There is not much of it except along the mountaintops, where all is white, but enough for a sledge to run on. It is October.

An important event is now imminent. Very soon the southward autumn migration of the caribou from the tundra to the mountains will begin. Great herds will go through the Anaktuvuk Pass during a comparatively short time. The Eskimos will then have to shoot sufficient caribou bulls, which until the mating season are very fat, to ensure our main fat requirements for the winter. Later the beasts become skinny, and without sufficient fat, people on a meat diet throughout a long, cold winter are in an awkward position.

One day there was unrest in the camp; three families began to pack their things and strike their tents. They had suddenly got it into their heads to seek a new dwelling place. Soon the sledges were disappearing along the valley. Another day passed, and there was a general breaking up. No one had given any orders; the Eskimos had not assembled to discuss the matter—some had gone, and others were infected. This is characteristic of the Nunamiuts; many of their most important decisions may be taken in an equally casual manner.

There is bustle and activity when an old camping ground is left in this way. The dogs tug at their chains, knowing quite well what is afoot. Grown-ups and children run to and fro, busily collecting the family possessions. They have an incredible quantity of caribou skins and other things, and it is equally incredible that room can really be found for them all on the sledges. The last thing to be loaded is the bundle of long, curved tent-posts, which stick up into the air on top of the load. Finally the whole family crawls about on the willow floor, poking among the twigs to see if anything has been mislaid.

Off they went, one family after another. The settlement by Raven Lake had been wiped off the face of the earth.

Our course was southwest, toward the other side of the valley. We had therefore to cross the Anaktuvuk River, which was not yet frozen. Qawwik, who was among the first starters, was unlucky here; he got into deep water, the dogs became entangled in their harness, and two of them were drowned.

We started at different times, and I happened to be driving alone, followed by the little boy Kanigjaq. After a time I reached the river. I stood where the trail ended and peered out over the chilly black water. Kanigjaq followed my hesitation with indulgent interest; then he pointed to the river and said, "Fine!" So saying, he splashed gleefully out into the ice-cold water, which reached to his waist. From time to time he turned toward me laughing, beating the surface of the water with his hands and having the greatest fun.

I put the film things into my rucksack and drove the dogs straight into the river. Sometimes they found a slight foothold, and sometimes they had to swim, while I waded behind them, steering the sledge, which either fizzed ahead or put its nose under like a waterlogged barge. Then we came to a flat place with a few scattered willows, close to a small lake. Here smoke was rising cheerfully into the air. This was Imairniq (the dried-up place), our new settlement. My eyes rejoiced to see dry willow sticks round about. Just behind the camp the valley sloped gently to the foot of the mountain. It was undulating moraine country with hard-trampled caribou tracks on which the beasts might be expected shortly. During the autumn trek there is usually a thicker stream of animals on this side of the valley.

In civilization one usually lives year after year in the same place, sweeping and washing and trying to keep away the dirt. Here it is rather different; we go away from the dirt. Our homes spring up on virgin ground, and on the floor we spread a fresh layer of sweet-smelling willow boughs. The eyes can take pleasure in a new view, and it gives a feeling of security to know that here there are new chances of obtaining fuel and warmth. When in the grey dawn we sling our guns across our backs, there is also something uncommonly pleasant about roaming over a new hunting ground. Yes, indeed, nomad life has its joys.

This year the Killik people had joined the Raven people. During the summer they had come over the mountains on foot; sledges and other winter equipment had been left behind in the camp at the sources of the Killik River. These things now had to be fetched. Some time ago a number of the younger men had decided to go, but the days passed and no one went. I asked why they were delaying, and they replied: "We're going to-morrow." Ten days later I heard that they were going to start next morning—then at last they set off, with a string of pack-dogs swaying at their heels.

Piliala was to be one of the party, but he took the affair very casually and remained in the camp till early midday. I said something about its being hard work for him to catch up to his

comrades, but the Eskimos smiled and said there was no difficulty about that, for he flew over the mountains like the wind. I
watched him when he set off. He glided forward with a supple
gait over rough ground and smooth, and pushed on without
slackening till I could only just see him as a black speck far
away across the hummocks.

The return trip would take ten days. As they had started so
late, it was doubtful whether they would get back to the settlement before the caribou came. It was hoped that this would not
matter much, for if the beasts came in their usual numbers, the
men's relations would have no difficulty in shooting as many fat
bulls as the families needed.

Those of us remaining behind now ranged far and wide up
the valley and into the mountains, on the lookout for caribou
all the time. The wilds have something fresh and fascinating
about them after the snow has spread its white carpet over
stones and rubble. It is like a picture book with droll animal
drawings, each telling its own story. Wolf, wolverine, fox,
ermine, and the rest, which were always around us unseen, but
of which we had only found occasional traces, now betrayed
themselves by their plain trails in the snow. We suddenly learnt
that there were numbers of red foxes in the neighbourhood;
hard trampled tracks in the snow led to the remains of a dead
caribou a little way from the settlement. On the hillside behind
us were rows of the bear-like footprints of a wolverine, which
could be seen a long way off. And in one place a wolf had been
fairly close to the camp, sniffing after a bitch that was in heat.
Wolf trails crossed the valley in every direction. A bear or two
was still about, and the ground squirrel was bustling about, although the time was come for it to settle down to its winter
sleep.

It was clear that the wolves were interested in a big moose
which had its abode a little to the south. It stood, no doubt, in
the densest part of some willow thicket, where it was safe. If the

wolves tried to get at it in there, they would come to a bad end. The moose would then rush through the thicket and fling the wolves against the trees. In the open it would be a different story; there a flock of wolves can deal with a moose without difficulty, even if the chase lasts some time.

The Eskimos are not troubling to hunt this moose, although it would be fairly easy to get it. In the course of the year they have allowed moose to pass several times, although they could have brought down a number without difficulty. As long as there are caribou enough the Nunamiuts are content.

In contrast to the Indians they care little for moose skin and rarely dress it. Formerly they sometimes used an extra outer sole of moose skin, but no one in the camp finds that practical. They consider that the sole gets too stiff, and it is easy for frost and damp to get onto the upper side. Moose skin is used chiefly for ropes.

Sometimes, too, a camp sledge (*qamûn*) is made from it. First, holes are cut along the edge for the rope which is to make the load fast; then the damp skin is forced down into a depression in the snow, shaped roughly like a bath. When the skin is frozen, the sledge is complete. It makes a smart little toboggan which slides beautifully on its smooth hair bottom.

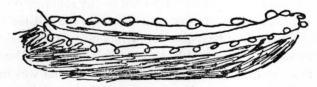

Sledge made of frozen moose skin (*qamûn*).—Drawn by the Eskimo Paniaq.

We are seeing more of the ravens than before—no doubt they find it a good idea to follow us when the snow keeps them short of food, for where we are there are always scraps of meat. "There's my uncle," Kakinnâq often says when he sees a raven close by, and has a good laugh. The uncle's name was Tulugaq (raven). This does not prevent him from shooting his uncle down when he feels inclined. The Eskimos firmly believe that the raven is a bird with strange powers. It is, as I have said, one of the chief figures in their mythology. But they have no scruples about killing it, any more than they refrain from shooting wolf or bear, which also have their souls and are personified in the old legends. The idea is that the animal's soul lives on and that it does not hurt it to be killed. On the other hand, the view is that the soul is offended if various ceremonies are not punctiliously observed. Any neglect in this respect might later cause bad hunting or other misfortunes.

One day I came upon fresh tracks of a large grizzly bear near the remains of a caribou which had been killed by a pack of wolves. There followed a long and tiring trail westward, into regions where I had not been before. What a fascinatingly wild and beautiful country! Mountain after mountain, a network of valleys, dark ravines with boulders and caves, and in the background snow-clad peaks like shining white spires.

Following a trail like this for hour after hour demands patience. From time to time the thought occurs to one, "Perhaps the beast will never stop at all." And I began to think of my return journey, and to fear that darkness would set in long before the settlement was reached. But fresh bear tracks in the newly fallen snow have an inspiring effect which overcomes all fatigue.

At last I saw his big, blackish-brown bulk moving up a mountain slope. But how was I to get near him? Above the slope rose a sheer precipice, and below it, beyond a flat piece of ground, came a steep drop toward the river. In other words, the slope was a closed area with just one approach, and that right under the precipice, the way the bear had gone. That would be all right if the wind were not in the wrong direction. But in any case the animal would have to take the same route back, and then there might be some hope of getting close to him.

Cautiously I stole forward. Then the bear suddenly rose on his hind legs and sniffed. What a magnificent great beast! I fired and missed. The bear dashed at full speed up the slope, then realized that the precipice was unscalable, swung round, and made off straight down the slope toward the drop. Suddenly he realized the danger and sat down hard on his rump to stop himself. But the slope was too steep and his pace too fast; he tumbled right over onto the ice-covered river. I did not see him come down, but it must have been a hard bump. A little later Bruin was lumbering along the moraine on the other side of the river.

Thus I was foiled of a magnificent skin and a skull of some scientific interest, but I did not feel any special bitterness about it. It was an amusing episode.

The country round is now practically empty of caribou, only an occasional small herd is to be seen. Aguk came upon six bulls at the foot of a cliff and killed three. They proved to be footsore beasts which presumably had failed to keep up. This happens fairly often; the continuous swift movement over rock and scree is very hard on the hooves. Sometimes they are torn; at other times sharp stones become fixed in them. Beasts which are injured in this way usually join forces. It is a curious thing that they generally lose the skin of their antlers much later than usual; we shot beasts like this as late as the beginning of November, and the bulls' antlers were still covered.

The cold is increasing. The river and the little pool close to the camp are covered with crystal-clear ice. The children were out upon it at once and are having great fun with a slide. They get up full speed while still on the shore and sail far out onto the ice. Sometimes they lie down on their stomachs, press their noses against the ice, and gaze down into the strange world of long-stemmed water plants and small creatures. Sometimes they catch sight of a fish, even a big one. Then they shriek with delight, and the rest of the children come tearing along and throw themselves down on their stomachs.

Bought food has come to an end. Next, the people have run out of tobacco; only a few have a little left. Some still have a little gasoline for their lamps, but most are out of that, too. We are lighting the tents in the old fashion, by burning caribou fat, using moss or scraps of cloth as wicks. There is not much dried meat either, and of fish there is practically none except for a few half-rotten ones which are to be eaten as a delicacy on special occasions. In short, we are living from hand to mouth. But crowds of fat caribou may come along any day, and then we shall be well off.

Last year the great southward migration began as early as the end of September, and it is now the end of October. Our eyes are turned northward. When we assemble in one of the tents of an evening, we talk endlessly about what can have happened. The trek of the caribou through the Anaktuvuk Pass is an annual event, but sometimes, very rarely, the herds do not appear. In the most favourable event this can be due to a local shift of the migration; the beasts may make their way into other valleys, westward for preference. Then the Eskimos are baulked of the fat they so sorely need; nevertheless there may be meat enough later on, for when the migration is over the herd usually trickles into most of the larger valleys. But sometimes, as I have said, the caribou suddenly and inexplicably remain absent from the whole mountain system.

Kakinnâq tells of the terrible year when the caribou failed altogether; it must have been at the beginning of the century. He was a boy then and lived with his father on the Sagavarniktok River. Five Eskimos starved to death there. Farther west, in the Anaktuvuk Pass, on the Killik River, and in other places, people died, too. Most of them were relatives of his and of Paniaq and Maptirâq. The last-named was just married at that time and remembered it all well. He can tell of similar earlier tragedies.

The days pass. The scouts who go out in every possible direction return with the same depressing reports. As far as we can reach into the valleys and mountains there is hardly a living creature to be seen. At last we cannot ignore the bald fact—*the caribou are not coming.*

CHAPTER 16

On the Trail

Paniaq lit his willow-wood pipe and said: *"Tainnagaluakkeatak qanuqsausîtsuq,"* meaning roughly, "It's no use crying over spilt milk." This is his regular expression when some irremediable misfortune overtakes him. But the situation is serious; he has a wife, four children, and twenty dogs, who have no food except what he can get by hunting. He wraps himself in a cloak of stoicism and refuses to worry.

The country is empty; not one caribou is to be seen, although we range far and wide. So we must move camp again. For such is the Nunamiuts' existence, a nomad life on the trail of the caribou.

We are now moving southward, along the valley for some distance, to a fresh patch of willows. Here we pitch our tents in a sheltered little spot under the lee of a round sandhill. This camping ground is called Kanngûmawik, i.e., meeting place, and the Nunamiuts have been accustomed to dwell here from ancient times. The name is derived from intercourse with the Indians; this is the place where the Eskimos often met them. They were here with the Chandalar Indians a short time before the bloody battle a little farther north in the Anaktuvuk Pass, an encounter which was described earlier in this book.

As we began to pitch the tents, the children swarmed round inquisitively, as they do at every new camping ground. They are incredibly observant and are continually discovering something funny. Suddenly an eager band came running up, pulled me aside, and pointed to something white in the moss. It was a skull. They picked it up and burst into roars of laughter at the sight of a wisp of moss which had grown fast to the chin and looked like a green beard. Then they began to kick the skull about. There are no inhibitions here; on the contrary, it is great fun to play football with a human head.

I examined the skull. There were a couple of damaged teeth; the others must have fallen out when wolf and fox had gnawed it. The temples projected rather boldly, and there was strength about the jaws. Eskimo or Indian? Perhaps he was a hunter. Not a soul now was interested in all the queer things which had gone on in the delicate network of nerves inside the skull. The hunter's excitement on the trail, his happiness in his tent, life among wife and children, cares, fear of the powers—all the mass of details which make up a human being were gone with the wind. The man had presumably died during his stay at this old camping ground. It was the custom in former times for the people to leave the dead man in his tent or turf hut and to move to another place. If a death occurred while the tribe was on the move, the corpse was left where it had fallen, sometimes covered with caribou skin. Equipment, weapons, etc., were laid by its side.

I carefully scraped away the snow where my tent was to be pitched. As I drove the spade down into the rich layer of moss, it struck something hard. I tried at other spots, and there appeared to be a level, hard floor where one would not expect to find anything of the sort. I peeled away a quantity of moss and found a rotten willow-bough floor: a family had had its tent there long ago.

The earth was frozen, so it was useless to try to dig any deeper, but I found a few trifles in the remains of the willow-bough floor—for example, some pieces of broken pots. The Nunamiuts used formerly to make clay pots for various purposes, among them for cooking meat. For this they were first filled with water, and red-hot stones were then dropped into them.

Pottery had its own technique. The clay was mixed with blood, ashes, and fine ptarmigan feathers or moss, and then laid round a form made of plaited willow twigs. When the clay was dry the form was taken out. It was important to use the right sort of clay. This was found in the Noatak area, so it was mainly the Nunamiuts living in the western regions who carried on pottery. The Eskimos still possess the art; they say it is an easy matter to make pots if they only have good materials.

I found a flint scraper, too, and a small piece of jade. This kind of stone was of the greatest importance in old times as material for implements. The Nunamiuts had flint enough; jade they acquired from the Kobuk Eskimos, in whose territory it occurs in considerable quantities. Beaten copper, which was imported from eastward, was also used to some extent.

Finally, I found a green bead of rock crystal. The owner must certainly have deeply regretted the loss, for this was about the most valuable thing an Eskimo owned. Not only was it a pretty ornament, but it also had magic power. Its price was high; only the finest skins would buy it.

The Nunamiuts had three kinds of rock-crystal beads—the green, the blue, and the white, which was called by the pretty name "tear." The women wore them in a string round the neck, in the ears, or in the nose; the men, in a strap round the forehead. They were also worked into labrets, belts, knife handles, etc. It is uncertain where they came from; a certain amount of evidence speaks for Siberia.

There is a legend of a woman who could not live with her husband. She left him and came to a strange land. There she saw a high mountain. Suddenly an opening appeared in it, and she went in. Roof, walls, and floor gleamed with crystal beads. She filled a skin bag and went out. The mountain closed behind her. Then she caught sight of a man fishing through the ice, and a strange feeling came over her. Suddenly he rose into the air, the fish-hook caught fast in her cloak, and she was carried with him through the air. They came down to earth just by his tent. She became the strange man's wife and had many children. So it was that crystal beads came to the Nunamiuts.

Agmâlik did not pitch his tent, but moved with his family into a turf hut close by. He had built it the year before, when the people spent a long time at this site. It is spacious and warm. The Nunamiuts have used the turf hut (*iwjulik*) from ancient times, mainly when it has seemed that they could remain a long time in one place. The older form was different from the present and was of three related types: long, with entrance on the long side (*akilliri*), long, with entrance on the short side (*siwunmuktaq*), and a more rectangular type about half as large as these (*iglupiaqtaqlik*).

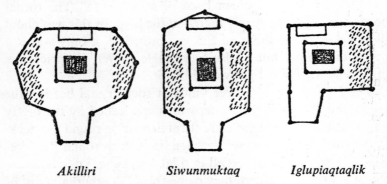

| *Akilliri* | *Siwunmuktaq* | *Iglupiaqtaqlik* |

Old types of turf house, seen from above. The black rectangle is the fireplace, behind it is a shelf for meat; the dotted area is the space for sleeping and sitting.—From a drawing by the Eskimo Paniaq.

The general principle was the same in all three types. In the centre of the hut four posts were rammed down into a small square and bound together above with horizontal cross-stakes. Outside this, and at a distance depending on the size of the hut, a number of shorter willow stakes were driven down into the ground. Each of them had an upturned fork formed of two boughs. Cross-stakes rested in the forks the whole way round. From there, sloping upward to the inner square, lay stakes packed close together; this was the roof. A close line of stakes also rose from the ground and rested aslant against the outer cross-stakes; these were the walls. The whole was covered with slabs of frozen moss (see drawing on p. 160).

The fireplace lay within the four stakes in the middle of the hut. Behind the fireplace was a shelf made of willow boughs (*quleruat*); on this the meat was placed. The sleeping places might vary somewhat according to the type of hut. The entrance had a passage on a level with the willow-bough floor; this did *not* go underground either wholly or partly, as with the coast Eskimos and others.

Sometimes, too, the frame of the turf house was constructed on the same principles as that of the dome-shaped tent. In that case the long curved willow branches were not dried, but bound together while they were fresh. A turf house of this type is called *qalurwigaq*.

One is constantly coming across old settlements in the Brooks Mountains, but the really old ones, overgrown as they are, are difficult to locate. On most of them tents or turf houses have stood, but now and then ruins of stone huts are seen; thus there are said to be one or two on the eastern side of the Anaktuvuk Pass. As I have said, stone huts are believed to date from the earliest Indians.

It is not so easy to find objects left by a nomad people, even if an old settlement is located. The Nunamiuts continually followed the caribou, seldom stayed long in one place, and were,

moreover, extremely careful to take their scanty belongings
with them. It was also their fixed custom in former times never
to live in an old turf house, but to build a new one every year,
sometimes several, according to the number of times they
moved.

The old type of turf house which the Nunamiuts call *akilliri*. In order
that the construction may be seen, only part of the turf roof has been
drawn.—From a drawing by the Eskimo Paniaq.

From an archaeological standpoint the Brooks Mountains
and the regions nearest to them are virgin soil. I might mention
that a Folsom arrowhead has been found on the Utukok River,
which shows that the very ancient Folsom people roamed
these parts. There are strong grounds for believing that archaeological investigations in the Nunamiut country would
throw light on problems ranging over a wide field.

We are now living for the most part on the remains of what
we shot earlier, eking this out with dried meat. Sometimes we
eat a wolf's recent kill.

At last one caribou has been shot, and it happened in a rather

Agmâlik, a little over fifty

Aqarwik and the Author

amusing way. Paniaq and I had been out on a fairly long hunting expedition and were returning to camp empty-handed and in low spirits. We were about a hundred yards from the willow thicket and the tents when suddenly a shot rang out just in front of us. We perceived nothing at the moment, but when we looked round a big bull caribou was lying just behind us, kicking up the snow in his death agony. And from behind a bush came the smiling Kakinnâq, gun in hand. The beast must have come up suddenly from the river just after we had crossed it.

The caribou which had been killed behind our backs was the cause of much chaffing and amusement; Paniaq and I were fine hunters indeed: we had been into the mountains hunting and had ourselves been hunted home to camp by a caribou bull.

During the day I noticed a small group of little girls sitting in a close circle, occupied with something which must surely be very important. I took a peep at them, and they were sitting round the caribou's stomach. They were cutting off pieces of skin, cleaning them a very little with a knife, and swallowing them. They looked up, chewing. Alasuq cut off a specially large piece of skin and handed it to me. It was a gift, and they expected me to value it. And I did.

One day we caught sight of a black streak gliding along far off in the valley: a man with a dog-sledge. The outlines grew clearer, and soon the team rushed in between the tents. It was Qawwik, one of the Killik hunters who had gone off to the people's settlement on the Killik River to fetch the winter equipment that had been left there. The others, who had been held up somewhat in getting the sledges into good shape, might be expected in a short time.

Qawwik is a brisk, stocky fellow of about thirty-five. He likes to be well turned out and make a good impression, and talks rather more often than the others about his dogs being the best. In the civilized world he might well be "a well-dressed man about town." He has a little black moustache, and unlike the others, wears a very dashing wolfskin anorak. This is a great luxury in the way of clothes, for it requires three skins, and for them he could have got a good deal of ammunition and tobacco by plane. He badly needs these things, for he is on his beam-ends like all the rest.

Qawwik went into one of the tents, taking with him meat from the sledge. People crowded in, and he sat there and was the central figure. He was a traveller from afar; there hung about him an aura of distant mountains and varied adventures. A hunter had come racing into camp full of new impressions—in itself quite an event.

Yes, they had come upon caribou far to the westward, tens of thousands of them. About Chandler Lake in particular there were multitudes. This was more or less what we had thought, but what should we do? Could it be of any use to go so far after them, or were our chances equally good if we kept to the regions farther east in the hope that the beasts would soon trickle in through the valleys?

Soon all the Killik hunters were back from the long journey. When the Eskimos come or go, they never use any greeting. This applies also to visits in the tents. When a party of men breaks up late in the evening, one suddenly sees a back at the bearskin door; one's guest has gone without a word.

When anyone has been on a long journey, he must be told as quickly as possible if any disasters have taken place while he has been away. Indeed, it is often customary to let him know by smoke signals before he even reaches the camp. If two fires are lighted so that the pillars of smoke run parallel before the wind, it means that two people are ill or dead. In this way, too, a man who is out on a fairly short trip can be recalled from hunting to take care of his family. The Nunamiuts also use smoke signals to report where the caribou are.

The busy little ground squirrels have all gone down into their holes now to begin their winter sleep, and the marmot, too. Fat and plump, most of the grizzly bears have also gone into hibernation. But ermine, wolf, wolverine, and fox have donned thick, glossy fur and are quite in their element in the mountains on the bitterly cold days.

The wind has swept away most of the snow, but there is enough for a sledge, though neither snowshoes nor skis can be used. Over wide areas the ground is an uneven mass of fairly high tussocks ("niggerheads"), frozen hard. This is slippery and difficult going, especially on returning to camp tired on a dark evening. But we take these and other difficulties patiently; they are a part of daily life in the wilds. Many things become a habit, and what is most important is to grow accustomed to accepting unpleasantness as part of the day's work.

The one and only thing which matters is caribou. After hunting at every point of the compass, we have established that the animals are not in our neighbourhood. So we must try another place, and push ahead until we fall in with the herds. We are to strike camp.

CHAPTER 1 7

At the Sources
of the Rivers

The sledges were loaded and the
women were busy harnessing the
excited dogs. Sledge after sledge sped out toward a new place
which might give new hope of caribou.

It was a fine sunny day, just cold enough, and the air was
clear as we pushed on into the mountains. We steered south, for
the most part following the course of the river, where the snow
was quite blown away. The sledges sped along on the crystal-
clear ice, slipping sideways now and again while the dogs strug-
gled to gain a foothold.

We were a queer procession as we drove along. First came
the hunter, with the big, heavily laden sledge, drawn by eight or
ten dogs. Then came the wife, with a sledge nearly as large, the
baby on her back and as a rule another child sitting on top of
the load. After her came the little wooden sledge, drawn by a
couple of dogs and driven by a small boy. Behind came the rest
of the children, running. There was liveliness and laughter all
along the line. Sometimes the girls perched themselves on the
loads in couples; they had profound secrets to chatter about and

plenty to giggle at. Now and again the procession was held up when there was trouble with harness or when a sledge skidded. Then a crowd of children dashed off to the river bank and began to hunt for small polished stones. When the dogs started again with a jerk, the children raced after them, their little legs going like drumsticks.

But far in the rear the puppy Animik came struggling along. Chalk-white, he was only a few months old. To run fast on slippery ice was terribly hard work for so small a puppy; he puffed and panted, with his tongue hanging far out of his mouth, and now and then whined pitifully. Soon he was only a black dot far behind us.

Close to the watershed (*narjaq*) we find a patch of willows, and we choose the outskirts of this for our new settlement. Here we are, hard by the sources of two long watercourses, the Anaktuvuk River, which winds northward along the wide pass toward the tundra and the Arctic Ocean, and the John River, which rushes southward toward the forests and finally joins the Koyukuk River in the Indian country.

Here there is varied and splendid scenery and a much wider view than before, for this is the place where many valleys meet. Northeastward runs the wide Anaqteqtuaq Valley. As a sentry at its mouth, a high curiously shaped mountain bulks large and attracts more attention than all its neighbours. Heaps of stones, sharply separated from one another, run up the coal-black slopes. They stand out as peculiar-looking strips of greenish hue. They have caused the mountain to be given the name Napâqtuâluit (the Mountain with the Old Trees). Southeastward runs Inukpasugjuk (Giants' Valley). Other valleys go westward.

Thus our settlement is favourably situated, for all these features of the landscape increase the chance of game finding its way to our hunting grounds. The autumn trek of the caribou is of course long past, and the beasts are now wandering far and wide over the mountains in herds of different sizes.

But something is wrong. Day after day we range far over the countryside in every direction but see nothing but one or two small herds of lean bulls. A few animals are brought down, and we keep going more or less, but meals are scanty for both men and dogs.

The shortage of fat is now becoming serious. The only form of fat we have is the marrow in the bones; it is eaten raw and is a dish more delicious in times like these than words can describe. But as a caribou has only four legs and few beasts are shot, not much of this delicacy comes the way of each individual. No, a diet of tough caribou meat with practically no fat becomes dismal after a time. It is a diet which gives one the same empty feeling under the breastbone as when one has nothing to eat at all. We can eat almost unlimited quantities without feeling satisfied. One's condition suffers accordingly; one feels the cold more: I have to make an effort to do things which otherwise would have been easy.

"It's rather like eating moss," Paniaq says with a smile as we attack the tough meat. And when we are out hunting together and look out from the heights over a wide area and do not see a living creature on the snow, only cold and nakedness as far as the eye can reach, he sometimes says in his dry manner: "A hungry land."

It is becoming common to borrow meat from one another. Here the Eskimos' sense of duty toward their nearest relations is clearly shown. When the hunter returns to the settlement with game, his wife immediately cuts off a few good portions of meat and gives them to her parents and parents-in-law. This diminishes the uncertainty which attaches to a single hunter's bag. In a way the community functions in hard times like a kind of mutual benevolent society.

I, too, benefit from this spirit of helpfulness. I shall not forget Unalîna's kindness in this hard time. She gives me a raw marrowbone now and again, although she herself has a large family and certainly no superfluity of good things.

Our situation would be more difficult if we had not a quantity of reserve provisions running about high up in the steepest mountains—the wild sheep. They are the bright spots in our existence. Leaving the lean caribou meat for the fat, tender mutton is like changing from bread and water in prison to the choicest dish at the Café de Paris. The sheep keep fat longer than the caribou, from the beginning of July to April.

Now and again we go out hunting sheep. But the beasts are rather scattered and in small herds, so even if we bring down some, they do not go far among sixty-five people.

One morning Paniaq and I were once again clean out of food. "We'll go out after a sheep," he said, and we were soon on our way up Giants' Valley. He had caribou-skin footwear as usual. I had put on my heavy ski boots for a change. They have stiff soles and felt uppers; I had not worn them before in the polar regions and wanted to test them here for the first time. I left my skis at home; there were too many stones and tussocks for me to use them with any pleasure.

We walked for some hours, crossed the trail of a huge she-bear with a cub, and at last reached a high, steep mountain. Having peered up it for a good time, Paniaq caught sight of two large rams high on the steepest part. The sharp-eyed beasts had seen us, but did not stir. "That's because they've never seen men before," Paniaq said.

Then a climb began which I remember with no pleasure. Large parts of the steep slope were covered with ice, and it soon became clear that my ski boots were about the worst things I could have on my feet. Paniaq's soft caribou-skin boots, which found a foothold even on small unevennesses, did him good service. I saw, too, how efficient the Eskimos' hunting sticks are in such conditions.

He made his way up with no great trouble. As for myself, I felt that the Eskimos must be right when they maintain that an evil spirit can sometimes get into things. Evidently a particularly malignant spirit had got into my slippery-soled boots. From my first step on the steep mountain slope the boots and I were on terms of enmity. I wanted to go up, the boots to go down. The result of this feud was that I continually had to put them out of action by lying down on my stomach. Then I took a grip of crevices and similar aids and hauled myself up. Finally, I was on a level with the quarry. The valley was far below me, and I had to cross a steep slope. Here it was of no use to wriggle forward on my stomach. The boots made me slip up three or four times and sent me sliding forward toward the steep drop. Then I had to cross a last unpleasant stretch of slippery ice; the boots had evidently planned to make the final descent from the mountain here.

But there was a report ahead, and I saw a ram in flight far away. The other must have been brought down, for Paniaq hardly ever misses. Since there was no longer any need to hurry, I took the opportunity to make a wide detour round the dangerous patch of slippery ice and reached the other side. There sat Paniaq, smoking his pipe beside a big ram.

We rolled and pulled the animal down to the foot of the mountain; as usual we ate the glands between the hooves and the dainty neck fat on the spot. The chalk-white winter coat was unusually thick and rich; a mountain sheep seems even better equipped against the cold than the caribou.

When I had at last got my mittens on after the cold work on the skin and meat in a temperature of 25 below, Paniaq said reflectively: "Let's drag the whole beast home to the camp, then we shan't have to come back with the dogs tomorrow. But it'll be heavy, I know that; I've done this before."

I now saw a new side of the Nunamiuts' old technique. First he cut the skin lengthways into two halves, and in each of them he placed the same amount of meat, evenly arranged for approximately the full length of the skin. Then he cut holes along the sides, in front, and behind, threaded a skin rope through, and laced each skin tightly together round its contents. The result was a long, compact parcel resembling a toboggan. We fastened our hunting ropes to the beast's muzzle, fixed the ropes round our chests, and trudged off.

Paniaq was right; it was an awful grind. About 100 lb. of meat and skin, and that with no proper sledging surface at all, but for the most part a mass of hard-frozen tussocks from which the snow had been half blown away. We bent forward to the harness and had to put all our strength into the task without a moment's relaxation.

Then darkness came, and with it an endless grind and every kind of miscalculation, so that our tow was continually sticking fast. Glittering northern lights crept up above the mountain to the east. I looked up stupidly and tramped on stubbornly through the darkness, panting, with aching shoulders. It seemed an eternity. I should have liked more than anything to cast off my load, leave the sheep where it was, and go quietly home. But it was to some extent a matter of prestige—if Paniaq could get his part of the beast to camp, I could bring mine.

As I towed my refractory half-sheep along through the untidy landscape, I remembered when, as a boy, I had dragged a quite ordinary Norwegian sheep over the mountains to a summer farm in the Hallingdal. It, too, was a refractory beast, but it was intact and had legs to walk on.

It was late in the evening when we reached the settlement. My back and shoulders ached and my temper was rather worn, but shortly afterward the world was bright and all my toil forgotten, for the tent was filled with the strong, delicious smell of fat mutton sizzling in the pot.

Little Wirâq, who is nearly a year old, crawls happily about the willow-bough floor of the tent wearing a short shirt. He sits down on the willow boughs with a bare backside and does not seem to be in the least cold. Outside it is nearly 20 degrees below freezing, and inside it is none too warm; I myself sometimes prefer to have my anorak on.

The Nunamiuts know what they are about in dressing the small children so airily. It hardens them. One of the older people said to me: "It's an old custom with us to let the children go for a long time with bad footwear or furs with holes in them, so that they grow accustomed to wet and cold." The meat diet also makes them strong and helps them to stand the cold. In addition, the young hunter strengthens his physique by exercise of various kinds—running, wrestling, jumping, etc.

Thus women and men in their childhood and adolescence have gone through the process which is called adaptation—the delicate, imperceptible changes which take place in blood, cells, and tissue when human, animal, or vegetable organisms suit their defence to their surroundings. The result is that the Nunamiuts as adults feel no discomfort worth mentioning even in temperatures as low as —60°. I never hear of an Eskimo being frostbitten. A thing which strikes me particularly is their capacity to work in severe cold for a long time with bare hands.

Agmâlik tells in his whimsical fashion of an old Eskimo who was quite exceptionally hardy. "It was some time ago," he says. "The old chap came on a visit to our settlement from another part of the mountains. At night he slept in my tent. It was so cold in the tent that thick ice formed on the water-pot, but it was too warm for him. He threw off nearly all the caribou skins and lay with bare legs. He had hoar-frost on his toes in the morning."

There are white men who are not inferior to the Eskimos in this respect; they are found mainly among those who have been hardened in their youth, farming, fishing, trapping, and so on. Typical townsmen often have rather less power of resistance. They can usually manage to exist in the Arctic regions, but suffer much discomfort.

Another characteristic of the Nunamiuts, as of the Indian caribou hunters I lived with previously, is their capacity to endure hunger for quite a long time without being weakened to any appreciable degree. It happens so often that game runs short and the Eskimos go hungry. In such circumstances it is of decisive importance to remain strong and alert; their lives depend upon it. Much the same thing is true of the polar dog, and a polar bear, wolf, or white fox can go without food for about a month and yet be at full strength when there is at last something to hunt.

The Nunamiuts are tough rather than muscular, except for their back muscles, which are unusually strong. A hunter can carry a fully grown caribou cow over his shoulder and can draw a heavy load. The muscular systems of his arms and legs are soft and long, as with a long-distance runner. His reflexes are often as quick as lightning.

I remember one evening in the tent of one of the Eskimos. The youngest boy was crawling about on the willow-bough floor, and trying to stand on his legs. The hunter himself was repairing his snowshoes; he was immersed in his work and did not look up. Just by the red-hot stove the child suddenly lost his balance. In a flash the father hurled himself forward and seized the boy. It was a matter of a tenth of a second.

In addition to this they know how to economize their strength. In the first place, the Nunamiuts in all their work have an elaborate technique which aims at securing the best possible result without wasting effort. Not least important, they have marvellous powers of relaxation. When there is nothing to do, they cast their cares aside and are happy. This is an invaluable source of strength and recuperation. It is a power which civilized man is losing more and more; even in repose the "motor" is at work, and the result is shattered nerves and stomach ulcers.

When I lived among the caribou hunters of northern Canada, we usually hunted with dog-teams. We stood on the back of the sledge and let the dogs race along after our quarry. Sometimes the caribou took a zigzag course, while the leading dog steadily kept straight on, so that we gained on our quarry. When we were close enough, we ordered the team to stop and fired from the sledge. This technique is practicable on the Canadian tundra, but is of no use in the Nunamiuts' mountain country. Here the caribou is hunted on foot even in winter.

Lean times have come. Day after day we go out in search of game. There are few caribou, and they are shy. If we come upon a herd, we usually have to run both fast and far. Even though it may look hopeless, experience shows that the chance of a shot often comes if only we hang on. The caribou is full of whims; he may stop or turn suddenly. During a hunt like this, when going at full speed, the Eskimos from time to time shout "Hi! hi! hi!" This often makes the herd momentarily halt.

Then there are patient hunters like Mikiâna, who can sit down in a favourable spot and wait in the hope of the quarry coming their way. A cold job.

I once met old Aguk far out in the countryside. We caught sight of two caribou-like little dots on the mountainside. It was late, and I said something about the deer perhaps being too far away. Aguk replied, "Caribou are never too far away," and off we went. This is characteristic of the Nunamiuts. They have inexhaustible energy in the chase even if the chances seem small. If it had not been so, they would have gone under long ago. It is in such circumstances as the present that the vigour and ability of the race are fully displayed. Storm, cold, dark, weariness— everything which can cause discomfort—counts for little against the one thing which matters—to find a herd of caribou and follow it ceaselessly up hill and down dale in the firm belief that in the long run an animal will be brought down. The Stone Age is once more on the trail.

CHAPTER 18

From Generation
to Generation

It was evening. The tent was full of hunters. Outside, a snow blizzard was driving through the darkness, and it was bitterly cold. It was just possible to see a few snowed-up tents and feel the blackness from the nearest mountains. Otherwise the wilderness was just a sheet of grey out of which the wind came rushing.

A belated hunter pushed the bearskin door aside, slipped in easily, and sat down on the willow-bough floor. Paniaq was sitting in the middle of the circle, telling one of the old tribal stories: the legend of the giant hero Ayaguwmalgalga, who created out of clay the first Nunamiuts and a large white dog to help the people. This giant had strange gifts. He could call animals; when he did so, caribou, wolves, foxes, and wolverines came in procession from the mountains. He was equal to anything except one evil man, who tormented the hunters and possessed their wives. Once Ayaguwmalgalga killed the man, but he came to life again. Many strange things happened to the giant. At last he left the people, but before he went he placed his

174

two great mittens against one another in the snow. "You will remember me," he said and disappeared. The mittens became a mountain by the Alatna River.

These are a few features of the story. They give but a poor impression of the terse, picturesque style, the primitive atmosphere, and Paniaq's vivid manner of narrating. This handsome, leisurely hunter was as carried away as if he had been recounting his own experience. His face reflected his story: at times he was intensely serious, and the words fell from his lips sharp and hard; at others, he brightened up at a humorous touch, and sometimes he burst into infectious laughter.

When he had finished, there was silence in the tent for a few moments. Then he said: "That was an inland story, one of the oldest. It dates from before the great flood."

Then he told of the great flood, when the water rose and rose. The Nunamiuts took refuge on the hill called Umiat, about a thousand feet high, by the Colville River. They were there for a long time, till at last the raven came to their help. It pierced a fragment of dry land with its spear, and the sea fell. The great sea beasts made their way out, and where they followed a tortuous course the rivers now run in zigzags.

Then Kakinnâq began to speak. He, too, is an excellent storyteller, but his style is different. Paniaq is rather the artist who dwells upon the fine points of the story. Kakinnâq is dynamic; there is something gripping in his speech.

His first story was of a woman who rose from the dead. Then he told us about Uqailaq (no tongue), a little child possessed of an evil spirit. Its mother always kept it covered up. Those who peeped at it by stealth fell dead at once; their throats opened, and their tongues came out under their jaws. The story ended tersely and creepily. "When the mother took the child down from her back, people saw that there was a gaping hole under the jaws and no tongue. It was a boy."

Kakinnâq said: "Just as nowadays people can die quite suddenly, so death came suddenly to our ancestors at the sight of Uqailaq."

There was a sort of competition between Paniaq and Kakinnâq as to who could tell the most stories, and many strange legends were related. Kakinnâq wound up with a humorous tale about a girl who did not get a husband.

There were three girls, and one of them was of the kind which must always command. They agreed each to get a husband. So they went out onto the ice, broke a hole in it, and took out lines and fish-hooks. Men lived in that water. A young man down in the water knew what sort of person she was; he filled his hair with tiny water creatures and ooze, made himself a moustache, and put on ragged clothes, so that he looked like a poor man. Then he bit on the hook, and the woman hauled in the line excitedly. When the ragged old man appeared above the edge of the ice, she became angry and threw him back.

Then came the turn of the other women. Each of them hooked a young man, hauled him up eagerly, and went home to the settlement with her catch. The first woman fished and fished, but did not get a bite. At last there was nothing to do but to go home. Then she heard a noise and turned round; there stood a young man by the hole in the ice, roaring with laughter and flinging taunts at her. She ran back to catch him, crying: "Wait! wait!" But he dived into the hole in the ice and disappeared. She had to go home without a husband.

Then Paniaq told a new story, and was so amused at it himself that he made a few sketches afterward to illustrate the action. Here is the story, with Paniaq's own illustrations.

Long ago there lived a man who was called Kinnaq. He made himself a kayak, paddle, spear, and casting gear—all of copper. It took him several years to make all this, for working with copper was a hard job. When he had finished, and the ice broke up, he wanted to try the kayak and launched it. It was a fine craft with a good turn of speed. So he started downstream.

Caribou being loaded on to a sledge. In background the "mountain with the old trees" and the beginning of the Anaqtiqtuaq valley

The country is alive

Qayaq has made sure of his dinner

The dogs have a rest after being driven for many hours

On the way into the mountains. The dogs are harnessed in pairs along a common middle trace, the lead-dog ahead. Other Eskimos often harness them in a "fan"

Dogs ready to start: tents have been struck and everything lashed on to the sledges

FROM GENERATION TO GENERATION

On his voyage he caught sight of a caribou, killed and cut up, close to the bank. He was very hungry, and highly excited, steered his boat straight for the kill. When the boat struck the bank, a large piece of meat fell down and remained lying forward in the bow of the kayak.

Kinnaq, the madman, paddles like fury to get at the meat which is lying in the bow of his kayak.

Kinnaq said to himself: "Good, I've caught some meat to eat." But he did not see how he was to get hold of it. He would have to paddle after it. So he paddled ahead, but although he toiled with all his might the meat was always in front of him. He grew hungry and tired, but went on paddling and paddling like a madman. At last he was quite worn out. The kayak upset and he was drowned.

The end of Kinnaq. The kayak capsizes and he is drowned.

All the Eskimos listened eagerly, even though they had heard the stories many times before and knew every sentence. Many of the old legends are full of suggestive strength, a curious mysticism, and a deep humanity. They derive fresh strength from the Eskimos' unshakable belief that the things related have really happened.

We broke up toward midnight; the wind had fallen somewhat, and a few scattered stars gleamed among dark clouds. There was visibility for a good way into the mountains; I had a glimpse of jagged peaks and black ravines. Every time the wind rose a little, a rushing sound came from the night. Filled with a curious emotion, I stood for a time in front of the tent, looking out across the wilds.

Throughout the winter and far into the spring I heard a multitude of old stories which I noted down or transferred to a tape recorder. They can be told after a successful wolf—or reindeer —hunt, but also when everything has gone wrong. It is as though the Eskimos want to gain strength to keep themselves going. Some of the stories have a direct function; after their telling good hunting can be expected. But the number of stories told in the course of one evening must not be uneven. There must always be "two legs to stand on"; otherwise they would be forgotten later.

Some of these old legends have migrated inland from the Eskimos on the coast. Others occur among the most diverse Eskimo groups, even among the people of Greenland, without its being possible to say anything certain about their origin. Influence from Indian and Siberian tribes can also be traced. But the greater number are the Nunamiuts' own. They bear the stamp of inland life, caribou, wolf, grizzly-bear, and wild-sheep hunting, and the grim struggle for existence in the mountains and on the tundra.

The stories are of many kinds; the most important group are

those which treat of dangerous spirits. Sometimes these spirits
are described as alarming, at other times they may take up their
abode in apparently innocent things. There are also different
types of evil spirits, which have names and special qualities. In
the course of the winter a whole procession of them passed by,
like a thrilling play in which grotesque forms appear out of
darkness.

There are stories of fire-breathing devils with mouths stretching to their ears, of rolling fire which pursues an Eskimo, of a
giant man-eating mouse, of dangerous dwarfs which travel
through the air with dog-teams, of fearful giants, of the little
devil Erâq, who eats his own mother, and of the man-killer
with whom only the hero Qayaqtuarneqtuq is strong enough
to cope. This last is an unusually long story, and according to
the Eskimos it would take a month to tell it all. Last and not
least, there is the story of the evil spirits which proceed from
human beings.

There is also a mass of stories of more mixed contents, in part
of epic character. We hear of a woman who finds a skull and
sleeps with it. In the night it becomes a man. Then there are
stories of half-men, and of a hunter who is a head without a
body and has tremendous strength in his hair. Women marry
dogs (Indians), human beings turn into animals and animals
into human beings. There are stories of journeys up through a
hole to an upper heaven, to two small stars which are called
Puyyutsâk because they are as close together as when the first
finger and thumb are held a little way apart, and of journeys to
the northern lights and the land of the sun.

Then there are mythical stories of the people's origin and
how the raven obtained the light of day for them. The Nunamiuts have also a variation of the widespread story of how the
sun and moon came into existence. In a turf hut where a number
of people slept, a young girl was violated night after night. She
wanted to find out who the violator was, so she dipped her finger

in soot and one night put a mark upon his forehead. When it grew light, she saw that it was her own brother, and was in despair. She cut off both her breasts, laid them on a flat stone, went into the assembly house where her brother was sitting,

The fire-breathing devil with his mouth stretching to his ears wears out his legs pursuing the poor boy (Iliapaluk), who has flown like the wind on magic boots. Finally the boy strangles the devil with his belt and brings his head to the wicked "rich man." The boy has previously undergone two tests: he had, unarmed, to kill first a wolf and then a big bear. These, too, he killed with his magic belt.—Drawn by the Eskimo Paniaq.

held out the breasts to him, and said: "Here is thy wife." Then she went out and rose into the air in circles that grew ever wider. Immediately after, the brother too went out and rose into the air in her "tracks." She became the sun, he the moon.

There are also stories of wars, voyages, and wonderful happenings of many kinds. And finally there are the light, gay animal fables. All kinds of creatures figure in these, from the louse to the mammoth, but the raven most of all.

There are various figures which occur repeatedly in different stories. Among these are the poor boy (Iliapaluk) and the old woman (Analûjaq) on the one side, and the "rich man" (Umialik) and his daughter on the other. The boy overcomes the greatest difficulties in many extraordinary ways. When the rich man's daughter announces that she will marry the man who lays a carpet of fine caribou skin across the river ice from the other's dwelling place to her tent, it is of course Iliapaluk who performs the feat. Another frequent figure is Kinnaq, the madman. Here a grotesque humour comes into play. Once he is without food and begins to eat his own flesh. The story ends: "Soon he has no more flesh on his bones, he has eaten himself up."

Often the stories clearly indicate how people should behave in order to avoid certain misfortunes; at other times the instruction is tacitly understood. Vehement passages of an erotic nature often occur. The stories are usually built up dramatically; the style is concrete and suggestive. Songs are often inserted into the text. Before a narrator concludes his story, he gives it a title which creates an arresting picture. One of them is called "The Man Who Rests on His Elbow."

Not infrequently the Eskimos offer precise confirmation of what is told in a story. For example, they can tell of dwarfs so small that they sewed themselves anoraks from the skin of caribou ears, and they tell where the ruins of their habitations can be found. It looks as if many of the stories must contain a kernel of truth, but often imagination has spun such a web round it that it is no longer visible.

One evening I obtained a curious proof of the origin of one of the Nunamiuts' most remarkable legends. It is the story of a giant mouse (*ugjugnaqpak*) which lived in a lake and killed people when they came paddling by. Two brothers, Illaganniq and Kuwjawak, wanted to destroy the beast. They were taller and stronger than all the rest, and there are many stories of their exploits. Illaganniq had skin between his toes and could swim under water like a seal. When they came to the lake where the monster lived, Kuwjawak paddled about to distract its attention. Meanwhile his brother swam under water, drove his flint spear into the giant mouse, and killed it.

This is a typical inland story, and the Nunamiuts take it very seriously. They even identify the lake where the giant mouse was killed; it is, they say, to the south of the upper part of the Colville River and is called Qarjuayât.

The evening this story was told Inualûjaq was among those present. He said: "The giant mouse has a queer head, just like a shrew-mouse's." I asked how he knew that. "I've seen it," he said. He told us that he and his father Paniulaq were once by the lake where the giant mouse was killed. He had just been married then, so it may have been about forty-five years ago. The skull was lying on a mound. It was large, almost high enough to reach a man's knee, and almost four feet long. The teeth had fallen out. His father took the skull with him in his skin boat when he went down the Colville River and sold it the same year to a fur trader named Charles Brower at Point Barrow. I later received confirmation of this in another way and heard that it ended up in a museum in the United States.

Probably the skull was that of a prehistoric animal. Such things not infrequently come to light in Alaska through the erosion of river banks and so on. In the great gold-fields near Fairbanks a number of animals from the Pleistocene era have been found: mammoth, giant bison, giant bear, giant beaver, tiger, horse, and others.

That this strange world of fantasy has come to be created is quite understandable. Here men live from the cradle to the grave in intimate contact with nature and in the hardest possible struggle for existence. Caribou, wolf, bear, mountain sheep—they have the whole wonderful polar life at their very doors. The mountains are wild, the abysses black, the snowstorms violent. Then there are the upper air, the stars, the face of the moon, and the northern lights, all living things to them. Death is always something near at hand, and there is so much to set the imagination working when men feel their own littleness.

One legend tells of the two old women who dragged their turf house and some of the frozen ground under it across the tundra. They were on their way from the interior and were bound for Point Hope.—The turf house is seen both from the side and from above. The lower part of the sketch shows the floor with the fireplace in the middle.—Drawn by the Eskimo Paniaq.

Many of their strange fancies seem to have grown up subconsciously, through dreams, suggestion, shamans' trances, or hallucinations—based on actual strange experiences. Thus the legends are valuable material for the psychologist.

They cover a wide range—from mythology to folk-lore and history. From the Stone Age upward generation after generation has made its contribution, and the whole accumulated tradition has been carried on. Vivid expression has been given the

instincts which are astir in the depths of the soul—especially
fear. Taken together the stories are something more than the
legends of a people. The ancestors' living words are themselves
the source of the descendants' beliefs and view of life.

At first glance these legends may give the impression of
chaotic imaginings which lead nowhere. The whole gives the
impression of a huge untidy patchwork to which generation
after generation had added its quota. But on closer examination
it is seen to be woven in distinct patterns.

The Nunamiuts believe, among other things, that every
flower, every mountain, everything on earth, has its spirit, and
that both men and animals have souls. This soul lives on after
death. Most species of animal have a chief who gives renewed
life to his kind. With human beings it is rather different. Some
remain under the earth, others wander about invisible among
the living. Paniaq relates that there is a settlement by the Utukok River where many Eskimos who died long ago still live.
But only shamans can see them. It sometimes happened, too,
that a people from the air arrived, went round a settlement and
took all the men and women who lived there away with them to
a good place. These are the Uiwaqsât.

An important feature of the old life was the Nunamiuts' relationship to animals, to whose souls great consideration had to
be paid. Various ceremonies had to be observed, most particularly when a wolf or bear had been killed—a subject to which
I will return in more detail later.

But it was above all the many evil spirits of the stories which
occupied the Eskimos' minds. Characteristically enough, good
was not represented by a definite spirit which the people wor-
shipped or relied on. Good was considered a matter of course,
while evil was something dangerous and surprising which called
for active resistance. And this applied not only to the spirits
which were in nature, but just as much to those which were at
work in human beings.

There were various instructions for self-defence. Magic phrases and magic songs were a good protection, so were amulets of ermine skin, hawk's feathers, wolverine skin, and so on. When a child was conceived, it received its amulet for life at once, and later it received more. The greenish-blue crystal beads were also a good defence, also the two large labrets of stone or bone which the hunters wore on their lower lips till quite recently. Paniaq relates how, when he was a boy, old Ayauniqpak once took these off and rubbed them hard against Paniaq's chin and teeth. Paniaq did not like this, but Ayauniqpak said: "Don't worry, for if I do this for a long time you will have a long life." As he continued to rub them, one of them broke right across. Then Ayauniqpak said: "After that I shall not live long." He died the same spring.

But the most important defence against evil spirits was the shaman (*angatkuq*), who was able to perform supernatural feats. Long apprenticeship and wide knowledge were required to become a great shaman. Others had expert knowledge in restricted fields. For this the apprenticeship was less exacting; "medicine" could indeed be bought, sometimes from the Indians. Women, too, could become shamans; in the previous generation there were many of them, and in earlier times there were probably more.

The shaman's field of activity was wide and wonderful. He could keep evil spirits away, look into the future, and know the right answer when an important matter was to be decided. Thus, he could say where herds of caribou were to be found, whether the Indians or the Barrow Eskimos were planning an attack, and so on. He could make long journeys up into the air or to the kingdom of the dead, turn himself into a bird or a blue fly, let himself be burnt to death and come to life again without a burn on his body, and much else.

His most important instrument was the drum, which had magic power in his hands. Another was the "medicine stick" (*qijuwautaq*), which has been much used in the mountains from ancient times. From it was hung a belt or a loop of hide; this was sometimes placed round the neck or foot of an Eskimo lying stretched at full length, sometimes only round a mitten. The shaman then tried to lift it up with the help of the stick. If he succeeded easily, no evil was to be apprehended, and there were bright prospects for the affair which was to be arranged or decided. But now and then it was done only with difficulty or not at all—a bad omen. Aguk says that he saw a shaman try to lift a pair of mittens in this way; he pulled so hard that the medicine stick bent, but in vain.

An idea which constantly recurs among the Nunamiuts is that one person can cast a spell over another. This was one of the shaman's most feared attributes and could cause people to become cripples, or die. This kind of power was sometimes used against unfriendly persons in the tribe, but most often against their enemies, the Indians and Barrow Eskimos. Distance was of no account; the shaman's powers carried a long way through the air.

But the Barrow Eskimos' shamans also had the power of casting spells on men and women, and they directed them at the inland people. It became, so to speak, an air battle, victory going to those whose power was the strongest. The evil spirit flew through the air like a great noose of hide, and if it was not stopped it laid itself about the settlement and pulled itself tight. Then a flint spear was driven into every man's stomach. It twirled round and round in the intestines, slower and slower till life was extinct. Afterward the skin was intact, without wound or scar. Sometimes a little blood might appear on the lips, that was all.

"The Nunamiuts' medicine was always the strongest," Paniaq says. "It has killed most of the Barrow Eskimos, or crippled them. Hardly any of the tribe which originally lived at Point Barrow are there now. Only immigrants." This last statement is correct in so far as terrible epidemics, especially measles, have cleared off a considerable part of the old Barrow population.

He gives the following example of the strength of the Nunamiuts' medicine: "Once the Nunamiuts' shamans saw a noose from Barrow come flying through the air. They seized their drums and brought their medicine into action. It was so strong that they were able to send the noose back. It flew to Barrow and struck the Eskimos there. Many of them were killed by the noose their own shamans had sent against the enemy."

It was a matter of course that the shaman obtained great influence in the community. He was often paid for his activities and might become the "rich man" of the settlement. Thus his position became doubly strong. The Eskimos' lack of independence, and the fact that the community had no chief, contributed to this end.

The wicked shaman meets his fate. He is placed close up to a fire with a flint spear against his chest and a flint knife against his back, and is burned alive.—Drawn by the Eskimo Paniaq.

"In my time everything was medicine," Paniaq's mother once said to him. This shows how everyday life was entangled in a web of religious superstition. The shaman's activities were only one link in the chain; in addition there were taboos and ceremonies of many kinds which had to be rigidly observed as prescribed in the old legends. Everywhere there were spirits. No, life was certainly not simple.

Woe to him who dared to offend against the precepts of the tribe. Taglugjaq tried to do so. His dead grandmother Maligiâluk, who was a great medicine woman, had laid upon him an intolerable number of duties. He could not eat from the same pot as the others, he could not do this or that, and he must be punctilious in observing a number of ceremonies. A small part of this he evaded. But it was the worse for him, Paniaq says. He became unlucky in his hunting; the caribou fled from him. All his toil was useless; misfortunes followed him all his life.

"This happened at Raven Lake when I was a boy," said Kakinnâq. His eyes were wide open and staring at the opposite wall of the tent, as if he saw something there. "Many hunters were sitting together in a turf hut. They saw a noose from Barrow, which came flying through the air to kill the great shaman Amaqtuq. Immediately he and others had recourse to their medicine. Then eagle's wings grew on Amaqtuq. He suddenly flew up through the smoke-vent with such speed that the beating of his wings put out the oil lamp. Ayauniqpak was there and many of our relations; they saw it all with their own eyes."

CHAPTER 19

The Wolves Howl

The ceaseless struggle for food means that the Nunamiuts have no time to continue trapping effectively. But at last a number of traps and snares are being set, and skins are beginning to collect in the camp.

Wolves, wolverines, and foxes are what they are after. The skins of these animals are their only means of obtaining ammunition and other things, so trapping is of great importance to them. They have not many wolverine skins left over when their own requirements for trimming cloaks, etc., are satisfied. Fox skins are not worth much. It is the wolf that counts; in his case there is a bonus of fifty dollars per head, in addition to the price for the skin. The whitish-grey skins, with their long, close neck-hairs, are well paid for by the coast Eskimos, who use them for trimming. Thus, the Nunamiuts are not only caribou hunters, but wolf hunters, too.

Skins have long been their most important assets in the barter trade with coast Eskimos and Indians. In old times, as now, the greyish-white wolfskins ranked highest; the black were almost worthless. Wolverine skins were also esteemed, likewise the skins of the silver fox and cross-fox, some of which were re-exported to Siberia. White fox skins had scarcely any barter value.

The Nunamiuts have a varied collection of strange legends about wolves, wolverines, foxes, etc., dealing not only with the hunting of these animals, but also with their souls! The wolf is the principal character in a number of fascinating stories. One of the most curious is "Magûla," a long narrative which in a detailed and peculiar manner attributes to the wolf the qualities and mental processes of man. The events are seen from the animal's point of view. One of the most important points to be demonstrated is that the wolf has an immortal soul and that men must observe a number of rules if it is not to be offended.

The story contains a thrilling incident in which the wolf Magûla and his brother wish to avenge the killing of their sister. They set off and come to a camp where the killer is staying; they recognize him by the black tattoo marks over one eye. But the brothers have no knife. They find out from an old man that a tribe farther down the river has flint knives. Magûla sets off to get hold of one. On the way he is caught in a snare. The hunter comes, flays the wolf, and cuts off his head. Magûla feels no pain, but is fully conscious and thinking clearly all the time. Then the Eskimo throws the carcass and skin across his back and goes off home. He crosses the trail of a menstruating woman and has to make a long detour.

When the hunter arrives at the camp, he goes round his tent once, stamps hard on the ground five times, and cries out so that all can hear him. This is the sign that he has caught a wolf. The animal is hung up beside the skins on a scaffolding a little way from the tent, and we hear what the wolf's thoughts are at the sight of them. The Eskimo takes off all his clothes, washes his body all over with a piece of skin, and puts on clean clothes. Then there is a feast in the tent. When the hunter eats, he puts out meat for Magûla's soul. Care is taken that the cooking-pot does not boil over and that no one touches the hunter's eating utensils. Nor may he eat fat or drink gravy. Before the hunters lie down to sleep, they hang up their most valuable things, even their crystal beads, and call to Magûla: "Take what you like!"

Magûla stays with the hunter for five days, then he has to leave. From the gifts hung up he chooses two flint knives and two forehead straps set with crystal beads. So he and his brother succeed in taking the murderer's life and can return to their parents, with the death of their sister avenged.

It was an unwritten law that a hunter might not catch more than five wolves, five wolverines, and twenty foxes in the course of one season. When these figures were reached, the traps and snares had to be put out of action and certain rules observed for a definite time.

The many effective methods of capture testify to a highly developed hunting technique. The commonest were snares or fall-traps. Sometimes a net of sinews was laid over the snow and bait placed in front of it (*poro*). A snow hut was built close by, in which the hunter remained under cover. When a wolf or fox approached the bait, he burst out and frightened it into the net, and then used his lance. For wolves and foxes they had, among other things, an infamous method of capture which was called *isiwjuaq*. A piece of whalebone was pointed at both ends, coiled

Pointed piece of whalebone for catching wolves and foxes (*isiwjuaq*). The old lengths were: for wolves, from the beginning of the wrist to the tip of the middle finger; for foxes, from the hindermost depression in the palm of the hand to the tip of the middle finger.

up, and smeared with liver, blood, and fat. It froze into a little, hard ball which was then laid out as bait. When the wolf swallowed it, the whole thing melted in its stomach, and the whalebone straightened out and pierced the animal's intestines. The effect was fatal, but often the beast had to be pursued for a fairly long distance.

This method of capture is no longer used. Wolves are now caught in scissor-traps or snares; for that matter, they are just as often shot. For foxes and wolverines scissors-traps or stone fall-traps are used.

Trapping results can fluctuate greatly from one year to another. This fluctuation is due partly to variations in the stock of animals, but not least to the abundance or scarcity of caribou in the region where the Eskimos are. If caribou hunting is attended with constant difficulty, the result is often that trapping has to be more or less neglected.

I was starting out one day to cross the valley and stalk three caribou which were grazing on the other side, when five wolves came down through a narrow gully and out into the open. They slipped along in single file with a light-footed gait peculiar to them, their bushy tails hanging down behind. The leader was coal-black, the others greyish-white. From time to time they sniffed the snow—the beasts were on the fresh trail of my caribou.

Well out in the wide valley they caught sight of the quarry. After the long chase they were at last at the end of the trail. As at a word of command, the wolves fanned out in line and increased their speed, their bodies pressed flat to the snow. Two moved out to each side, while the black wolf remained in the middle, almost directly on the trail of the deer.

The caribou perceived them and dashed off in alarm. They did not run far, but stopped short on a hillock and looked back. The wolves were gaining on them. Suddenly the caribou were off again; then they broke into a nervous trot, now in one direction now in the other, as if uncertain where to go.

Two wolves appeared over the nearest hillock, right on top of them. This worked on the caribou like an electric shock. Two

Kimmâq, a coquette of eighteen, a danger to susceptible young hunters

he limestone cliffs in the Anaktuvuk Pass recall in many ways the mountains of
Svalbard (Spitzbergen)

Arnâtsiaq (little woman)

of them sped down the valley like the wind, while the third, which had lagged behind a little, must also have got the scent of the wolves approaching along the river, for it dashed up the slope above the valley. Now everything happened in a flash. The two wolves covering the upper flank shot forward like lightning— one snap at the hock tendons and the caribou fell. Once only, the deer half rose in a feeble effort to escape; then all was over. Soon the whole pack was there, biting and tearing the warm flesh, a grey and black circle on the white snow. . . . Two ravens planed down from the precipice above.

This is one of the many dramas which are played out in these wilds. There are masses of wolves in the Brooks Mountains. They are continually after the caribou herds and give them no peace; they destroy several thousand beasts every year, and in winter the remains of kills can be seen everywhere. If caribou are abundant, the wolves sometimes kill indiscriminately and eat only the tongues. One can safely reckon that *one* wolf destroys about fifty caribou every year. By hunting the wolves, the Nunamiuts save the lives of at least two or three thousand caribou yearly, sometimes more.

The wolves in the Brooks Mountains are of the same sort as on the north Canadian tundra, big beasts which may weigh up to 140 lb. and measure about 6 feet from tip of tail to muzzle. Their colour is greyish-white, black, dark blue, red, and on rare occasions grey. The animals are most often in packs of three to twelve. Now and then there may be about twenty in a pack. The pure-white wolf of the north Canadian islands and northern and eastern Greenland is rare here.

As a rule beasts of prey run away from men, but one can never be quite safe. Uinniq had a rather disagreeable encounter. He was out caribou hunting on a misty day with fairly dense snow squalls. He caught sight of a herd and began to crawl slowly toward them. Suddenly he felt the weight of a heavy animal on top of him, and his arm was caught by a double row of teeth. Wolf. He kicked and hit out, and the beast suddenly let go and disappeared. The whole affair had probably been a misunderstanding. The Eskimo was crawling forward in his brown skin anorak fairly near the caribou herd, and the wolf had taken him for a calf and then realized its mistake.

The Brooks Mountains are typical wolverine country. There are plenty of precipices, steep gullies, and heaps of stones, all ideal for these animals, and there is usually plenty of food where the wolves have made a kill. Sometimes the wolverine takes to hunting; then it jumps upon a caribou's back and bites through its throat. It also kills a good many mountain sheep, and in hunting sheep it has an advantage over the wolf in that it can follow the sheep on precipitous slopes. But most often it lets the wolf do the hunting and helps itself to the remains of the kill. Stocks must be fairly large; every time we move to a new place we always find a number of wolverine families in the neighbourhood. The male's tracks are long and almost like a bear's; those of the female are rounder. It is a cunning beast and not easy to catch. The skin in these regions is fairly dark.

As mentioned earlier, there is a good stock of red foxes in the Brooks Mountains. The white fox, on the contrary, is rare. On the coast there are many from time to time; their stay there has enabled the Nunamiuts to give me much interesting information about the animal. In early summer the white fox usually comes a little way inland; there it makes its earth, where the cubs are born. In autumn the animals are to be found on the coast. If there is an abundance of lemmings on the tundra, or a dead whale has drifted ashore, a large number of the white foxes may stay on the mainland throughout the winter. But it often happens that many of them make their way out on to the sea ice as soon as it is safe. Here they find dead seals and whales, or regale themselves on the remains of polar bears' kills. When the spring comes, they feast on the young of the common seal.

Blue foxes are very few in number, scarcely 1 per cent. This is quite understandable, for life on the tundra and the sea ice demands a white protective colour.

As for the grizzly bear, which, like the wolf and wolverine, was the object of an elaborate cult in earlier times, the Nunamiuts hunt it primarily to get skins for the tent doors and intestines for the windows. The meat, needless to say, comes in handy as well.

The hunter creeps up to the grizzly bear to stab it with his lance.—Drawn by the Eskimo Paniaq.

Bears are now shot, but a generation or so ago it was customary for the hunter to attack the beast with the lance (*pana*). The shaft was made of birch, the point, of a bear's legbones. It was necessary to get at close quarters. Sometimes the bear was irritated by arrow shots; sometimes the hunter raised his clenched fist slightly in the air over a hillock and attracted the bear by imitating the "chit! chit!" of the ground squirrel. Then, when the bear rose on his hind legs and attacked, the hunter placed the shaft of his lance at an angle with the ground and let the bear run right onto the point. It often happened that the hunter afterward had to dance round with the bear, driving the lance in deeper all the time. Not infrequently he was injured, and sometimes the bear was victorious. A similar method was employed in bear hunting in Norway until some time in the last century.

The coast Eskimos used to attack the polar bear with the

lance held loose. With them the whole procedure was easier because dogs took part in the hunt; they danced round the bear and diverted its attention from the hunter. As late as the 1880's,

The bear rises on its hind legs and attacks. The hunter places his lance against the ground at an angle, and the animal flings itself against it.— Drawn by the Eskimo Paniaq.

Norwegian trappers in Svalbard (Spitzbergen) killed the polar bear with the lance without the help of dogs.

The grizzly bear is the animal for which the Nunamiuts have the greatest respect. There are many dramatic accounts of fierce encounters between the great beast of prey and the mountain people's cool, agile hunters. Farther south in Alaska, indeed, almost every year a few people are mutilated or killed by grizzly bears or by the great brown bear. I myself came up against one of these brutes, and still shudder at the thought of it.

It is early in the morning. I have just put on the cooking-pot and am sitting shivering, waiting for the warmth to spread through the tent. Then I slip out into the semi-darkness for an armful of wood. It is bitterly cold, but still. I can faintly discern the mountains behind the settlement. Smoke rises gently into the air from the tent chimneys. The families are just up and sitting about half-dressed on the caribou skins, having their breakfast. Now and again a woman comes out of a tent to fetch an armful of wood.

A wolf's howl rises and dies away. It has a thin, distant sound; it must have come from somewhere in the mountains far to the east.

The camp is transformed in a trice. It is as though the howl were the starting signal for a race. In an incredibly short time the hunters have pulled on their anoraks, grabbed their hunting bags and mittens, and hurled themselves out of the tents. They fasten on their snowshoes, seize their rifles, and one after another, speed away eastward toward the mountains.

Late in the evening they come back. One wolf has been shot. The hunters' chances would have been far greater had they worked as a team, but they do not trouble to do this. Each man hunts for himself and becomes the owner of the beasts he shoots. "We ought to have a chief," Agmâlik said one evening in vexation, when they all returned empty-handed.

When the wolves howl, they may be giving expression to feelings of various kinds; the Eskimos maintain that they can sometimes distinguish differences in tone. When the beasts are hunting in a pack and have at last brought down a caribou, they often howl two, three, or four times before they begin feeding in earnest. This is probably a summons to those wolves which have not yet reached the kill, but may be continuing to hunt the rest of the caribou herd. Amity usually exists among wolves in a pack, which often consists of a mother and her cubs. The howl is used also as a signal for assembling after an unsuccessful hunt. In the mating season the howl has its special significance. It can also express fear: if a wolf is suddenly scared, it may utter a raucous bark. Lastly, the howl seems to express a less easily definable mood: the naked wilderness lies spread under the stars—the wolves raise their muzzles skyward and give vent to a discordant series of melancholy howls.

The Nunamiuts have from ancient times been accustomed to decoy wolves by imitating their howl, especially in the mating season. They are past-masters at producing blood-curdling wolf-howls.

One day two of the Eskimos came in with great news: far south in the valley there were thousands of caribou, streaming northward toward our settlement. We all brightened up; now at last our starvation diet would end.

Next day I climbed up into the mountains to reconnoitre. In the distance the snow was covered with small, black spots, like flies on a sheet of white paper. There must have been thousands of caribou there. But their pace was slow; they were probably grazing their way northward by slow degrees.

In the evening all the hunters discussed the matter in the tent. It was universally accepted that we should not approach the caribou; if we did, we should run the risk of scaring them away from the valley. Sooner or later they would come; we must arm ourselves with patience. It is another rule that when the caribou arrive in a stream, the leader and the first part of the herd must be allowed to pass without being fired at. If they are frightened and turn in their tracks, the multitude behind will follow them, and they may flee for a great distance. When the leading troop has passed, shooting matters less, for then the caribou will most likely settle down in our region and remain there for months.

CHAPTER 20

The Main Herd
Turns Away

The thousands of caribou were still a good way off down the valley, taking it easy, grazing and sleeping, and just moving on a little when the fancy took them. Nevertheless, the mass of black spots on the snow had become clearer; every day the main herd was coming a little nearer. We waited.

One morning I went out hunting up a side valley west of the camp. If I should be lucky enough to come upon caribou in there among the steep mountains, I could safely shoot without scaring the main herd, which was in quite a different area. We could, indeed, reckon on plenty of meat in the immediate future, but the present supply was practically nil, and every scrap that could be procured immediately would be a blessing.

The valley I entered was a deep and curious one. Steep limestone mountains rose into the blue; at the far end I had a glimpse of a gully full of boulders and scree. The deep shadows, the steep mountains, and the puzzling way in which the valley ended made me feel that this was a place where anything could happen.

I followed the northern side close to the mountains. At once I began peering up the slopes, and after a time I sighted a small family of sheep—an old ram with big horns, his mate, and a little lamb. They had ensconced themselves upon a ledge in the steepest part and seemed to be making themselves comfortable there, but how they had managed to clamber up was quite incomprehensible. At any rate it was hopeless to try to secure them.

Farther up the valley I crossed the trail of a grizzly bear, out and about although it was now November. Bruin, too, had gone into the mountains. I looked up toward the top and reflected a little: first I must go up that mountain, then perhaps down on the other side and up another. It would get dark; I should probably not get home before nightfall and should have to dig myself into a snowdrift. If I shot the bear in the depths of the mountains, there would be no hope of transporting the flesh and skin. Besides, thousands of caribou were expected at the settlement quite soon. Such is the reasoning of a hunter who is weak and wants to avoid the trouble of tracking a bear up a steep mountain. Argument is skilfully added to argument till it becomes quite clear that the most comfortable solution is the best.

Near the bottom of the valley I lighted a fire, made tea, and grilled a few pieces of meat on a spit. Here I had the company of an ermine—a chalk-white little beast of prey, big-eyed with astonishment. It danced about my camping ground, peeped out from behind stones and tussocks with its head on one side— charmingly graceful, a delight to the eye. The creature stared and stared and never tired of watching the strange new being which had intruded on its solitudes.

Thus I had some company as I went along, but it was not very much. Not a caribou was to be seen. The empty countryside undeniably depressed me. I was the first man to try his luck up there, and I had been so sure that a chance would come my way.

I set off homeward with a dismal feeling of empty-handedness; my progress over the rough ground was slow and wearisome. One feels so entirely different when one has managed to wrest some meat from the country at a time when men and dogs are short of food. Then a difficult road homeward and a heavy burden are child's play. Each step brings one nearer to the joy of the surprise and the story.

I went along over the hillocks on the north side of the valley. Visibility persisted, but darkness was beginning to fall. Then my eye was caught by something new, something alive and moving along the heights on the other side. It was caribou—in multitudes! In long compact lines the beasts were streaming out of the main valley, swinging round the steep hill at the corner, and continuing straight into my valley. They were moving at a good pace, as if disturbed.

Now or never! Could I dash across the valley and get into position in time, before the beasts had passed? I set off at the best pace that straps and cloth would bear, over tussocks and rocks and river ice from which the surface water spurted up all around me, and then up the slope on the other side of the valley. I flung myself down behind a rock, panting. A great number of caribou had passed. I saw them swarming over the mounds farther up the valley; there was a smaller herd straight in front of me, but the range was long. Perhaps this was the rearguard, perhaps more would come—in any case I ought not to take any chances, so I fired. Four caribou fell.

I set about flaying the animals, while mist and darkness fell rapidly. As I was busy with the work, I suddenly started; there was a gentle pattering in the snow. Then I perceived a row of caribou's heads turned toward me; the beasts stood there side by side, almost on top of me, staring. Suddenly they melted into the darkness, and for a short time I heard muffled hoof-beats in the snow. It is incredible how quietly these creatures move.

It was not the rearguard I had fired at. Fresh herds came along continually through the darkness; it seemed that there would never be an end to them. Some passed just below me, others along the slope above, a swarm of living creatures, a ceaseless procession of shadows. Sometimes the deer stopped close beside me and then started aside in alarm; others I only just saw. Most were hidden by the darkness; I heard only their soft trampling. There was a nervousness about them, all seemed to be in a great hurry to get on.

At last I finished flaying and cutting up the big bull caribou. I put the tongues, a quantity of marrowbones, and some liver in my rucksack and set off home. A fresh wind sprang up, and in a short time the mist had vanished from the landscape. The night was clear under friendly stars.

On the slopes above me I saw lines of caribou making their way in, all uneasy and hurried. This must be the end; in the direction of the main valley not an animal was to be seen. Yes, over a long moraine a string of seven or eight beasts, seen in sharp outline, was passing. But these were not caribou; they were wolves. No wonder that the herd was disturbed.

When I reached the camp toward midnight I was received with smiles, and the Eskimos' pleasure on hearing that a good wad of meat would soon be driven into the settlement was unmistakable. But as usual there was no suggestion of praise; a hunter bringing down a few caribou is never anything to make a fuss about, even if food is short.

Our pleasure was somewhat mixed. The Eskimos immediately confirmed what in my heart I had feared. It must be the main herd I had met, all those beasts for which we had now been waiting so long and which we had confidently expected to stream along to the regions round our settlement. Scared by the wolves, they had rushed up the main valley for some distance and then swung sharply into the side valley. And now they were certainly far beyond the mountains.

It was a severe blow, but as usual the Eskimos would not let their disappointment get the better of them. Not much more was said about caribou that evening. I mentioned the bear's tracks I had seen, and so the conversation turned upon Bruin.

Kakinnâq declared that there was nothing peculiar in a bear being out and about so late. The year before, he had shot a bear in January. These are the bears that have failed to excavate places for hibernation before the ground is frozen hard, and after that it becomes practically impossible; so they have to potter about in the cold and snow till winter is over, and have none too good a time. Their only food is the remains of wolves' kills. The bears become hungry, thin, and bad-tempered; a bear of this kind is to be avoided, the Eskimos say.

The year before, Tautuq came upon a winter bear in February—a monstrous animal entirely covered with a thick coating of ice: hardly anything of its fur could be seen. He fired, but the bullets had no effect on the beast's armour, and it padded quietly on. He fired off almost a whole packet of ammunition and must have scored a number of hits, but without result. Tautuq was frightened and hurried home.

It may also happen that wolves dispose of one of these winter bears, if it is not one of the cunning "old hands." There are various stories to this effect, and Kakinnâq has had personal experience of it. He sighted a bear which seemed curiously languid; he got close to it and brought it down without difficulty. At the sound of the shot four wolves sprang up a little way off and fled. It was found that the bear had been severely bitten, was losing a great deal of blood, and would not have lasted long.

The conversation then turned to bear hunting with the lance. Paniaq was not particularly impressed; he thought that he and other hunters would be able to deal with bears with such a weapon if necessary. "No, Tulukkâna's hunting was quite another thing; he killed a bear once with a stone club. He was my father's uncle and the most daring hunter in these mountains, so steady of hand and swift of foot that no one could compete with him."

Then he told of another encounter between Tulukkâna and a grizzly bear. It was by Raven Lake. The people had hunted a large herd of caribou onto the lake, and from their kayaks had stabbed many deer with flint spears. They were busy flaying the carcasses when a big bear came sauntering up the flat valley. Everyone wanted to kill it, but there was no cover, and it seemed hopeless to try to get within range with bow and arrow. Then Tulukkâna rushed off like the wind, right toward the bear. It flew at him furiously, but he danced out of the way. This was repeated time after time, and they came nearer and nearer to the other hunters on the shore of the lake. As he danced round the beast and teased it into pursuing him he uttered wild howls and sang weird songs. At last the bear was brought quite close to the other hunters, who shot it with their arrows.

One winter Tulukkâna made a trip westward to the coast, to the Eskimos' old trading place Kotzebue. His worst enemy, who had sworn to kill him, went there too. One day, when many people were assembled together, Tulukkâna said so that all heard it: "People say someone means to kill me. I should very much like to know when he is going to try." With these words he made a gigantic leap, as lightly as a feather, right over a caribou-skin tent and two skin boats.

Thus we shortened the evening in the tent with stories about one thing and another. It was true that thousands of caribou on which we had reckoned with certainty were no longer approaching our settlement and that our food supply was as insecure as before—but this thought we had smothered. We had expelled the bitterness from our minds before it had had time to take root. New days were coming and something would certainly turn up, for with caribou it was as in the old Eskimo stories—they might suddenly appear when least expected as though by a miracle.

CHAPTER 21

Daily Life

We continue our restless existence, moving camp constantly from one place to another, now down the John Valley, now into the mountains to the east and west. The hunters leave the settlement every day in an unrelenting struggle to get meat enough for men and dogs.

From time to time single Eskimos go out on long reconnaissances. Aguk reports that far south, close to the forest, there are a number of caribou high up in the mountains, possibly driven there by the wolves. But it is no use seeking our quarry on the steep ground near the mountaintops. The meat has to be transported home. We are not fastidious about ground; the dogs are driven over incredibly rough country, but there are limits. We talk of going out onto the tundra to the north; the caribou sometimes settle down there in winter. This happened a few years ago; the Eskimos followed them and got both caribou and wolves.

The temperature is usually between —10° and —40°F. This would not be bad, for a polar country, if it were not for the wind. It blows continually; the north wind from the tundra and the Arctic Ocean is especially severe, and it is worst in the John

Valley, where the river is called Atsitnaq, meaning "the blowing river." In most polar regions the air is usually fairly still
when the cold is acute, but not in the great northward-running
valleys of the Brooks Mountains; here the wind is really in its
element when the temperature is about —40°, lashing us with
blizzards of snow. Before Christmas the valley was blown fairly
clear of snow, and rocks and black tussocks stuck up.

When the storms sweep the valley, they have their own way
of dealing with the tents, whirling round and sweeping the snow
up into steep drifts, so that we have to dig ourselves out and,
soon afterward, in. I myself have a spade, but most of the Eskimos use caribou horns in the old manner, and then it is a slow
business. I now realize what an excellent dwelling the Nunamiuts' dome-shaped skin tent is. There is nothing for the storm
to take hold of, and the drifts all round are not nearly as large
as outside a modern tent. Within, it is snug and so warm that
only on really cold days is there ice on the water-pot in the
morning. The inside of the caribou skins is seldom covered with
rime, but they collect a good deal of moisture and soon become
heavy to transport. But this is a minor defect when one has
plenty of dogs, compared with the advantages such a tent offers.

My tent is in a different class. It is a modern living tent, of
thin canvas, the only one I could obtain at short notice. I have
reinforced it with caribou skins, but when the snowstorms are
at their worst I sit in a thorough draught. Of a morning the inside surface is thick with rime. If the storm rages for several
days on end, a coating of ice forms which becomes so firm that
it is almost impossible to remove.

On raw, black mornings I defeat the cold successfully; I light
the stove and start cooking breakfast from my "bed." Chips and
wood are arranged in a neat pile in the evening; I need only lean
forward, heave them in, and light the fire. The kettle, full of
snow, and the cooking-pot, which has an inch-thick coating of
ice over the meat it holds, are slung over it. Then I bury myself

in the sleeping bag again and do not stick my nose out until the stove has begun to give out a delicious warmth. The rest of the business is quickly done. I dress and pull on my anorak in a twinkling. Then I slap the roof and walls so that the hoar-frost drops down inside and the driven snow tumbles off outside. I brush the hoar-frost off my sleeping bag and other things, take my big knife, push my arm out of the tent door, and cut a few chunks off my "reservoir," a great hard block of snow which I have placed close to the entrance. I push the bits down into the kettle, in which they melt very quickly. I use some of the water for my morning wash, the rest for my tea. At last the good smell of cooking meat fills the air, I throw a few slices onto my plate, and breakfast begins.

It is still dark when I creep out of the tent. All round lie the dogs, covered with driven snow. I look out across the valley toward the black mountains, take note of wind and weather, to decide in which direction I am to go out hunting.

I look into Paniaq's tent, where the whole family is sitting round the meat dish. There is no morning surliness here; all meet the new day with smiles. Then off hunting. That tireless septuagenarian Aguk is away into the mountains already, and now I see one hunter after another slip out of the tents, fasten on his snowshoes, and disappear into the grey half-light. Some rush out with their dog-teams at full gallop; they are off to inspect their wolf and wolverine traps. The driver stands behind, grasping the steering handles and manœuvring skilfully along the narrow track between the willows, the heavy sledge skidding round at the bends.

Agmâlik, as usual, has his wife, Kaliksuna, sitting in the sledge, a broad, comfortable figure. It is not that they are particularly inseparable; but she can always make herself useful. The wife's help means much to a hunter, for while he is seeing to the traps or dashing off after a herd of caribou, she looks after the dogs. This means double work for her, inasmuch as she has to toil at dressing skins, sewing, and much else till late at night.

I make my way into the mountains in the grey morning light, peering about me. The wilds promise so much. So the days begin, full of expectation and joy in life. Behind us lie other days with many disappointments, but they are forgotten every time we set out afresh. The wilderness has its own way of giving men confidence in the future.

The Nunamiuts are never afraid of going into the wilds alone; on the contrary, it is the rule that the hunters stroll about the country by themselves. Only very bad weather will keep the men at home in their tents when food is short, especially as it is in a blizzard that the caribou are most easily approached.

To press forward against the wind on a really rough day in twenty or forty degrees of frost requires a good deal of concentration. One's face comes off worst. One must run a mitten over one's nose, ears, and chin frequently, rub extremely carefully, and at the same time feel if any part is frostbitten. If slight frostbite has occurred, the best thing to do is to place the bare hand over it till the blood begins to circulate again. The common idea that a frostbitten place should be rubbed with snow is quite wrong; it causes destruction of tissues and painful after-effects.

I have seen no cases of frostbite among the Eskimos. As for myself, I have managed all right except on one occasion. It was an exceptionally cold day, and I had had to tramp into the teeth of a hard wind for five or six hours. The result was peculiar. For a couple of weeks I went about with rather a different face from that which I have been accustomed to all my life. The girls looked at me with mingled surprise and disgust; the hunters laughed. This white man who had changed his face was the funniest thing imaginable.

Nor does the darkness seem to bother the Eskimos. The

hunters often return to camp late in the evening, many hours after darkness has set in. When we move camp, tents frequently have to be pitched in the dark; the Eskimos do not even see any advantage in reaching their destination while it is light. When the tents have to be pitched, one's fingers have to grope for innumerable little things, and fuel has to be found in the black willow scrub. But everything goes almost as smoothly and quickly as in broad daylight.

I have found a similar attitude of mind among other primitive peoples, and it certainly was so formerly. The popular belief that when darkness set in the Stone Age people huddled in fear about a fire, which was kept alight as protection against wild beasts, is hardly consistent with the mentality of primitive people and their capacity to fend for themselves. The danger of attack by beasts of prey is usually exaggerated, and the effectiveness of flint implements underestimated. No doubt the natives then, as now, felt equal to a situation which was an everyday affair to them. This is one of the many respects in which the Stone Age people are misjudged.

Like most natives, the Nunamiuts are most skilled at finding their way. I never heard of one losing his way in snowstorm, fog, or darkness. This is due partly to the knowledge of the country and to keen powers of observation. They have grown accustomed from childhood to notice a multitude of details in the landscape, and these are remembered. That their recollection is so exact is due in no small degree to their possession of a marked capacity to form mental pictures of concrete things— rocks, mountains, grass, snow formations, etc. As guides they also use the wind, snowdrifts, and the stars.

Their knowledge of the stars was once considerable, and they still know a dozen stars and constellations of which they make some use. These have descriptive and amusing names. The Turf House (*iglupeaqtalik*) is a combination of the constellations Orion, Auriga, and Gemini. The Sealskin Bag (*pûgjaq*) is the constellation Cetus. The Hunters (*tuwât*) is the name of the constellation Sagitta. They are also well acquainted with the Great Bear, Cassiopeia, the polestar, etc. They know, too, the variations of individual stars in relation to the seasons.

I go across to Kakinnâq's tent. He is washing his hands vigorously, having just skinned a wolf. The Nunamiuts wash their hands several times a day; as far as I could make out, water is seldom applied to their bodies. This is also the case in summer, for there is no question of bathing, the lakes and rivers being too cold. There are no bad smells, either from people or in the tents. The few vessels are washed after every meal. People seldom spit on the floor.

Compared with white people, their standard of cleanliness is not very high, but it must be remembered that the dirt which comes from a healthy life in the wilds cannot be compared with town dirt.

Two Killik hunters come into the tent. They are clean out of ammunition and want to try to barter a packet or two from Kakinnâq, the "rich man," who usually has some available. A good business talk ensues; they are old hands at the game. Kakinnâq is in a class by himself; he knows exactly what he wants for his things and sticks to his price.

The Nunamiuts' keen trading instinct has its roots in tradition. In former times well-to-do Eskimos had "business partners" even in other tribes, far away. They sent one another goods from time to time and maintained a profitable business co-operation. But if an Eskimo has an unconquerable desire for something, he throws his business instincts to the winds. He *must* have it and does not shrink from paying an absurd price.

For that matter, most Eskimos in northern Alaska have a practical business sense. This is undoubtedly of great value to them now that they are becoming civilized. On the whole the Eskimos seem to have qualities which make it easier for them to adapt to the culture of the white race than, for example, the Indians. I have been strongly impressed with this fact during my travels about the country. By and large the Eskimos become reliable and efficient workers—on the whole a valuable element in the civilized part of Alaska.

The burning question at every new encampment is how to get fuel. Sometimes we camp by a patch of willows where the Eskimos have recently been, and then the place is usually cleaned out; not a dry stick is to be seen. So we have to transport all our wood by dog-team from another place, and sometimes we have to go a long way for it. Quite a lot of fuel is needed when so many tents have to be kept warm in severe cold.

Once in a way it happens that we stumble upon a virgin patch of willows with an abundance of dry bushes. Then we feel that we have struck it rich. But most often we have to search both long and hard to find enough. Before the snow came, there was a good deal of drift-wood by the large rivers. But now it is buried.

The wood problem was obviously still greater in earlier times, when the Nunamiuts were more numerous and exploited the various available supplies more fully. At Chandler Lake, where the Raven people had a settlement a few years ago, no fuel is left. The Eskimos helped themselves by mining coal a good way into the mountains, but ordinarily they fetched all their wood from about thirty miles to the southward.

This inexorable demand is continually made on me: Wood must be found, carried, or driven. A lot of fuel is needed to warm my draughty tent. A load is consumed in a short time, and more has to be fetched. I get no peace.

In this the other hunters have a great advantage over me.
They have wives. So I not only have to find wood in places
where every dry stick has to be sought for intensively, but have
to do so in competition with the experienced older ladies of the
camp. There is Angayik, who can smell out a stick of wood
right through the snow, hawk-eyed Kaliksuna, and all the rest.
It is no joke competing against a bunch of determined women.
It often happens, too, that mothers bring all their children to
help them, a downright unfair form of competition.

In the beginning I had a difficult time. When I arrived, the
women had usually stripped the best patches of dry wood. But
something had to be done. So I pulled myself together, thought
the problem over thoroughly, and by degrees became wise. I
began my wood-collecting from the outer edge of the patch of
willows and worked gradually inward toward the settlement. I
had farther to go, but I found untouched supplies all for myself.
The women searched first for everything that was nearest to the
tents, and then continued gradually outward. It was their habit,
and any other method of work would call for a revision of the
feminine mental process, which is much too difficult. There are
other tricks, too, and I learnt the art of judging where dry wood
was to be found.

The gathering of wood is subject to certain rules. As long as
it is lying about or rooted in the ground, it is common property,
but if it is flung together in a heap, a family has acquired rights
of ownership over it, and such rights are always respected, even
if the heap is so far off that it would be possible to help oneself
without anyone knowing who had done so.

The willow is used not only for fuel, but for the most varied
purposes, and occupies a central position in the Nunamiuts'
material culture. Snowshoes are made of it when birch cannot
be brought from the forest; it is used for tent-poles, handles of
stone-hammers, trapping gear, pipes, and much else. And not
least is the willow valuable for making tent floors. All things

considered, it can be said that the Nunamiuts have a kind of "middle culture," which has features derived both from the forest and from the tundra.

Not so very long ago they used stone lamps for lighting the tents, and to some extent also for cooking. The fuel used was seal's blubber, sometimes caribou fat. Most often they made the lamps themselves of a kind of sandstone, but some large soapstone lamps were also in use for lighting and cooking; these all came from the country east of the Mackenzie River. Blubber was obtained by barter with the coast Eskimos to the north, and had to be transported over long distances, so that the Nunamiuts could only carry a limited quantity with them. Not infrequently necessity compelled them to eat the blubber. Generally speaking, the oil lamp could never replace the willow.

A settlement in the wilds has a peculiar quality: it is a smile among savage mountains, a place where one can feel secure among other men and women. When one comes home tired from hunting, one feels more cheerful at the sight of grey, dome-shaped tents, with smoke rising into the air. They are homes just as much as town dwellings, but the impression they give is fresher and more vivid. Red-cheeked children fly in and out. There is always something they cannot find. They tumble down among the bundles of skins at the back of the tent, poke about, and then dash back to their games and fun in the cold and snow. The wife sits on the willow-bough floor, dressing skins or sewing, and has her hands full. Evening comes on. From time to time she takes a turn outside and looks out over the mountains. Will he come soon? Has he shot anything? At last she makes out a little spot, something living, far across the snow. A feeling of safety and happiness runs through her, and she hurries into the tent to put the meat-pan over the fire.

CHAPTER 22

We Lose the Sun

So far everybody has kept pretty fit, and only in one or two cases of slight indisposition has there been any use for the popular art of healing. That is very simple. The Nunamiuts know only very few medicinal plants. One is called *awingaq* and is used as a cure for rheumatism. Aguk says that he learned from an Indian of a plant which was good for pains in the back and elsewhere. It affected the skin so strongly that a piece of cloth had to be laid between. It is curious that the Nunamiuts have so few medicines derived from plants, while the Indians have so many.

The Eskimos' two most important methods of treating illness are surgery and the light massaging of the stomach with the finger-tips. Paniaq is the people's doctor; he is sent for immediately and sets to work giving massage (*saptaqtoaq*). He says that he tries to straighten out quite small knots in the stomach or intestines and thinks that this is useful for most illnesses.

How true this may be I cannot say. I may say that in the spring I took the temperature of a feverish boy just before and just after such massage and found that it had fallen from 103° to 102.4°. Paniaq complains that his hands have not the same power as before. "I have taken the strength out of them with too much massaging," he says.

HARRISON COUNTY
PUBLIC LIBRARY
105 North Capitol Ave
Corydon, IN 47112

Then something did happen. Kimmaq, one of the prettiest girls in the settlement, was suddenly taken seriously ill. It appeared to be an inflammation of one of her jaws. Half her face swelled up violently, and she had a high temperature and severe pains.

Paniaq set to work with his stomach massage, but this time it did no good. What were we to do? Several days passed; the poisoning spread downward and her breast, too, swelled up. It looked bad.

We assembled in the tent where Kimmaq lay moaning under the skins. Beside her sat her sweetheart, Tautuq, a good-looking young fellow. He was rather dejected but did his best to conceal it. Her father, Aguk, was also very anxious, but as placid as ever. A number of men and women were sitting round, for it is customary for people to assemble when someone is ill.

"Perhaps we ought to try cutting," someone said. The other hunters nodded. I melted some snow in a cooking-pot, brought the water to a boil, and put a hunting knife into it. The Eskimos looked on in astonishment and asked what it was for. I tried to explain about disinfection and suddenly discovered how difficult it was. I endeavoured to make the matter simple and said that on a knife like that, which was not boiled, there might be more tiny little dangerous animals than there were caribou in all the mountains. The Eskimos looked at me, and I saw how foolish my explanation must seem. Some grinned faintly, as much as to say "We can't swallow that."

Then I gave the knife to Maptirâq. It was agreed that he should be the surgeon, for he had had the most experience with the knife, they said. He ran a dirty finger along the edge to try it, and then cut. The girl uttered a piercing howl of pain. The knife was too blunt, the cut not deep enough. So the whetstone was produced. No nonsense about boiling the hunting knife this time; a fresh cut was made. The girl screamed again, worse than before. This time the cut was deep enough, but no matter came out, only a torrent of dark blood.

A few days later she was in a miserable state, and we thought she would die. Something had to be done. I told the Eskimos that the best dog-drivers ought to set off due south toward the forest until they met people. They were to carry with them a letter asking that a plane might be sent to fetch the girl and take her to Fairbanks.

The proposal saved the situation. The hunters had indeed talked about the necessity of getting help from the civilized world if Kimmaq was to be saved, but here again the trouble was that the community had no leader. There was talk but nothing more.

Next morning four sledges set off southward. They had a long way to go, but the worst part of it was the deep snow in the forests, with the dogs as thin as they were. Nor could much meat be spared for the dogs' food on the journey.

In the grey dawn a fortnight later we heard a distant humming above the noise of the wind. The dogs were harnessed at top speed; the sick girl was placed on one of the sledges and driven off to a lake where we had marked out a landing ground in the middle of the ice with willow rods. Kimmaq was carried aboard the plane, the engine was started, and the plane vanished into the grey sky. We stood by the dog-teams, looking after it.

At last the messengers came back with exhausted dogs. They had been to the little place called Bettles on the Koyukuk River, where they met people who took charge of the telegram. They were full of stories of the Indians' country.

Kimmaq was taken to Fairbanks, where she received medical treatment. She recovered her health, and in the spring was flown back to the mountains.

It was November. This month the Nunamiuts call *Tarraqsiorwik,* which means, in abbreviated form, "the time when the ram chases his own shadow in the moonlight and thinks it is a sheep."

The old Nunamiut names for the months are different from those of the coast Eskimos and to a great extent bear the stamp of inland life. I give them here because they throw light on an essential part of the people's way of life and habits of thought:

January	(*Siqinnâtsiaq*)	New sun.
February	(*Siginnâsugjuk*)	High sun.
March	(*Paniqsiqsîwik*)	The lean time.
April	(*Qajgilirwik*)	The ptarmigan come.
May	(*Suwlorwik*)	The rivers break up.
June	(*Erniwîk*)	The young are born.
July	(*Itsawik*)	The gander moults.
August	(*Nirlâligit itsawiat*)	The goose moults (has had her young).
September	(*Amîqsiwik*)	Loses skin (the caribou bull sheds the skin on his horns).
October	(*Nuliarwik*)	Mating time (for caribou).
November	(*Tarraqsiorwik*)	Follows a shadow. (The ram chases his shadow in the moonlight and thinks it is a sheep.)
December	(*Siqinirilaq*)	No sun.

The days are growing shorter; one notices it from week to week. The sun hangs low over the mountains. The feeling that we shall soon lose it becomes stronger as the light falls so low that large parts of the valley remain in deep shadow even in the middle of the day. Our range of vision is reduced.

The sun seems to be in a hurry. It is as though it wanted to hurry through its last obligatory tours of duty up here in the north in order to undertake more important duties on the other side of the globe. Finally, it throws a flood of light only over the highest peaks. Then it is gone. It still sends a greeting to us, for there are days on which the afterglow gleams through the clouds and becomes a sort of red roof over the darkening country. But soon this colour display is over; the black days are coming.

Darkness. In the middle of the day we have a bare four hours of grey half-light; otherwise it is night. The atmosphere of the wilderness is changed. The world has narrower limits; things seem different from what they were. Even our camp is not the same. When we drive into it, the eye is no longer met by the cheerful view of the camp as a whole; it sees only the vague contours of a few tents through the greyness. At the same time the settlement plays a greater part than when the wild country lay round about bright and vivid, offering richer pleasures. In the darkness one feels more strongly how good it is to have a home to take refuge in and what it is to meet men and women.

The Nunamiuts carry on with their hunting and work with the same cheerfulness as when the sun was there. No one seems noticeably oppressed. I, too, am quite happy in the half-light; there is enough employment for one's hands and no time to be down in the mouth. Those who write dramatically about the horrors of the time of darkness are usually people who keep indoors in a tent or hut. For them the darkness is something threatening which gets on their nerves. If one goes out into the open and fights the darkness, it is not half so bad. There is a peculiar subdued atmosphere. Gradually more details appear in the landscape, the eyes are adjusted to the view, which extends as with the opening of a shutter. When there are thick clouds or a snowstorm everything is more difficult; but there are clear days with stars and flickering northern lights, and they make up for a great deal.

But sun is sun. The thought of it can be pushed deep down into one's consciousness, but it burns there like a glowing ember. This longing for the light is the undertone of one of the

Nunamiuts' most beautiful legends. It tells of a people who journeyed to a land where the sun never set. When the days began to grow short, a large snow-white owl descended noiselessly upon the settlement. All the people climbed up on it and crept in under its feathers, where there was plenty of room. The owl rose into the air in wide circles and then flew right away. The country far below changed; the travellers saw snow no longer, but a land of summer. They came to strange parts and a new people who received them hospitably. For a long time they lived in the sunshine. Then the northland called to them. They summoned the owl, and immediately it came gliding down. Again the people crept in under its feathers, and were carried northward toward the bright Arctic spring.

Hunting in the few hours of half-light is no easy matter. It is hard to discover the scattered caribou herds and no easier to bring them down. Judging the range is a special problem.

It is becoming clear that with game as scarce as it is the whole people can no longer keep together. There are too many mouths to feed here in proportion to the small number of caribou to be found in a limited hunting area. By degrees a number of families have disappeared from the common settlement and are seeking their fortunes elsewhere. A large number of the Killik people, with old Maptirâq at their head, are pitching their tents a little south of us in the John Valley, at a place called Qayaq. Here two large rivers run into the John River from the west and northwest; they are called the Ikiaqpak and the Qalutâriaq. One or two families are roaming about in the mountains elsewhere without my always knowing exactly where they are. They usually return after a time to one of the larger settlements. The five families of the Raven people mainly stick together, and I go with them.

One day the boy Uinniq whirled into the camp with panting dogs and new harness of grizzly bear's skin. He came from the

Killik people's settlement and had a surprise for us—a cargo of fresh fish, grayling. Two hunters had come upon a strip of open water a little way up the River Ikiaqpak. The Eskimos put a fence right across; into the bottom they drove stakes set close together, leaving an opening in the middle, where they placed a bow-net. Then they drove the fish against the fence and into the bow-net. But the fish are small, and all things considered, a modest contribution to a kitchen for several families.

"It's certainly coming soon; she's got a bit of wind," said Paniaq. He had just gone over and given his daughter Qutuk stomach massage; a new citizen was expected in the wilds. A little later I went over to see her. She was sitting with her hands in her lap and gave me a forced smile. I have always liked Qutuk; there is something rustic and intensely primitive about her. A robust woman, not positively pretty, but with a motherly charm of her own, so attractively unconscious in every little movement, in every shifting expression.

She had visitors the same day; two hunters and one or two women from another settlement came to see her. At once she was the housewife, set to work to cook food for them all, bustled about arranging things and talking, till the guests left toward evening. No one should see that she was in pain; that was not seemly.

The birth was slow; Qutuk, I am told, is the only woman who has had difficulty in the last stage of her pregnancy. Then one day she and her husband, Aguâq, got busy striking the tent, packing the sledge, and harnessing the dogs. They were going off to try their luck as hunters somewhere else. No one saw anything odd in their moving like this just before the baby was born. It is nearly forty below.

A few days passed, and then one of the boys drove up to the settlement with weary, frost-covered dogs. He had come for the "midwife," though in fact among the Nunamiuts it is the older

hunters who deal with births. This time it happened to be old
Aguk; he is very clever with his hands.

It was a girl. She was called Ayapana, after her grandmother.
It is customary to name children after their grandparents, or if
their names will not go round, after some other dead relation.
Children can get an additional name later on. There is no difference between men's and women's names; for example, a boy
can be named after his grandmother. Indians are often unwill-
ing to tell their names to strangers. The Nunamiuts, on the contrary, give their names readily, and that was the custom in earlier times.

As a rule births take place normally; complications are exceptional. The Nunamiut women have a good deal of pain, but
as far as I could judge it is less acute than with white women.
There is reason to believe that this is due more than anything to
the Eskimo women's attitude to birth. They face it as a simple
matter of course, without strain.

The caribou are in a hurry. The few we see are going as
swiftly as if they had to arrive punctually at an important meeting. We have to be quick when a herd is sighted, for it will be
gone in a twinkling. The animals are practically all young bulls,
and all are thin. At this time they usually wander about on their
own, but the Eskimos say that however far they go they can
find their way back to the main herd at any time.

We piece together all the reports we have from the different
hunting parties of the direction in which the animals are wandering, in order, if possible, to get a line on the whereabouts of
the main body. The result is confusing. No one can understand
this animal. One gradually comes to regard the caribou as
something mysterious. The Eskimos' most fantastic legends of
the caribou begin to sound quite reasonable. Kakinnâq says:
"Once the caribou had shining white incisor teeth just like a
wolf." I am quite ready to believe it.

Windy Camp

It was a dark evening, and we had driven a long way with heavy loads. Suddenly a willow thicket appeared just ahead of us. One after another the dog-teams burst through it and halted at an open spot. We were tired, and a bitter wind was blowing.

Before we set about pitching camp a fire was lighted; we poured scalding tea down our throats and ate a little raw, frozen meat. All the Raven people were there and also the Killik hunter Mikiâna with his family. We were again on the move.

Tents were pitched, and I, who work alone, had a good deal of trouble with mine. The rushing wind flung itself eagerly upon the canvas, blew it up into the air, or made it flap about with a smacking sound. Then, when I went off after fuel, I found only a few miserable sticks. A windier hole and one poorer in wood it would be hard to find. We are to remain here for some time, and we shall return here after a stay somewhere else. Why the Eskimos choose to settle in such an inhospitable place is not easy to understand, when there are better camping grounds with equally good hunting prospects. The settlement is called Qalutaq, after a small river which runs into the John River from the east.

These dark windy days do not worry the young ones. One day when a storm was raging I was out after wood, when I perceived something unusual on one of the hard-blown drifts by the river. I went closer, and found it was a group of four quite small girls, stretched out on their stomachs with their heads together. They looked up at me quickly, but did not allow their important conversation to be disturbed. They giggled and had great fun together as the tempest raged over them.

One of the hunters has returned from a sledge trip far to the south, and tells us that there are still few caribou there, but a good many lynx tracks. The lynx is a typical forest creature and does not usually thrive in the tundra. But it may sometimes come a long way north, the Eskimos say. Several years ago great numbers came right down to the Arctic coast. This is confirmed by Charles D. Brower.* Migrations like this depend upon food conditions. The lynx's main food is the snowshoe hare, of which the numbers increase greatly over a period of seven years, until the countryside swarms with them. Then sickness suddenly attacks them, and so many die that there is hardly one to be seen. Then the lynx is in a bad way and has to range far in search of food.

The days passed. The results of our hunting were as meagre as before, apart from occasional flickers of encouragement when a small herd of caribou hurried past. I came upon one of these, at fairly long range, brought down two deer, and went after the others at full speed. There was a report ahead of me; two caribou fell, and the rest disappeared. Out of the greyness came Aguk, smiling, rifle in hand. This old hunter is incredible. If there is game about, in some queer way or other he is always there.

Wolf hunting is rather better, though none of the men have time to look after their traps properly. There are a lot of cubs about; it is a good year for wolves.

* *Fifty Years Below Zero,* Dodd, Mead & Co., New York, 1948.

In trapping there are no personal rights. If a man has luck in a new area, it is not long before two or three others set their wolf and wolverine traps there—sometimes quite close to the first man's traps. No one has any objection. When I once said that white trappers had the right to keep other people away from their trapping areas, one of the older men said: "We Eskimos will not allow a man to think only of himself."

It looked as if the Eskimos meant to stay at Qalutaq indefinitely, although we had to transport fuel a long way by dogsledge. Then one evening, with his usual suddenness, Paniaq made a decision. Next morning he was going farther south with his family. Would I accompany them?

It is not easy to understand clearly what mental processes precede the Eskimos' decisions on important questions; for example, where moving camp is concerned. The matter is relatively clear when it proves impossible to kill enough game from the old settlement. Then a family may go to a new region because its relations and friends are doing so. At other times it is the primitive man's childish delight in change which sends him away. As a rule the decision is made on a sudden impulse and takes effect at once. Long-term plans do not exist for these people, nor thorough preparations. When, for once, they do make serious plans for moving camp, say, in three days, it is most likely that the plans will come to nothing. It is almost as if the Eskimos refrain from acting until the pressure of circumstances becomes so strong that no act of will is called for. These circumstances can be of many kinds, often not the sort that would weigh with us. The influence of suggestion from relations and friends is of special significance.

Early next morning we set off through the darkness. It was something new for me to be moving with only one family. A pleasant, peaceful feeling it was, too, for I get on very well with Paniaq, his wife, Umialâq, and the four children.

The "mountain with the old trees" at the entrance to the Anaqtiqtuaq valley

One of the caribou bulls shot by the Author on the occasion when "the main herd turned away"

My little friend Uyarâq, ten years old and a "regular tease"

A journey with Paniaq is varied and interesting; that I knew from shorter trips. Not only has he a fund of knowledge of the wilds and of old times, but he enjoys telling stories when he is in the right mood. And there is always a cunning humour behind it all. The most valuable information I rarely get by direct questioning, but when he is discoursing variously, it emerges as if quite by chance.

We followed the John River southward. There were four sledges; first came Paniaq with the big sledge, then Umialâq with one nearly as large, then I with the little girl Sikiârjuk sitting on my load. Finally the wood sledge and the little boys. Heavy loads and hard work for the dogs.

Umialâq is small and light and had the little boy on her back, but she managed the heavy sledge cleverly and tirelessly. I could not help admiring Paniaq's way with the dogs. He hardly ever hit them, rarely shouted at them, only put in a few quiet words where they were needed. If he wanted a rather quicker pace, he started a gentle whistling, to which the dogs reacted at once.

In places there was good going. The dogs trotted across the ice, while we sat on the loads and had nothing to worry about. Paniaq told me one or two things about these new regions. In his mother's time a good many Eskimos had starved to death there. In those days things were much more difficult, he said; guns were slow in coming inland, and the people were always so short of cartridges that bows and arrows were used as well for a long time. A hunter who had ten or twenty cartridges was reckoned a wealthy man. They charged their cartridges themselves and took care that the charge was not too strong for the bullet to remain in the animal, so that it could be removed and used again.

The valley became narrower, the terraces on both sides of the river higher. Suddenly the dogs picked up a scent and quickened their pace. They swung into a sledge track which led to a

little patch of willows. Smoke rose into the air. It was the Killik
people's settlement, Qayaq.

Men and women came out of the tents; there were smiles and
pleasure at meeting again. Many of them we had not seen for a
long time now. Several of the girls were there, and certainly the
camp up north had seemed rather empty when they went away.
Old Maptirâq, erect as ever, invited us into the tent and treated
us to the best he had. The others sat round and we chatted.
Then we went on southward.

A river cut in from the east deep down between moraines.
Here we swung off uphill toward a narrow valley the contours
of which could be faintly seen in the darkness. This valley is
called Oqûluk (the sheltered place). We pitched camp by a
thick patch of willows.

It was long since Eskimos had been there; scarcely an old
axe-mark was to be seen. There were masses of dry wood, a
delight to the eye. The north wind did not reach us there; it was
like the stillness of a church after the eternal wind at Qalutaq.
The snow was deep indeed, and in places it was difficult to move
about, but we could put up with that when so much else was
good.

Food had to be found, and we devoted all our energies to
hunting, each in his own direction. The first day I saw no caribou but sighted a pack of wolves, fourteen of them in all. On my
way back I splashed through the surface water of the river and
was rather sorry for myself, for there were forty degrees of frost.
To get one's legs wet is one of the worst things that can happen
in the polar regions; I had bitter experience of this when I lived
with the Indians of northern Canada. There we wore stockings,
duffel socks, and moose-hide moccasins without hair; if this
footwear gets into water, it all becomes sopping wet at once,
then freezes hard and becomes icy cold against the feet. After I
had a winter foot-bath of this kind on the Canadian tundra,

Corporal Williams of the Royal Mounted Police had the pleasure of slicing off a good piece of one of my big toes. This kind of surgery he always enjoyed very much.

I therefore anticipated the worst after my foot-bath in the Alaskan mountains. I ran home. To my astonishment I did not feel cold, and when I reached my tent and took off the wet kamiks and caribou-skin socks, there proved to be nothing the matter with my feet. I mention this to illustrate the excellence of the Eskimo footwear.

We did not get within range of a single beast. This would not do. Here we had everything—fuel, no wind, a beautiful valley—but not what mattered most, caribou.

Christmas was near at hand, and we were to take a trip back to Qalutaq. But just before the start Paniaq went off to take up some of his traps. On his return he said that he had seen about twenty sheep high up in the mountains just behind the camp. We were in a dilemma; the sledges had been loaded and the dogs harnessed. If we went into the mountains after the sheep we should be delayed for one day, perhaps several, and miss the great Christmas festival. But twenty fat sheep . . . !

We went to Qalutaq. It was a delightful trip in quiet, bitterly cold weather. We continually saw ptarmigan in the patches of willow along the river, sitting hunched up like white buds on the branches. At one point we "flushed" a caribou, which dashed up the moraines and vanished in the grey distance.

The little girl, Sikiârjuk, sat on Paniaq's load the whole time; not once did she keep herself warm by running. She was terribly cold. It was the first time I had seen an Eskimo child suffer from cold at all, and it was really bad. She cried—not as though demanding that anyone should help her, but silently and bitterly. Her hair hung down over her face in strips white with frost; through it I could see her tear-filled eyes.

Paniaq flung the heavy tent-skins off, laid the little girl out-

stretched upon the rest of the load, heaped the caribou skins on
top of her and lashed the whole fast. Sikiârjuk was now completely covered up.

It was quite dark when we drove up to the settlement. Nevertheless the children were aware of us some time before we arrived. They came running in a crowd toward the sledge, laugh-
ingly jumped aboard and gave the dogs extra work in dragging
the loads over the last stage. Then, when I was about to pitch
my tent, they streamed along and gave me a hand both in fetching willow boughs for the floor and in shovelling snow.

Almost the whole people was to assemble in Kakinnâq's tent.
He had made it a good deal larger by moving the tent-poles outward, but nevertheless I could not see how so many people
could be squeezed in. "It'll hold them all right," said Paniaq.
"We have an old proverb, *Tupiq qâlaitsuq* (a tent never
bursts)." And he was right; there were about sixty people, but
we all sat down, though it was a bit of a squash. Mikiâna, from
the coast, conducted the service, and hymns were sung vigorously.

Then the feast began. It was simple enough; everyone had
brought with him the best he could in the way of food. But as
the great majority had not much else besides lean caribou meat,
it did not look as if the Christmas fare would be particularly
varied. But then Kakinnâq rose, and to our astonishment he
laid upon the floor a little heap of fragments of dried caribou
fat, saved from the autumn! We sat staring. I at once began to
make a rough count of the pieces and made sure that there
would certainly be one for each of us. It was hardly believable.
Yes, Kakinnâq was a man to look up to in the community. Once
more he had justified his reputation as a man of great wealth.

After the meal a little skin bag filled with presents was produced. They were modest enough, but gave pleasure and
amusement. One man got a fox skin, another a pinch of to-

bacco or a few matches neatly tied together with sinews; the women usually got a few needles, sinew thread, or a piece of fur for trimming, and so on. I had put aside for the occasion a quantity of bought articles for the children and girls; the glittering hair-slides, rings, and games were a tremendous success. I myself received one or two surprises, things carefully chosen with a thought to what would give me pleasure. Ayaunik had made the sweetest little mittens and leggings for a doll I had been given earlier for my daughter Benedicte. Kaliksuna gave me a piece of fat. Maptirâq gave me an old box for fish-hooks, carved from a mammoth's tooth.

It was hot in the tent, where we sat packed like sardines. Outside it was crackling cold and for once quite still, with moonlight. The bearskin door was tied up, and the opening was a white patch of frost-haze. On the threshold sat the two young girls Tatqawina and Sisualik, with their arms round one another. Behind them the moon stood like an orange wall—it was as if they were leaning against it.

The next evening we were in a different era. The drums beat; the people gave themselves up to strange songs and hectic dancing. The spirit of the Stone Age was still alive.

CHAPTER 24

The Country
Comes to Life

I was paying a visit to Aguk's tent early one morning. He said: "Today the sun turns." I asked how he could know that. He took me outside and pointed to two small stars which stood right above one another in the northeast. "That's Agjuk," he said. "The first time they are seen over the mountains the days begin to grow longer. Soon we shall see the great star Uwlureaqpak, which tells us of it." It was December 23.

The sun! Suddenly we had something to look forward to. January came in sharp and cold, —50°F. None the less there are a number of birds which stand the winter here, north of the timber line. One day the pretty little Siberian grey siskin flew about close to the settlement. The other birds which pass the winter in these regions are the raven, Arctic owl, ptarmigan, dipper, tit, jay, and sometimes a woodpecker or snow bunting.

I now get much pleasure from my skis. It is delightful to be able to glide away far up the valleys and shoot down the hillsides. The Eskimos watch my manœuvres with wonder; the small boys are particularly interested. Now and then they borrow the skis, and it is astonishing how quickly they copy me.*

One evening Kakinnâq was tremendously busy, sitting over in the corner of his tent and working intensively on some quite small object. I asked him what he was making. "A tooth—to go here," he answered smiling and pointed to his upper jaw, where there was a gap left by his having lost both his front teeth. Soon he had finished, and with an air of great seriousness placed the new tooth in his jaw. His work did him credit; it was a beautifully shaped tooth of walrus bone—a dental mechanic could not have done better. It was, indeed, the only restful element in Kakinnâq's mouth, in which all the other teeth stuck out in one direction or another. He has, moreover, fathered a brand-new idea in the odontological field—that of replacing two teeth by one broad one. How he made it stay in I cannot say, but he did, except when laughing uproariously, when it was inclined to shoot out.

At last he said: "You see, I shan't use this tooth for chewing; I've plenty of teeth for that. It's a windscreen, so that I shan't get too much cold air right down into my stomach."

When Eskimos come into a tent, they are very careful to brush or knock snow and hoar-frost from their skin clothes. If footwear or an anorak needs drying, it is carefully turned inside out and always hung up well away from direct heat. An important matter, for the skin can be damaged beyond repair by the slightest carelessness.

The women are always busy mending or making new footwear, especially for the many children. When they grow tired of making new boots for these rascals, they have recourse to what is called an *âktâk:* the skin on one of the caribou's hind

* After his return to "civilization" the author had twelve pairs of skis and sticks sent to the Nunamiut children from Norway.

legs is torn off, the lower part is sewn together, and the leg, turned inside out, is stuffed tight with caribou hair or moss while it is damp. When the skin is dry, the moss is taken out, the leg is reversed again and the "boot" is finished.

It blows and blows, but the wind can drop suddenly as if switched off, and the dark country spreads itself in gentle outlines under the stars. The northern lights glide up in the east, tentatively at first; then they gather strength and build a fairy bridge in red, green, violet, and gold across the valley from mountain to mountain. No wonder that they have set the Eskimos' imagination working, and that strange stories have grown up to explain this fascinating play of colours across the winter sky.

The clear days with northern lights or moon affect the dogs, too, and they howl. It is the same with the wolves. Sometimes dogs and wolves howl alternately, answering each other and seeming to enjoy it, and a pack of dogs can make a good deal of noise. Seeing that the dogs are tied up close to the tents and that two hundred throats are pouring forth all the noise they can, one's eardrums have to stand a pretty severe assault.

That the uproar can to some extent keep the caribou away is another matter. It makes little or no difference when many deer have definitely settled in the valley; then a wolf can howl there and the caribou pay little attention to it. But if the herds are on the move, and especially on cold days, there is danger of their turning away from their course when they hear the noise of the dogs. The old Eskimos say, too, that their fathers never let the dogs howl or yelp. Indeed, some preferred to drag the woodsledge themselves rather than run the risk of the dogs' making a noise on the way and perhaps ruining a chance of hunting. The Eskimos fully realize that it would be an advantage to have the dogs better disciplined, but seem unable to overcome a slackness which has persisted for some time.

Something happened which disturbed people for a time. A hunter from the Killik settlement to the south of us came on a visit and told us this story. Old Inualûjaq was out hunting and brought down a large black wolf; it did not move and appeared to be dead. He went toward the animal and was quite close to it when it suddenly jumped up and ran away. Inualûjaq fired four or five shots at such short range that some of them must have been effective, he being so cool and sure a marksman. But the wolf ran on quite unaffected and disappeared. Inualûjaq followed the trail for a good while, but in vain. Next day he took a dog and continued the search, but it was as if the wolf had sunk into the ground. There was a strange, gloomy atmosphere in the tent as the hunters sat discussing the affair. I was rather surprised, but did not ask any questions. Then Agmâlik said, so that I, too, should understand the significance of the event: "When strange things like that happen with animals, it's always a bad omen."

"What can happen, then?"

"Perhaps Inualûjaq will die."

Said Mikiâna: "Last winter, on a sledge trip, Inualûjaq killed two of his dogs. He stabbed them with his knife and covered them with snow. Next day one of the dogs came into camp. Soon afterward one of his grown-up sons died. A strange thing happened at our old settlement, too, that year. In the winter we often heard a fox barking in a queer way just behind us on the mountainside. Once we heard the hoot of an owl which was quite different from what it usually is. That summer we lost two children."

Both Paniaq and Agmâlik had stories of similar things which had happened to them, and in each case a near relation had died shortly afterward. "Everyone knows it is so," said Paniaq. "Sometimes I can hardly believe it, but I can't help believing it all the same."

A week later Inualûjaq came on a visit to our settlement. He

was taciturn and looked miserable. He remained healthy and
active all the time I was in the mountains. But a month after
this event his new-born granddaughter died.

The light increases; a warm redness filters up and gleams
through driving clouds. Sometimes sky and snow acquire a delicate green tone; it reminds one of the clear colour which meets
the eye when one looks down over the side of a boat on a large
fresh-water lake. As changing lights on a stage influence one's
moods, so it is here. Willows, rocks, mountains, and snow-clad
slopes with rows of drifts like stiffened waves, emerge from the
greyness with new contours and seem different from what they
were before. The richer impressions give new life to our
thoughts; we feel that the light is falling on them, too. We have
happy expectations. The sun will come soon.

The children's games are a good calendar; now they go ahead
in earnest with outdoor games of many kinds. Sometimes they
play soccer (*arjaujaqtut*). The ball is of caribou skin, and the
rules are simple: sometimes the ball has to be kicked into a
goal, but most often the object is simply to send it as far as possible out into the countryside. Soccer is an ancient sport with
the Nunamiuts, as with other Eskimos. It is mentioned in many
of the old legends. When they describe a man visiting a settlement, it is almost a regular feature that he first hears lively talk
and laughter from people playing soccer. The hero of the story
(often the poor boy) may surprise the rest by running more
swiftly with the ball than anyone else. It is a fine thing to be a
fast-running soccer player.

The children play stick-ball, too. There are two sides; one
player throws the ball, and one of the other side hits it away
with a stick. This player then has to run to a fixed point and
back, while children of the other side seize the ball and try to
hit the runner. The Norwegian Lapps, who were brought to
northern Alaska at the turn of the century to teach the coast

Eskimos how to manage reindeer, taught them stick-ball, too. On their annual journey to the mouth of the Colville River the Nunamiuts associated with the coast Eskimos; from them the inland people learnt the game, and they liked it so much that they continued to play it in the mountains.

Thus, all was well except for the caribou. What had become of the main herd? From time to time a fair number of caribou would come along, and for a few days the cooking-pot was fuller than before, but what good was that when the beasts were away over the mountains in a twinkling as if the devil were at their heels? Not infrequently we saw caribou dashing away with wolves in pursuit. One day a panic-stricken herd of caribou came rushing right into the camp, among the tents and dogs; it was an extraordinary scene. Aguk was on the spot, as usual, right in front of the deer, and he shot three.

A little excitement may be a good thing, but when for days on end it is just a question of whether one's stomach will be filled or not, one can do without it. Our most important source of fat, marrow, now failed us altogether. The caribou had so consumed their reserves that there was no longer any marrow in their bones, only a thin, blood-stained fluid without nutritive value.

Paniaq's thoughts take a quaint turn sometimes. One evening he frankly apologized for the caribou being so few. This was not meant as a joke; he spoke as a hospitable Eskimo. A foreign hunter from a distant country had come to his people, and he felt a kind of responsibility for his having a good time. Next moment he said confidently: "If the caribou disappear altogether, we've got plenty of skins." He told me that many times he had had to eat the skins. "They taste good when they're boiled," he said. It is such a common thing for the Nunamiuts to be on starvation diet that they have a name for this dish (*disaruaq*).

"If the caribou don't come at all . . . ," I said one evening when the hunters were sitting together. Mikiâna shrugged his shoulders and began to talk about something else. That day there had been bad hunting for everyone, but their temper was unchanged. I never hear the Eskimos discuss the possibility of going anywhere for help. They will let things go pretty far before they think of such a thing. The hunters have a blind faith that a miracle may happen, that the caribou will come in thousands at any moment. So, in earlier times, they have often let things go too far: people and dogs have at last been so exhausted that it was hopeless to set out on a long journey to seek help from coast Eskimos or Indians.

Then something encouraging happened; the Eskimos for the first time in a long time saw *nurrarik* (the Eskimos' common word for cows and calves). This was a good omen; the main herd could not be far off. But the frozen wilds remained as devoid of life as ever.

The incomparable Kakinnâq, that well-spring of rebellious cheerfulness and solemn narratives, had his own omens. He said: "Just wait till the moon grows small and lies like a basket in the sky, for then it will be filled with caribou. Then when it swings down toward the mountains, the beasts will stream out over the country. You will see."

It was a bitter, windy day. I was sitting in the frost-covered tent, thinking. Behind the stove lay a frozen knuckle of meat, and I had just settled the problem of whether I should cook it or not. I also had a small piece of a caribou's stomach on the staging outside, if the knuckle should not be enough. For that day I was safe, but next day's food—well, that was still walking about on four legs. But I was brooding over secret plans. I had had a sight of a promising valley a long way off where I was sure no one had hunted before. The more I thought of that valley the more faith I had in it. I knew in my heart that I had thought like this about no end of places before and been disappointed, but every time I told myself that the new place was something quite different.

Suddenly the skin which hung over the entrance was thrust aside, and little Ayaqiujaq, in his white sheepskin anorak, tumbled in. Breathless and round-eyed, he burst out, *"Tuttuwagjuits!"* (a great number of caribou). I pulled my anorak over my head, shot out of the tent, seized my rifle, buckled on my skis and sped off up the side of the valley. The other hunters were all on the move, dashing along at full speed on snowshoes. And in our wake the children came trotting, while a number of the women climbed up onto a hillock.

I had not been going long when I came to a sudden stop. It was incredible: there were caribou everywhere. They were swarming along the slopes of the valley and on the flat—thousands of beasts, some near and large, others black spots in the far distance. And up in the mountains they were pouring along, a broad stream of brown-grey caribou from the highest pass down to the bottom of the valley. The whole country was alive.

And low over the mountains a quarter-moon lay like a basket in the sky. "There you are," said Kakinnâq. "It was full of caribou, just as I said."

CHAPTER 25

Song

When a number of hunters assemble of an evening and talk about hunting, I sit and listen to the music of their speech. It has a controlled strength, running on in an even rhythm.

The Eskimo language is certainly not easy to learn; there is a great deal in it that is strange to a white man. Take, for example, the following sentence from one of the Nunamiuts' old legends: *Inuit tuqunniaraluarâgigât tuqutaulaitsuq,* which means: "People tried to kill him all the time, but he never got killed." Element by element, however, the translation runs as follows:

Inui - t tuqun - niar - aluar - âgi - ga - a - t
People kill - try - though - always - (participle) him, he
tuqu(t) - ta - u - lait - su - q.
Kill - ed - be - never - (indicative) - (singular).

As is seen, the meaning is expressed by, among other things, the addition of the most varied endings. Endings may, according to their meaning, correspond to English verbs, adverbs, adjectives, pronouns, prepositions, or conjunctions. They may also express subtle shades of meaning which are not usually expressed in our language. Many Eskimo words contain a long string of such endings.

It is important to me to get stories, etc., reproduced in phonetics corresponding exactly to the pronunciation. This is a very difficult task for anyone who is not a trained linguist. To capture the curious, often closely related sound is sometimes like catching a fluttering butterfly with one's hands.

I have sought help from various Eskimos. Kakinnâq had to be rejected at once, for he talks like a rushing torrent. When I asked him to talk slowly and clearly, he looked at me in astonishment, and the torrent of speech continued. Then I tried one of the pretty young girls in the camp. As soon as I returned from hunting she came to my tent and we set to work. This aroused a good deal of interest; the married women smiled knowingly. It would have gone quite well, however, if the children had not continually disturbed the work. They were always dashing up, poking their heads through the caribou-skin door and staring inquisitively. Then they tittered and made comments wholly unconnected with linguistic studies. At last I found an Eskimo who gave me quiet, valuable help. But it was arduous, for every single word had to be repeated an intolerable number of times.

With much toil and trouble I made a fairly good job of the spoken language, but when it came to the reproduction of the Eskimo songs I was all at sea. The queer tones and rhythms offered greater difficulties than I could cope with.

I set my hopes on Sig Wien. I had asked him some time before to bring up a recording machine by air, but it is a long way, and as president of an aircraft company which serves the whole of north Alaska he has his hands full. The chances did not seem great.

He came. A shining little plane appeared between the mountaintops. We thought it would land on a lake a mile or two away, but it did not. The experienced bush pilot steered straight down toward a narrow strip between the tents and the moraines, and the plane landed there as certainly as a car driving up to a door.

A smiling giant clambered out of the plane—Sig Wien, the Eskimos' friend not only here, but all over northern Alaska. He is the Nunamiuts' firm support, for, as I have said, he flies in a quantity of things several times a year and takes away their wolfskins. He makes nothing out of it worth mentioning, but he is fond of these primitive people. Moreover, he had found time to obtain and bring with him a recording machine and transformer.

Next day he flew back southward. Then a time of great activity began. As soon as hunting or other work was over, I set my marvellous machine working and recorded songs, old stories, vocabulary, etc., on the tape. The recording machine was a success from the start—"Almost like strong medicine," said one of the older men, smiling. On it the Eskimos were able to hear their own speech and their own songs; they laughed heartily and thought the whole thing a queer, amusing game. But strangest of all was the "shining glass" which came with the machine and which I hung from one of the tent stakes. It was the first time they had seen an electric lamp.

Curiously enough, the Eskimos have taken to the microphone as if it were the most natural thing in the world. Their manner of telling stories is as fresh and impulsive as before; they sit on the willow-bough floor and hold forth like experienced broadcasters.

Now there are floods of songs; I find, indeed, that this isolated people in the depths of the mountains has preserved a mine of them. They love singing—through it they express the changing moods of daily life; they abandon themselves to it with a kind of intoxication. A hunter may be sitting in his tent gazing in front of him, when suddenly the urge to sing comes

Iluppak, a dashing young hunter

Aguk, just home from hunting with a few stories to tell

Alasuq having a good meal of gadfly grubs, which in spring cover the side of the caribou's skin nearest the flesh, and are considered a delicacy

Spring is approaching; the caribou move northward to the tundra where the calves will be born. Each herd is led by a cow

Paniaq and the Author

over him. When he begins, the others—men, women, and children—join in from time to time. The chorus grows stronger and the tempo quicker; a storm of strange notes fills the skin tent.

The Nunamiuts speak of their great composers of former times with the same veneration as we speak of Bach, Beethoven, and Grieg. Some of the best known are Qallayauq, Kumak, Masuâluk, Nasarniq, Suwaliq, Qungusialuk, and Tatpâna; the latter is probably the most famous. The people still has its composers; the leading one is Maptirâq.

Good music travels far beyond language boundaries. Thus, other peoples' songs have in the course of time found their way to the Brooks Mountains and there taken a new lease of life. The Nunamiuts have songs from the Kobuk Eskimos to the south, from the Eskimo groups along the coast of northern Alaska and Canada, from the Diomede Islands in the Bering Strait, and even from Siberia.

It is of special interest that the Nunamiuts have preserved a number of Indian songs. These date from the time when the Indians also hunted caribou in the mountains. Most of the tunes have no doubt been learnt from the Koyukuk people, with whom the Eskimos have associated from time to time for feasts and races.

The Eskimo songs are of many kinds. There are a great number of festal and dance songs, which are sung in chorus and are usually accompanied by drums. As I mentioned earlier, there are four groups of them: *atûtiqpak, atûtipiak, sayûn,* and *atûgaujaq.*

Then there are songs connected with the shaman's activities or with various ceremonies, protective songs, love songs, lampoons, hunting songs, children's songs, humorous songs, songs to the northern lights, the moon, etc., animal songs, songs which accompany stories or are linked up with particular events, and so on. There are said to have been war songs, too, but they are no longer remembered. There are no dirges.

A good many have words, but they are often hard to interpret. Old-fashioned language survives, and also, no doubt, abbreviated sentences or special combinations of words have definite associations for the Eskimos. Many of the songs have no words, only meaningless syllables which coincide exactly with the rhythm.

With some songs the words are sung in turn by two men. With others another person has to break into the song at set places with a wild *Hoi! Hoi!*

Most of the songs are still the common property of the people, as they were in the past. But a few seem to have become a kind of private property. This was more emphatically so in earlier times, especially as regards "strong" songs—for example, hunting and trapping songs whose object is to assure the hunter of success. The right to use them can sometimes be bought.

An essential part of community singing is the drum, a cari-

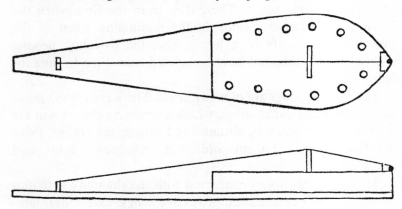

The Eskimos' one-stringed instrument, *kasagnaujaq,* was about sixteen inches long and was held against the left side.—From a drawing by the Eskimo Paniaq.

bou skin stretched over a ring of willow wood. In times past the Nunamiuts had another instrument, a kind of one-stringed mandolin which they called *kasagnaujaq*.

The Eskimos' music reveals something fundamental in their character. It also contains features derived from the people's cultural history, pointing the way back into the past and to other tribal groups. But it is not easy to interpret this peculiar music. There are things unfamiliar to a white man's ear, strange rhythms and intervals, nuances unlike anything a modern instrument can reproduce. But even to a layman it is clear that they betoken a musical people.

I recorded on the tape about two hundred songs. The composer Eivind Groven, one of our foremost experts in the field of folk-music, has been through the greater part of them. I give below a selection which he has scored. Further, he gives the following interesting comments on Nunamiut music:

Hearing Helge Ingstad's comprehensive collection of records of Eskimo and Indian tunes from Alaska was an interesting experience. A first impression of the singing was that it is monotonous and peculiar. But that was due mainly to the manner in which the melodies were sung. When one became accustomed to the timbre of the voices and the "text," gradually the shape of the melodies appeared and the sense of the music became clear. And the better one gets to know it, the more one realizes that this is material of enormous value, not only from the scientific but also from the artistic standpoint.

The records show that the singers certainly have a good ear. They sing true without going sharp or flat. And the repetitions are exact. Even minor details of rhythm and tone are exactly reproduced. It can therefore be taken that the people is highly musical.

The melodies bear witness to a sense of consistent style. Each is composed as a compact whole, and some phrases stand so high as music that they can hold their own as valuable material for musicological development.

The tunes cover quite a wide tonal range, and the rhythm is also varied.

The typical Eskimo melodies can be classed as pentatonic (five-tone scale) with a major tendency. But the five-tone scales are not completely consistent. It is found that several types of pentatonic major are represented.

The Indian melodies have rather a minor tendency, usually with an element of the pentatonic, but have a freer scale. We find the same freedom in the Siberian songs, where the five-tone scale with a major tendency is the foundation, but the keynote is undefinable. The scale is six- and often seven-tone.

The melodies in many cases lose their character when played on a tempered instrument, for example the piano. This is especially the case with the "Song of the Man Who Made a Kayak of Human Bones . . . ," in which the third and sixth are at least a comma over the normal pure minor third and sixth and about thirty millioctaves above the corresponding tunes on a tempered instrument. Something similar occurs in rhythm sample no. 1, *atûtiqpak,* in which the third and sixth in pentatonic major are one comma lower than in our scale.

Rhythm sample no. 2, *atûtipiaq,* rather suggests natural scale (willow pipe and cow-horn) in that the fourth flat above the keynote, especially in the two-time section, is sharper than in our scale. The three-quarter tone degree up to C seems to be clear.

Individual tunes show a marked relationship to melodies of different origin.

"Old Eskimo Song from Kobuk" is related to the leading motif of Tchaikovski's Fifth Symphony (first movement).

Eskimo song from Kobuk

Tchaikovski

One finds tunes which resemble each other so closely that one might think they were variations of the same melody.

The "Song from Herschel Island" (Canadian Eskimos) has a certain similarity to a hymn tune from Telemark:

Eskimo song from Herschel Island

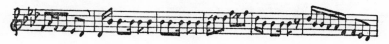

Hymn from Telemark

There is, too, something in the syncopated rhythms and the slightly enlarged intervals in the pentatonic-major melodies which is not far removed from well-known Negro tunes. For instance, rhythm sample no. 1, *atûtiqpak,* and the "Song of the Man Who Made a Kayak of Human Bones . . . ," seem closely related to the Negro song "Tramping" (especially as sung by Marian Anderson).

It will be seen that in the scores I have in some places put dashes before the head of the note. These indicate a deviation from the normal interval. If the dashes run upward, it means that the note is sharper, if they run downward it means that the note is flatter. Single dashes indicate a deviation of at least a quarter tone. Double dashes indicate a deviation of one-eighth tone (one comma).

Helen H. Roberts * uses a similar method in her copies of Eskimo tunes. She puts the dashes *through* the head of the note, but I think it is clearer to place them before it.

The following selection of songs (Mr. Groven says) were all recorded among the Nunamiuts:

Examples of rhythm in four types of Nunamiut dance song.
(From the Nunamiuts.)

1. *Atûtiqpak*   Syncopated two-time.

2. *Atûtipiak*   Five-time and three-time.

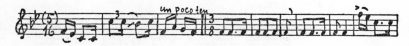

3. *Sayûn*   Three-time tendency throughout.

4. *Atûgaujak*   Almost rhythmic march.

* *Eskimo Songs,* Report of the Canadian Arctic Expedition 1913–18, Vol. XIV.

Old Dance Song.
(From the Nunamiuts.)

æ eng ja æ ange jange jæ enga ja enge enge jæ-æ

æ ange jenge æ hange ja ange næ jange jange ei

enge enge æ ja hange jange ja hange ja jange jange ja ei

æ ange jange ja hange-æ ange jange ja hæ hæ ange hæ ja

ange ja anga ja jange ja ænge nga enge enge enge ja

Song of the Man Who Made a Kayak of Human Bones and Human Skin.
(From the Nunamiuts.)

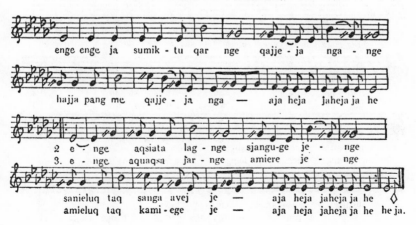

enge enge ja sumik-tu qar nge qajje-ja nga-nge

hajja pang me qajje-ja nga — aja heja jaheja ja he

2 e nge aqsiata lag-nge sjangu-ge je - nge
3. e-nge aquaqsa jar-nge amiere je - nge

sanieluq taq sanga avej je — aja heja jaheja ja he
amieluq taq kami-ege je — aja heja jaheja ja he heja.

Love Song.
(From the Nunamiuts.)

enge enge ja   enge jæ   enge jang æ   ja jan ge ja jange ja   ja ja

ange ja jange ja   jange jange jaja ange   jange jange ja   eng eng enge ja

ja jange   ja jange jange   ja jange ja jange   ja   ja ja   ange ja

jange ja   ange ange ja ja ange   ja ja jange   ja ja

Old Kobuk Song.
(From the Kobuk Eskimos.)

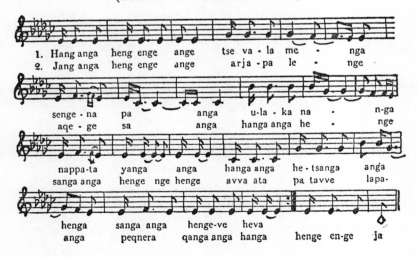

1. Hang anga   heng enge   ange   tse va - la me -   nga
2. Jang anga   heng enge   ange   arja - pa le -   nge

senge - na   pa   anga   u - la - ka na -   n-ga
aqe - ge   sa   anga   hanga anga he -   nge

nappa - ta yanga   anga   hanga anga   he - tsanga   anga
sanga anga   henge nge henge   avva ata   pa tavve   lapa -

henga   sanga anga   henge - ve heva   henge en - ge   ja
anga   peqnera   qanga anga hanga   henge en - ge   ja

Song from Herschel Island.
(From Canadian Eskimos.)

enge enge enge enge ja   aja ja ja ja ja ja jange jange ja enge enge--e ja

a ja ja ja ja   ange jange ja   aja aja ja ja ja jangejangejangeja

e - engé - e ja aja a ja jeng ' ja jam nge ja   a - ja ja ja

jange jange ja   ja - enge - eja   enge - eja

The Dying Indian's Song.
(From the Koyukuk Indians.)

Jå ni ka tien ni sjiu hå Ja alla le Ja   alla

le Ja — alla le Ja — alla le Jo elli

kout Jutta ta ni sja — nga jutta ta jutta ne

sjånk Ja ha je ja Ja ha je ja   alla le

Ja eli kou Ja alla le

Siberian Song.
(From the Eskimos at East Cape, Siberia.)

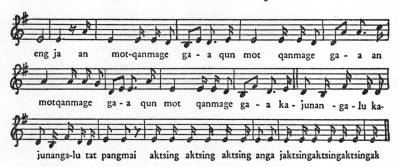

eng ja   an   mot-qanmage ga - a qun mot   qanmage   ga - a an

motqanmage   ga - a qun mot   qanmage ga - a ka - junan - ga - lu ka-

junanga-lu tat pangmai   aktsing aktsing aktsing anga jaktsingaktsingaktsingak

We had had a musical evening in the skin tent, with gaiety and laughter. One Eskimo after another had taken the microphone and sung, and a few of the women had participated, even the reserved Kaliksuna, who had sung an amusing ptarmigan song. The children had made their contribution, funny little verses and jingles, followed by outbursts of laughter. Then I turned the tape back and let the Eskimos hear their own voices, to the delight of all.

Then I said to Paniaq: "Now call the animals as you do out hunting." Paniaq took the microphone and started. He gave an animal concert so astoundingly true to life that we might have had all the beasts of the wilderness about us. He called caribou, moose, mountain sheep, fox, raven, owl, yellow-billed loon, ptarmigan, ground squirrel, and all the rest. Last came the wolf. And the wolf's howl rang out, so perfectly true to life in its harsh dissonance that I felt a chill down my spine.

Suddenly he received an answer. The dogs which had lain asleep in the snow outside the tent woke, raised their muzzles to the stars and howled, too.

CHAPTER 2 6

Ill-omened Qalutaq

The thousands of caribou had settled down in the neighbourhood, and at last the beasts seemed to have become quiet. If we took a turn down by the river as far as the nearest moraines, herds were to be seen in almost every direction. Bulls, cows, and calves were pasturing along the slopes of the valley as peacefully as cattle in a field. We shot what we needed without difficulty. Even if we were still short of fat, we had the pleasant feeling before each meal that we could now eat just as much as we liked.

But the wretched settlement Qalutaq, which till then had embittered our lives with shortages of food and fuel and ceaseless gales, had not quite done with us yet. The caribou had streamed in over the countryside, it is true, but men can be made to suffer in so many ways. It is strange indeed how all manner of difficulties accumulated at that settlement. One of the Eskimos said seriously: "I've felt all the time there was something wrong with the place."

An aircraft came with men from a world far south, where there were other occupations besides hunting the caribou and wolf. It came from Fairbanks and had a curious cargo: a fur-dealer and an Eskimo woman and her two quite small children. The fur-dealer wanted to find out whether it would eventually be possible to do business with the Nunamiuts. It was significant of the isolation in which they had lived that this was the first time a fur-dealer had made his way into the mountains. Other natives of Alaska had had regular communications with the traders for a long time. The Hudson's Bay Company has been working among Indians and Eskimos in the wilds of northern Canada for two hundred years.

The fur-dealer's arrival among these people was a depressing sign. It was ominous of chewing gum, sweets, bad clothes, and many of the other blessings of civilization. The shining white teeth would decay as those of the coast Eskimos had decayed; diseases would take a hold. The people's mentality would change; experience shows that this happens pretty quickly when the outriders of civilization begin their work.

The Eskimo woman and her children were attractive, but what a difference there was between them and the Nunamiuts! It showed clearly what a swift change takes place in primitive peoples under the influence of civilization. The woman seemed out of place in the caribou-skin tent, and the two Eskimo children were like delicate flowers compared with the robust, vital mountain children. They were completely lost on the uneven willow-bough floor of the tent and burst into tears when they had to cross it.

After two days our visitors moved on. It would take some days for the new influence to wear off, but the many demands of daily life would help and I should soon slip back into the old routine and be at peace.

But no, there was no peace, for the scourge of civilization had suddenly fallen upon us. Almost every one of us was laid low with severe influenza and whooping cough at the same time. The sickness spread to the other settlements. There were scenes of utter misery in the tents all round. Many people had high temperatures and most of them violent coughs. At the same time we had trying weather; for week after week storms or strong winds swept down the valley. The immediate surroundings of the tents, and the ground between them and the river, were completely changed during this time; the snowdrifts, hard as stone, had grown so high.

At the Killik encampment south of us in the valley, two children born in the course of the winter died, and some of the adults could only just keep going. Paniaq was one of those who were most ill. He lay day after day by the stove like a sick wolf, wrapped in caribou skins. He had a great deal of pain. Now and again I could hear a piercing yell from his tent. With a faint gleam of his old humour he said: "When I have really bad pain, I yell as hard as I can. It does me good."

I myself did not escape, but I could not waste more than a few days in my sleeping bag. Of course I did not have, as the others did, a wife to fetch wood and meat, to cook and manage things. The unmarried women, too, were fully occupied in looking after their own families at this time. So I had to go out after wood in all weathers, and sometimes hunting. In this I was unfortunate, for time after time when I had crept up into position I had a volcanic outburst of whooping. This quite new noise made a deep impression on the caribou; seldom have I seen them run faster.

Outdoor life proved to be an indifferent cure, and I was unwell for quite a long time.

This was another example of the risks the Nunamiuts run through contact with civilization. They are so untouched that they have little resistance to the sicknesses of the white race. As for myself, I had established on earlier visits to the polar regions that a certain degree of immunity against chills and similar minor ailments rapidly diminishes. It may be that in this case my powers of resistance were particularly reduced by the shortage of fat.

Before all the sick had recovered, the Raven people suddenly decided to find a new dwelling place farther north. It was as though they wanted to flee from the curse that lay upon Qalutaq. Kakinnâq and Agmâlik, who were in perfect health, set off ahead with their families. The rest of us followed at a more leisurely pace. Paniaq lay on top of the load like a flaccid caribou carcass, and I myself was not in particularly good fettle.

We came to a bright and pretty spot. We could see from the snow that the wind was gentler there. And in the thick willow patch there was an abundance of tinder-dry trees, which told us how delightfully warm it was going to be in the tents.

Once more we were close to the watershed in the Anaktuvuk Pass, a little south of one of our early winter encampments. The tents were pitched in the valley on the broad, level banks of the river. To east and west we were flanked by high moraines, and behind them began the slope toward the mountains, several miles in extent. As soon as we came up from the river we had a wide view over the fascinating open landscape, which I have described earlier. But it was some time before we got the sun, for the high mountains shut it out. For a long time a red glow had been playing along the edge of the sky and growing stronger daily. There were times when crinkly clouds over the mountains became such a flaming marvel that no words could describe their play of colours. We waited hungrily for the sun itself, and at last, on February 3, it shed its light upon our settlement.

All was suddenly changed. The time of darkness now seemed far away, almost like something we had dreamed.

The men were out hunting every day, even those who still felt the after-effects of illness. Caribou were everywhere in thousands. Large areas of the valley floor and of the slopes were trampled hard. When we drew near to the grazing herds, we could see their hooves strike the hard crust of the snow and send a dainty shower of glittering snow crystals into the air. Then, when the beasts moved on, the ground was turned up as by a harrow, and the reindeer moss peeped out here and there from its white shroud.

The caribou came from the east. The distribution of the herds usually changes with wind and weather: in fog and snowy weather the animals do not move about much, but they gather speed before a storm. Always when migrating the herd has a leader, most often a cow. It keeps a hundred yards ahead of the others, which gives the herd a better chance should there be wolves ahead. When suspicious, every single beast usually stops, stands quite still, listens, and watches. This is a useful common reaction, for on the march there is a good deal of noise from the many hooves trampling the snow crust. The Eskimos declare that the caribou can tell the difference between the steps of a man and a caribou.

At this season it sometimes happens that we shoot a beast which is very fat, most often a cow without a calf. The news goes round the settlement at once, and a good many people drop in, quite casually as it were, at a suitable time before the cooking-pot boils. At this time I was served with a dish I had not met before: small, fat intestines with their contents in them, properly cooked. It is called *aminlilik*.

There is an art in judging at a distance which beasts in a herd are fat, and equally in concentrating on these and not, in the excitement of the hunt, shooting others which may be temptingly near. Aguk is a master of this art. He says to me: "If you see a bull with antlers which are flat at the tips, don't shoot him. He's a thin beast. But if you see a bull with antlers which are round and jagged at the tips, shoot him. He's a fat one. And if you see a cow with low-branching horns with many notches, shoot her. But you must look at the skin, too. It must be glossy."

The Eskimos also have a remarkable capacity for judging the age of a caribou at a glance (the number of notches in the horns signifies nothing). When I ask them how they set about it, they reply: "Why, we know the beasts. It's very much as with people. You can tell from so many things how old a man is." Moreover, they have different names for the caribou of different ages.

One has to be content so often with an approximate statement of the weights of wild animals that some exact figures may be of interest. Here are the weights of a few caribou, taken a short time after they were shot.

Weight of caribou bulls in February:
      2 years old   145 lb.
      4 years old   234 lb.
      5–6 years old   281 lb.
Weight of caribou cows in February:
      2 years old   148 lb.
      2 years old   147 lb.
      7–8 years old   204 lb.
      12 years old   215 lb.

These are the total weights, with intestines and without substantial loss of blood. These lean winter animals will weigh about 30 to 40 per cent more in the autumn. The ages are as given by the Eskimos.

One of the things the Eskimos most enjoy is visiting each other's settlements. They have a grand time chatting about the many little things which have happened in the world of men and beasts since hosts and visitors last met, and having a good laugh in the new surroundings.

One day I went on a visit to the southward, to the Killik settlement, Qayaq. Of course the sharp-eyed children detected the sledge when it was still far off and also knew at once who was coming. As usual they shouted the visitor's name all over the settlement and were in a fever of excitement. The people swarmed out of the tents at once—first the girls and wives, then the hunters. When the dog-team drew up, they stood there smiling at me; I had the pleasant feeling of being welcome.

We went into one of the tents, where the best that could be offered in the way of caribou meat was served. This came first and talk second. Maptirâq set the tone. First he asked me to excuse his having nothing but lean caribou meat. Then he said he was glad that I had wished to live with his people that winter.

We talked about old times, and I heard many arresting stories of his youth. In those days a hunter always carried a piece of jade in his belt; that was his file for sharpening his tools. Flint and willow-cotton were always in use; of matches and other bought goods there were very few. Then he fetched a skin bag from the corner of the tent and fished out of it two old labrets carved from white stone. The front of each was about two inches in diameter, and a greenish-blue rock crystal was glued fast to it. On the back there was a short, rough stem and a smaller plate to be forced through a hole in the lower lip. He handled them carefully. These were heirlooms and his greatest wealth; they were not for sale at any price. It is not so long since the Nunamiuts wore plates like these, an important defence against evil spirits.

Maptirâq told also of tattooing, which was formerly general among the Nunamiut women. They wore three stripes of tattoo-marks down their chins. The men tattooed themselves only when they had killed a man, and then they made a spot a little way from the corner of the mouth. The tattooing was done by running a sinew, smeared with soot and grease, under the skin.

We had a long talk about times past. "In my young days," he said, "there were still a few men who hunted with bows and arrows. Times were often difficult. If the caribou came to an end, life came to an end, too."

At last we got to the story of the great flood which the raven made to subside so that the earth appeared.

"The earth must be great," said Maptirâq, "and where it ends no one can know. I have heard of Eskimos who live a long way off and whom I have never seen."

"What do you think the earth looks like?"

He looked at me and said: "Why, we can see that with our own eyes."

"Perhaps it's round," I suggested cautiously.

Maptirâq did not reply; he went on hollowing out a willow pipe and obviously did not think it worth while to examine such an idea any further.

"Some people think it is," I continued.

Maptirâq lit his pipe carefully, then he looked at me in astonishment and said: "That's a thing everyone must understand, that the earth is flat; otherwise the rivers would run off it."

It was late evening and moonlight when I parted with the Eskimos and went off upstream. I sat in the sledge and let the dogs trot. It was still and cold. Due north, over the row of bushy tails, glimmered the northern lights.

What strikes one most of all when one associates with the Nunamiuts is this—that there is no essential difference between them and other human beings, whether they live in New York or London or Oslo. They love, hate, are unhappy or happy, and strive to master their fears as we do. And their capacities are like ours.

On the one side are the characteristics common to men generally, on the other the special features of the race, which are determined by environment and other causes. Here there are various circumstances which may surprise one.

During my intimate association with the Nunamiuts, in good times and bad, I have gradually acquired a fair knowledge of their mental processes. Much which at the beginning could not be discerned became clear by degrees. It is like going into strange country: first a vague general picture appears, but as one walks about, a multitude of details gradually emerge, and one begins to realize how much one does not know.

One of the Eskimos told me how Aguk had just been insulted and added appreciatively: "Aguk didn't fly out, but just sat quite calm." This is characteristic. The Nunamiuts aim at self-control, or, to put it more correctly, they so armour their senses that unpleasant things may penetrate them as little as possible. This is so with death. There are exceptions, for example Una-lîna, who grieved long and deeply for her little son; but sorrow is often short-lived. They also accept other disagreeable occurrences with equanimity, as when the caribou have failed and they are threatened with death by starvation.

Much that is unpleasant is forgotten. Sometimes injuries seem to be remembered objectively, as it were, without the bitterness that we feel. It once happened that a number of Eskimos were living by a big lake. On one side of the lake Ulîqse and his family had pitched their tent; on the other side lived Makkalik. Makkalik was married to Ulîqse's sister; he was a rather peculiar fellow in many ways. There was an agreement between the two families that if anything happened they should set up a pole with a strip of skin at the top. When this signal appeared, the hunter on the other side would paddle over at once.

One day Ulîqse came on a visit to his brother-in-law's camp and found only his sister in the tent. She was ill, with a high temperature and severe pain. It appeared that her husband, for some incomprehensible reason, had moved over to his mother in the neighbouring tent. It was impossible to have speech with him. Ulîqse could not see his sister neglected, and despite her miserable condition, transported her across the lake to his own tent. Soon afterward she died.

Ulîqse hoisted the signal to bring his brother-in-law across, but no one came. So he had to dig a grave for his sister in the frozen ground all alone. It was a hard task; he worked at it for three days.

Twenty years passed. All this time Makkalik and Ulîqse

were constantly together, hunting and in camp, but not one word was ever said about what had happened.

Then there was a funeral. Each of the hunters took a shift at digging down through the hard-frozen earth; and it came to Makkalik's turn. He set about it vigorously, while the others stood round. After a time he said cheerfully and with a hint of bragging: "It isn't nearly as hard to dig a grave like this as people say it is."

Ulîqse replied quietly: "Oh yes, it is hard work. I know, because it took me three days to bury my sister."

Makkalik immediately flung away his tools, clambered up out of the grave, and lay down on the ground.

If many injuries accumulate, the suppressed feelings may burst out explosively, but it takes a great deal to make this happen. On one point, however, the Eskimos seem to be very sensitive—where the insult is of such a kind that they are made to feel inferior as human beings. In such a case there can be an instantaneous and violent reaction. This can easily happen when an inexperienced white man is tactless in his behaviour. Without intending any scorn, he can hurt an Eskimo most deeply by the tone of his voice or by doing something that is quite ordinary in the civilized world. If a white man is foolish enough to show that he thinks himself better than an Eskimo, it takes very little to make the latter blaze up. I believe this to be the explanation of several of the cases where Eskimos have murdered white men on the coasts of Canada and Alaska.

As a rule the Nunamiuts have no wish to hurt one another; on the contrary, they are anxious to maintain a friendly tone in personal intercourse. Backbiting is rare. Every man or woman is respected—even when quite young people talk, everyone listens with interest and in silence. And hospitality is an unwritten law. These rules are sometimes broken, of course, but not often.

The Nunamiuts' smile is illustrative of the good companionship among these inhabitants of the wilds. An Eskimo's smile, however, can mean a good deal. Most often it expresses cheerfulness and cordiality, but it can also conceal embarrassment or other feelings which it is not always so easy to discover. When we sat by the death-bed of the little boy Tullaq, and his father, torn with grief, burst out: "His legs are beginning to grow cold. Soon I shall have no son," he was met with a smile from the Eskimo who was sitting opposite.

A striking feature of the Nunamiuts, as of other Eskimos, is their self-depreciatory manner of speech. For example, they offer a guest a delicious meal and say, "Here's some kind of food." Something similar can be observed when they are telling of a successful hunt. Never a word of boasting, but usually one or two remarks which reduce the whole thing to a lower plane.

The causes of the peculiar Nunamiut mentality are not easy to discover. A great many factors are involved, and much is lost in the mists of a remote past. But a few main features of their psychology can to a certain extent be explained. One of the most important is this—that their environment and way of life in many respects have given their mentality the shape that is best suited to their hard struggle for existence, in the same way as the physical characteristics of men and animals have from generation to generation been adapted to Arctic conditions.

That an Eskimo does not allow grief and worry to make too deep an impression seems sensible, for sorrow weakens, and a man needs all his strength to maintain his existence. When they set store by cheerful companionship without friction or even pass over an injury in silence, the reason is roughly the same. It is evident that few things are more important than to maintain good relations in a small community like theirs, where all are more or less dependent on one another. It would take so little to overturn the boat.

They have great respect for white men, but are not impressed by either their knowledge or their inventions. The first aircraft certainly gave the Nunamiuts a surprise. But this was soon changed into interest in the plane's working. These people have a peculiar bent for mechanics. Nor is it very easy to surprise an Eskimo. To people who firmly believe that men journey to the stars and can be changed into bears or birds there is nothing so very remarkable about aircraft.

When we sat together in one of the tents late of an evening and talked about one thing and another, I sometimes contributed to the entertainment by telling them something about civilization. I held forth about the skyscrapers in New York, about cars, trams, steamers, and the crowds of people down south. I made an effort to give clear pictures. There was seldom any reaction from the Eskimos; the whole thing fell flat. What the Nunamiuts have not seen has for them little interest.

There are many different currents in the Eskimo mentality, and one should be cautious in judging these people by their smiling exterior. Deep down in their minds there may be bitter thoughts of which only a glimpse is now and then obtained. This may often be due to their mutual dependence and feeling of littleness in the face of the powers that rule them.

The most essential characteristic of the Nunamiuts, and the one which is most conspicuous after long association, is a good one—their kindness and helpfulness, and the natural, humorous manner which makes them easy, pleasant company. These people are at peace—they have developed a way of life which exactly fits the demands made upon them by nature. There is much in this to make a visitor from civilization reflect. Here are primitive people who own nothing but what they can load onto a sledge, whose life is a continual struggle against hunger and cold—and yet they are as happy as men can be. They meet the morning with a smile, and cheerful sounds issue from the tents till they roll themselves up in their caribou-skin blankets and go to sleep again on the willow-bough floor.

Sun over the Mountains

This is the time for wolf hunting.
I write at the beginning of March,
their mating season. We often see them sneaking about over the
snow, now chasing terrified caribou, now sleeping on hillocks,
occasionally rising to peer cautiously around. The Eskimos
have their scissor-traps out, but wolf shooting is a fine and
stimulating sport. Great skill is required, for these beasts are
very cunning.

In the Giants' Valley there was a large white wolf which was
so swift-footed that it could almost keep pace with the caribou.
The Eskimos say this happens only rarely. Most of us had seen
the beast, but it was not to be caught. Then one evening Kakinnâq came home with something bulky on his sledge. There was a
peculiar air of pride about him as he unharnessed the dogs. He
lifted the animal up and dumped it in the snow; it was the white
wolf—a large, handsome beast, yellowish-white all over, but
for a few small grey patches.

A more persistent wolf hunter than Paniaq I have never met.
When he has suddenly got it into his head that now is the time

for shooting wolves, he gives himself no rest, but goes on with
it day after day, paying no attention to his traps or anything
else. The whole of his mind is concentrated on one thing—putting a bullet into a wolf.

He once went on like this for several days without result. His
zeal was certainly not cooled by the fact that his father-in-law,
Kakinnâq, had disposed of three wolves in the same period. In
the darkness of early morning Paniaq was off into the mountains; he hunted till late in the evening and came home to the
settlement long after the rest. But ill luck pursued him.

It happened that I wanted meat at that time and brought
down two caribou in one of the valleys. When I looked in at
Paniaq's tent that evening he had just come back from wolf
hunting, having been at it for twelve good hours. He seemed
remarkably taciturn. In a few moments he burst out: "How am
I going to get any wolves when you're blazing away down in
the valley?" This was a most unreasonable criticism. It is an
everyday affair for people to shoot caribou; besides, he had not
given any indication as to where in the mountains he was going
to hunt. I said something like this, without taking the thing too
seriously.

I mentioned the matter afterward to one of the other hunters.
He laughed heartily and said: "When Paniaq wants a wolf and
doesn't get it, he's angry; everyone knows that."

This was the only time during our long association that there
was even the slightest friction between us. When we met next
morning all was as before. That day he got his wolf—in fact,
two. He shot them, as they ran full speed, at a range of two hundred yards; I helped to bring them in and so was able to check
the tracks and the range.

Another time he was on the trail of a couple of wolves when
he saw a great brute in one of his traps. He did not want to spoil
his hunting by firing a round, so he took a primitive ice-chisel

which he had left behind in the trapping area on a previous occasion and went for the beast with that.

Agmâlik is building himself a spacious turf hut after the old design. This takes quite a lot of work, but quick and clever with his hands, he has it finished in a couple of days. It is 11 feet 4 inches by 16 feet 7 inches and much warmer than a skin tent.

The children enjoy the light days and are now playing games which are proper to this time of the year. They play darts (*napâtsaktut*). The dart is a spike put into a willow shaft, and it is thrown at a log of wood. The little girl Alasuq is a crack player; she defeats one boy after another. I, too, suffer ignominious defeat, to her great delight.

The children are also busy tobogganing and sliding down the steep moraines on both sides of the flats by the river. They are continually playing about on the high ground; seen from the settlement, in their long cloaks, they look like marionettes against the white background. Most of them have quite small toboggans made by their fathers, on which they love to slide down on their stomachs at breakneck speed. Those who have no toboggans slide on a caribou skin or on the seats of their trousers. Then there are some who prefer rolling down; they are great at rolling.

The ptarmigan have come. There are large flocks in the willow thicket quite near the camp, or in the snow. They rise in a white cloud as we drive the dogs forward. These multitudes of birds are a sight when, coming home from hunting in the evening, I reach the moraines and have the valley with its rust-red willows below me. The ptarmigan sit close together in rows in the treetops and on the branches; the willows seem to be bending under the weight of great white fruit in the evening sunlight.

The children are active in hunting and catching ptarmigan. The girls set snares along a fence of boughs erected in the snow, just as in Norway. The boys stalk the game with bows and arrows and are great hunters. Even little Ayaqiujaq wants to try his luck, but he is so small that both he and his bow almost disappear in the deep snow. He pushes on stubbornly, scares up flock after flock, never shoots anything, but is always well pleased with his hunting.

It not infrequently happens that the girls make captures of another kind when they are out snaring the ptarmigan. It is sunny now, and instincts are awakened. Eyes shine brighter and blood runs swifter. All round lies the willow copse, with open places where no one comes, most inviting for two who want to be quite alone.

I was chopping wood outside my tent one day when one of the pretty girls of the camp went off to look at her snares. She moved off on her snowshoes with a light, springy tread, her long cloak fluttering round her. Golden sunlight fell into the willow copse and upon the mountains; it was a lovely day.

Soon afterward a young hunter came out of another tent; he looked keenly in the direction in which the girl had disappeared, buckled on his snowshoes, and slung his rifle on his back. Then he sauntered off as hunters do when they are after caribou and nothing else.

Some time passed. Then the girl came back with two ptarmigan dangling from one mitten. Oh yes, she had been working hard and tending her snares; the inquisitive women who were peeping through the bearskin doors would see that. She was not walking at all fast, a little too slowly in fact, so that all could see that she was just back from catching ptarmigan and from nothing else. A little later the young hunter came along. He passed my tent. "Any caribou?" I asked. He shook his head, but on his face was the contented expression men wear when hunting has been good.

The Nunamiuts' view of such things differs from ours in many ways. Sex life is regarded as something plain and natural.

If two people want to have intercourse—very well; no one troubles so long as no personal rights are injured. If, for example, a wife is unfaithful, there is trouble at once, not because the husband feels any moral indignation, but because she belongs to him.

To all appearances, the Nunamiuts' liberal view of relations between man and woman contributes to a good balance in the community. That does not mean that it is necessarily suited to other communities. The Eskimos' view is based on certain preliminary conditions, and one of the most important of these is their healthy attitude toward life.

The Nunamiuts' sex life is not entirely uncontrolled; regulating forces are at work. These are not always very easy to define, but can be seen, for example, in the behaviour of the young girls: they mean to be won by a man they like. As for the boys, there is sometimes a certain shyness about them. An elderly hunter, talking openly to me about his amatory experiences, declared that he had never had intercourse with a girl till he was nearly twenty. "I was very shy," he said; "besides, hunting came first with me." Few wait as long as this, but his attitude is illustrative all the same.

All Eskimos, from the ten-year-olds to the old people, talk quite openly about everything connected with sex life. There may be coarse jesting, but there is always an undercurrent that is fresh and healthy in their discussion of such matters.

It was a shock to me at first when little girls of ten or twelve held forth without reserve about the most intimate matters, but it became a matter of course. Some of the people's old stories too are strongly tinged with sex—some, indeed, to such a degree that they leave nothing unsaid. They are told even if women and children are present and are always received with much laughter. These legends are of considerable psychological interest. Some describe peculiar occurrences—one, for example, tells of a woman who will not sleep with her husband because she constantly has intercourse with an evil spirit when he is out hunting. Other stories deal with more ordinary events, for example, a married man's infidelity. Thus there is a tale of one who when out hunting is continually unfaithful to his wife with two women who live alone in a turf house. They are called Puwitse and Singitse. The story ends with the wife killing them both as a warning to people like them.

The Nunamiuts are sexually mature at about the same age as white inhabitants of the north. Their sexual instincts also seem to be more or less similar. Homosexuality does not exist; one of the older men did not even know what it was. They talk of a certain perversity which formerly occurred among the Barrow Eskimos, and of relations between fathers and daughters among other Eskimos. When these things are mentioned there is no question of the Nunamiuts being shocked; the matter is discussed humorously, as something funny.

I had a fairly long talk with an Eskimo one evening about relations between men and women. His last words were: "I've heard from an airman that you whites look at such things differently from us; in fact, he said that you can't even talk about everything when women are there. Why is that?"

The light days make life easier for the women in many ways. From early morning until late in the evening they have their hands full, sewing, skinning, fetching wood, driving dogs, and doing other things which may be difficult in the dark days. It is almost incomprehensible how they have managed to continue sewing all through the winter, for most of them have had no light in their tents but a wick set in caribou fat. And fat has been such a precious thing that they have always had to save it. Nevertheless they have carried on their work steadily, and the stitches have been as fine and even as ever.

Some find time for rather finer sewing. They make borders for the tops of the kamiks (footwear) or along the lower edges of the hunters' anoraks. For this they use scraps of caribou skin, cut to shape, in black, white, and brown. They are put together in various patterns, as the drawings show.

The Nunamiuts' life is so exacting that there is very little time for art, and there is even less interest in it than formerly. In the past, for example, the men made fine carvings in walrus and mammoth bone, and the women spent more time decorating footwear, bags, etc. They undoubtedly had a considerable gift for such work. If I ask an Eskimo to draw something for me, he can immediately make a vivid sketch, while Umialâq swiftly cuts out the most delightful caribou-skin animals as toys for the children.

It is still cold. Sometimes it is very cold; then the snow is like sand, and the sledge runners are iced. In former times sledge runners were covered with strips from a whale's jaw, but this has not been the custom since communication with the coast Eskimos was broken off.

There are many fine days with the sun glittering on the white waste, but one must always be on one's guard up in the mountains. Often there are avalanches on the steep slopes, and many hundreds of caribou are killed by them yearly. Qawwik found twenty dead caribou beside an avalanche, and there are sure to have been more under the snow. Storms come up quickly from time to time, and then there is fog.

Fog can set a hunter a number of problems. One day I was caught a good way from home in fog as dense as a wall. I had just shot a caribou bull when the grey vapour trickled in over the mountains. My compass had been broken some time before, so I had to find my bearings in another way. There was a slight breeze, but that was of little use as a guide, because of the many currents and cross-currents from the side valleys. I knew, however, that the caribou had fallen with his head toward the west; so I took my bearings on the strength of that, and set off. I said to myself: "You've been in this fix before, and you know what to do; but you must mind your right leg. Don't take too long steps with it, or you'll go in a circle." I walked and walked down the empty valley, thinking hard of my right leg. At last I caught sight of a black heap quite close to me, which I thought must be the big stones which run along the river close to the camp. I was pleased with myself. I took a few steps more—and tripped over the caribou bull.

So I had to start again, and a wearisome business it was, walking till nearly midnight. At last I had had enough, and I was just beginning to search for a suitable snowdrift to spend the night in, when in the distance I heard the blessed sound of the dogs barking in camp.

Iluppak was in difficulties the same day in another part of the mountains. He chose to lie down in the snow and spend the night there without a sleeping bag. Next day he arrived at the settlement, smiling contentedly as if nothing had happened.

One of the other Eskimos said: "My father gave me this advice. Always put on your under anorak and take your rifle with you both summer and winter, even if you're only going a short way from the camp." Wise counsel. A storm can spring up in a trice, and one can meet animals anywhere. I mean not only the animals which are useful for food, but also those which can be dangerous to men. It is, too, a strict rule that no Eskimo ever fires off all his ammunition even if he has an obvious chance of killing a caribou. "You never know when you'll meet a grizzly bear in a bad temper," Kakinnâq says. Another rule is that snow must never be eaten, because it is weakening.

Toward Spring

It was a quiet, chilly morning. The sun had just risen and a flood of light fell upon snow-white slopes and mountains. The smoke curled slowly from the settlement chimneys and stood pillar-like against the blue sky.

I was sitting in the tent, waiting till breakfast was ready; the pungent smell of the cooked meat tickled my nostrils. Suddenly I heard singing, pushed the door aside, and looked out. Paniaq stood before the tent singing to the sun and the mountains. His head was thrown back slightly, and his deep strong voice rang out over the wilderness.

Yes, there was something in the air. And at last, at the beginning of April, the incredible happened—the sun gave warmth, just. I was out with the dog-team when I first noticed it, something like a gentle breath down my neck. Spring was coming. Strange thoughts rose in the mind.

The weather was fine, and the air between the blue sky and white snow was clear. The caribou had long since abandoned their leisurely life on the valley slopes, where thousands of them had been grazing, and were now moving off in long strings toward the tundra. Week after week they passed in procession along the moraines, dwindled to black dots in the wide pass, and disappeared.

We were not yet free of the after-effects of the sickness which had laid us low in the winter. Kakinnâq's adopted son Anga, eighteen years old, had been ailing for a long time and was now very ill. His face was thin and yellow, and his cough was terrible. From time to time he had the most violent convulsions and wandered in his speech. His father and mother sat by him day and night; they were weary and depressed. When the attacks came, Kakinnâq sometimes burst into tears. It looked as if the end was near.

I sent a message asking that the lad be fetched by plane, also that penicillin might be dropped if he could not be fetched at once. But no plane came. Each morning we wondered if Anga was still alive. We gazed skyward—the penicillin *must* come now.

Then suddenly one day we saw a large two-engined plane to the northward. It's not coming to us, we thought; such large planes never come to us; they stay high up and are on long-distance flights. But it dropped sharply, steered straight for our camp, thundered along over the willows and just over the tents, while the dogs yelped skyward. At the same moment something with a long red tail shot down through the air. Then the plane was gone in a flash.

Children and hunters dashed off among the willows like a pack of hounds. Soon they all came back at full gallop, headed by old Aguk. He held up something in triumph, a box fastened to a long red strip of cloth. *The penicillin!*

Paniaq and I immediately gave the patient an injection and continued them systematically. The dangerous attacks passed away, and it looked as if we had kept death at a distance, though the boy was still very ill.

The wolves now sleep for the greater part of the day. At about ten in the morning they lie down at a lookout point, and

they do not start hunting before five in the afternoon. They
sleep very lightly, and it is extremely difficult to approach them
by stealth, not least because our steps make more noise on the
snow than they did before. To move forward silently, a few of
the Eskimos use large bearskin overshoes with the hairs outside, as in bygone times. They are called *seagjuitnatârutik*.
Sometimes the hunters have luck and shoot several wolves at
once.

During the winter the beasts have roamed far and wide after
caribou, but the Nunamiuts declare that they return to their
home district for the mating season. The cubs are born in May
and June, and then comes a time when the male kills more caribou than before. At this time in particular the Eskimos keep a
sharp lookout for their lairs in order to kill the cubs later. Some
are well-known of old, for example, a large cave on the Mountain with the Old Trees.

The Eskimos have killed fifty-two wolves in all, this winter. A
poor bag, owing to their difficulties with the caribou hunting.
A capable fellow like Mikiâna did not get a single one. This
certainly means that they will not be able to get so much ammunition and other things by barter. The previous season was
even worse, only about forty wolves being taken. 1942–43 was
the great time for wolves; then the Eskimos got a hundred and
twenty-five.

Of the wolves caught this season five were black, one red, one
almost white, one grey, and forty-four whitish-grey. They
varied in weight between 55 lb. for a year-old cub to 108 lb. for
a fully grown male. But practically all the beasts were very thin
and would have weighed considerably more in good condition.

Now follow glorious days, with long runs on skis and with
the dog-team. The skis glide exquisitely through a mountain
world bathed in sunshine. The farthest white-clad tops stand
out sharp against the blue.

The most beautiful of all the valleys is the Giants' Valley. I often go there. I have seldom seen a limited area in which there is always so much game. Great herds of caribou, occasionally wolves, and scattered herds of sheep up on the mountainsides. In some wild gullies there are also quite a few wolverines.

One day I went to the far end of the valley and down the steep slope on the other side of the watershed. There something quite new met my eyes—spruce firs, a whole family of them. It was like greeting old acquaintances. A message from a land in the warmth of summer, which had quite slipped out of my mind after a daily life spent amid naked mountains. I could not resist going up to one of the trees, smelling the green needles, and running my hand down the trunk. The Eskimos call this beautiful country Sawinjaq, and here must lie the headwaters of the North Fork River.

On the way back I rested on the edge of a patch of willow, lit a fire, and quenched my thirst with scalding tea. Evening was drawing on, and all was still. As I sat there, a large herd of caribou passed close to me—bulls, cows, and slender-legged calves. Slow-moving beasts in glittering snow, and sunset over the mountains.

Sledge journeys can be beset with difficulties at this time, when there are caribou nearly everywhere. For instance, I want to go with the sledge to fetch home a load of meat, and suddenly a hundred caribou come along. The stupid beasts cross right in front of the dogs' muzzles, only fifty yards or so away. The dogs whine, and in a twinkling they are off at full gallop after the game, while the sledge bumps over drifts and sometimes skids far out to one side. To stop such a wild pursuit by eight big beasts, all mad for the chase, is not easy. My technique is to upset the sledge, fling myself into the middle of the team, and catch hold. This sometimes works; at other times no power in the world can stop them.

When meat has to be fetched home at rather short notice, we sometimes borrow a dog-team which is standing harnessed after a quick trip of some kind. This may cause some trouble, for as soon as the dogs notice that it is not their own master who is giving them orders, they do their best to shirk the job. One day I left the camp at a brisk trot with someone else's team, while a number of hunters stood looking after me. When I had driven a quarter of a mile or so, the dogs thought that was enough; they turned round, and it was no use my saying anything. We returned to the camp at a furious gallop. The hunters were still standing there. They had a good laugh, especially Aguk.

A few days later no less a personage than Aguk had a similar experience, or rather a worse one, for he was far out in the countryside when the team ran home. Late in the day he himself came pottering into camp on foot, not at all cheerful. It was clear that this time he saw nothing humorous in the incident.

Our cuisine is now agreeably reinforced by spring dishes: newly grown horns and gadfly larvae. The bulls' horns are about a foot long and covered with green skin. The soft part at the tip is eaten raw and tastes really good. The grubs are found in masses on the side of the skin nearest the flesh and in the throat and nose passages. They are eaten alive and have a sweetish taste. The children often sit down by a newly flayed caribou's skin, dig into the blood and tissue, and have a good feed. One small child can eat an incredible number of live grubs.

It was evening in the skin tent, and as usual most of the hunters were assembled there. Paniaq said: "On the tundra north of us there are many strange things to be seen. There are shells left by the great flood. In the frozen sandhills by the Colville River I have seen big fir trunks, so there must once have been forest all over this country. In many places oil bubbles up out of the earth. The Nunamiuts knew about this oil long before the white men.* We have an old story about it."

* About 35,000 square miles of tundra in the north have been set aside by the United States as an oil reserve, with the designation Naval Petroleum Reserve No. 4.

Then he told a story about a little girl and a little boy from Point Barrow who always wanted to play for a long time in the evening and were late in going to bed. Their father grew angry and said that they might just as well stay out. In despair they began to wander inland through the dark wintry country. The girl carried a little oil lamp which gave just enough light for them to see in front of them. Now and then she spilt a little of the seal oil, and that explains why there is oil (*anga*) at many places on the tundra. The boy was killed by a bear, the girl went on through dangers of many kinds. At last she came to a turf hut and found there an old woman and her five sons and twelve people who were halves, cut in two lengthways. The girl married the eldest of the sons. One spring she went to Point Barrow and visited her family there. Afterward there was constant communication between the Barrow people and these strange inland people. "That happened long ago, and the inland people were Indians," said Paniaq. "The story shows that there is Indian blood in the Barrow people. That's a thing everyone knows. There must also have been a lot of mammoth (*kiligwak*) on the tundra," he continued, "for at many places on the riverbanks the Eskimos have found huge teeth and sometimes frozen flesh. That was an important animal for our ancestors."

I asked how the mammoth was hunted, and he replied: "The mammoth often lived underground. The hunter searched for a depression of the right size. Then he shot his arrow into the ground. A year afterward he came back, and there lay the mammoth. Dead."

Here Kakinnâq interrupted: "Sometimes, too, the mammoth flew through the air." He went on to tell a dramatic story of an Eskimo who saw a mammoth come flying through the air pursued by a few huge dogs and behind them a party of hunters. They hit the ground. There the mammoth was killed. The people of the air flayed the beast and cut it up, loaded the flesh onto the dogs, and then vanished into the air the same way as they had come.

Then Paniaq told the tribal legend of the musk ox. As mentioned above, it is extinct in Alaska, but it must formerly have
been abundant there. We are told of a group of Nunamiuts who
in old times lived by the Colville River, a little way south of its
confluence with the Killik River. They lived mainly on musk
oxen. It was customary for the hunters to drive the beasts up
to the settlement and kill them there. One day they sighted a
large herd and began to hunt it toward the camp with the usual
shouting and hallooing. There was a girl there who was menstruating. She had to go out and urinate, and as the custom was,
she held a piece of skin before her eyes, because if a woman in
that condition saw anything of what was happening it would be
disastrous. When she heard the shouting of the hunters who
were driving the oxen, she could not restrain herself, but peeped
out inquisitively from behind the piece of skin. Immediately
both hunters and musk oxen were turned to stone. Those stones
can be seen by the Colville River to this day.

So we sit and talk on a light evening on the verge of spring.
And the peculiar atmosphere which the old legends always cre-
ate sets our thoughts roaming. I observe in the Eskimo mind a
groping for an explanation of life and its forces—a humble
wonder at the things which are beyond human understanding.

CHAPTER 29

Farewell to the Nunamiut

During April the sun really ac-
quires strength. First it breathes
away, as it were, the snow from the moraine hillocks, where the
first green blades soon shoot up at the edge of the snow. Then
it sets to work in earnest on the snow carpet which covers the
rest of the country. Patch after patch of grey and golden-brown
appears on the white sheet; the mountains are striped with black,
the brooks murmur down the slopes.

On April 14 I saw the first ground squirrel, sitting in front of
its hole, drinking in the sunshine, and enjoying life after its long
winter sleep. The grizzly bear gets under way about the same
time. I often come across its huge footprints, sometimes followed by quite small ones. A big fellow in the Anaqteqtuaq
Valley is an intolerable nuisance to Arnarniaq; it finds its way
to all his traps and eats the bait. Both bear and ground squirrel
are fat now. The Eskimos say that the bear's stomach has grown
together in the middle during hibernation; they think this has
something to do with its being able to remain in its winter lair
for so long without food.

The migratory birds are beginning to come. The pair of
eagles on the Mountain with the Old Trees are back in their
familiar haunts; the snow bunting twitters from boulders and
tussocks. Then there is a little brown bird which the Nunamiuts
call the "little eagle" (*tingmeaqpaujak*), and which they think
must come from Siberia. Nor should the robin be forgotten; it
sings in spring as no other bird does. But the ptarmigan are
leaving us; they move to the Arctic coast to breed.

There is a new atmosphere about the settlement. In front of
the tents the earth is clear of snow, with willow-scrub and moss
and frozen clusters of cranberry, trampled flat. A heap of splin-
ters from the winter's wood-cutting is whitening in the sun. The
tethered dogs no longer lie tightly curled with their muzzles
under their tails, but stretch themselves at ease with legs
asprawl. And the puppies dash about madly everywhere, their
stumpy tails in the air.

The bearskin doors are wide open, so that sun and light slant
into the tents; the wife or one or two of the children are usually
sitting on the threshold. The old willow-bough floor is thrown
out, and smiling girls come with their arms full of fresh sweet-
smelling boughs which are laid side by side on the earth. Outside the tent, women are busy crushing bones with a stone hammer. Afterward the bones will be cooked and fat extracted from
them.

The interior of Agmâlik's turf hut is like fairyland. From the
willow branches on which the turf rests, long shoots have sprung
up, with delicate sprouts and lush foliage. One sits under a
canopy of the tenderest green.

Sledges come and sledges go. There is always something or
other to be done. But no one hurries over his work. It is spring
now. If a hunter is inclined to laze in the sun for a day or more,
he does. Then he pulls himself together energetically and makes
himself useful. Some go to the trapping area with their dogs or
fetch home wolves and caribou, and then the women are busy

skinning the beasts. Others are engaged in hauling lumber from the forest limit, a trip which generally takes a couple of days. This is to be their fuel for the whole summer, so that many loads are needed. When there is no longer a snow surface for the sledges, the fuel problem is a difficult one in these regions.

Large piles of stakes gradually accumulate by the tents; later they will be transported still farther north, to the summer encampment.

At this season some of the lads are just as busy visiting other settlements as making themselves useful. Some run after girls; others are just eager to race off with the dogs and let everyone see what a rattling good team is theirs. The older people shake their heads and say: "The young fellows weren't like that in our time."

When nothing particular is happening, we can sit down in front of the tents and busy ourselves with all kinds of things for our diversion and amusement. One day Paniaq showed me how the Nunamiuts used to carve flint arrowheads. First he fashioned a little hammer (*natqiun*) with the head made of a piece of caribou horn and the shaft of willow wood (see photograph following p. 120). Then he held a piece of flint in the left mitten and gave it swift, sure blows with the hammer, turning the flint round all the time as the shape of the arrowhead or the stratification of the stone required. Afterward the arrowhead is cut fine with a curved bone (*kiglin*).

He told me that he had learnt the art from an old Eskimo when he was young. "There's no difficulty at all about making a fine arrowhead," he said. "No, not when one can do it," I thought.

He told me that the arrowhead was just as often made of caribou horn; it could have as many as four notches, he had never seen more. Then he went into the willow copse and returned with a dry stick green with verdigris. "A stick like this was used to colour the arrows with. We call it *kangruaq*," he said. He told me about the different marks the hunters used on arrows, bows, and other hunting equipment. Here are some as cut by Paniaq on a willow stick.

Three bow marks.

Aguâq is making a large ladle of sheep's horn, an old art with these people. Much work and great care are required. The horn is boiled from time to time to make it soft. In the lowest part a cut is made lengthways, after which the inside is scraped out with the curved knife. Then the lower part is turned inside out, carved level, and polished. The ladle is a lovely thing when it is finished (see photograph following p. 120).

I look in on Aguâq from time to time and see him at work. It is always pleasant to go into his tent, where Qutuk is the hospitable housewife. My little girl friend, three-year-old Puya, is there, and the baby girl Ayapana, who was born in the time of darkness and has a black tuft of hair on her head. They make a tremendous fuss over her. Indeed, the father has actually composed a special song for the baby; she giggles delightedly when he lifts her up and sings it.

The people are assembling. From the other settlements to the south and north families come driving with all their possessions loaded on the sledges and a string of children in their wake. It is hard work for the dogs when the sledges must cross the bare patches, but they seem to acquire fresh strength when they know camp is to be pitched soon.

There is noise and bustle when people come—dogs yelping, children shouting. The tents are quickly pitched; willing hands help to carry twigs for the floor and cut turf, which is placed round the base of the tent.

Piliala, the great runner, settled down close to my tent. I went in to see the family; it was a long time since we had met. He and his wife are so young and bright, and their child is delightful. Apart from the bare necessities of life they own only a few wolfskins. A poor home—but they do not seem to feel it.

When Inualûjuq and his large family arrived, there was much activity. He quickly set about making a new sledge of spruce brought from the forest. The implement he uses is the adze; only the blade is a steel one instead of jade as formerly. He uses it with great skill and it will be a fine sledge. Afterward he will paint it all over with the red dye (*iwisâq*) which the people find near the Killik River.

For the first time since the early winter the Raven and Killik people are together again in one settlement.

Two of the sledges brought a heavy load, the bodies of the two babies who died in the time of darkness. They were in coffins made of roughly hewn planks. Their parents had carried them about with them all the winter; it is not customary to bury the dead until the ground is free from snow.

The mother of one of the children was Tugli, a woman whose married life was not easy. She seemed quiet and resigned. No doubt the child was the bright spot in her life and reconciled her to much else. When I heard of the child's death, I sent the mother some trifles by a dog-driver, and this she did not forget. One day a boy came into my tent with a large piece of delicious knuckle-fat. It was from Tugli.

Mamaraq, the very old, thin dog with the tired, red eyes, was still alive. Unalîna would not hear of his being killed. In the course of the winter he had a hard time following us about from camp to camp in the wilderness, although he was always loose. He often arrived hours after camp had been pitched, quite worn out. Now he lay in the snow for the most part, or just stood gazing in front of him as an old dog does. But when the other dogs were harnessed, Mamaraq woke up, moving over to sniff at the harness and sledge. Then, when the team dashed out, he stood alone in the middle of the track and watched it go.

One brilliant spring morning Mamaraq lay stiff in the snow. A sledge-dog's saga was at an end.

May 2 is a red-letter day in my tent; for the first time ice has not formed in the cooking-pot during the night. One feels now that it is spring, with warm sun, murmuring brooks, and wide areas of melting snow in the valley and on the slopes. Heather and willow spring into life and lift their buds to the sun. The mornings are bright and promising, with the sweetest bird-song in the willow-scrub. From time to time a skein of geese makes its way northward high in the sky. Gulls sail over the valley on white wings and seem to have decided to stay.

Nothing is as it was; it is like turning the pages of a new picture book. Everywhere is growth and life after the oppressive winter. The movements of the wild creatures are different. Wolf, fox, wolverine, and all the rest are with young, and are busy preparing for the new life. The birds are pairing. I come to a little pool of melted water over light-blue ice. There two ducks are resting close together, the sun reflected in the green sheen of their wings.

The Eskimos have the spring in their blood, too. The young ones are lively and restless as they have never been before. All through the light spring nights they scour the settlement or roam out into the wilderness in bands. Sometimes I see three or four girls, arm in arm, far away over the hillocks. Quite often they are liable to pay me a visit in my tent at two or three in the morning. It never occurs to them that there can be any objection to such nocturnal visits to a solitary man in bed.

I may wake suddenly and see Kunnâna, Kimmaq, and the widow Paniulaq sitting smiling at me. I lean forward in my sleeping bag and put fuel into the stove; then the ladies grill some caribou meat and we have a cheerful meal. Then they slip out, and half asleep, I hear their laughter die away in the distance.

The smallest children are busy digging up roots in the sandy soil. A little green food certainly tastes good after nothing but meat for months.

Caribou now pass less frequently. It looks as if the greater part of them have reached the tundra after the endless migration northward. The few beasts which pass from time to time are moving very fast. They are in a hurry to get to the place where their calves are to be born.

The great river is open, and there is more bare ground than snow.

It will soon be time for me to part company with the Nunamiuts and leave the wilds behind me. My thoughts are turned abruptly to the world where I belong. It has become remote and unreal. A faint picture of streets full of hurrying swarms, noise, and tired faces rises in my mind's eye. I think how few really happy people I know down south.

I look round me: there is the Giants' Valley, the nameless hillock where I saw a bear's track not long ago, and there the strange peak of Soakpak stands erect against the blue spring sky—familiar features which delight my eye every morning when I creep out of my tent.

Laughter rings out from one of the tents. On a caribou carcass not far away sits the tiny boy Ayaqiujaq, gnawing a raw knuckle of meat. He looks up and smiles broadly, his face smeared with blood.

We were sitting in the tent, talking a little about my departure. Paniaq said: "We will give you the mountain which stands at the beginning of the Giants' Valley. It shall bear your name, and we will remember you." Then he added, in a matter-of-fact way: "Our people remember such things for many generations."

The tone of his voice, and the thoughts which I knew lay behind his words, made me feel that this was a real and great gift from these simple people. We went out of the tent, and he pointed to the mountain. It must be about six thousand feet high. The top is snow-clad for a great part of the year and is often used as a landmark when the Eskimos are coming from the north. I knew it well, I had so often hunted wolves and caribou there; there is always a great deal of game in those parts: a fine mountain, indeed. And I had got into good company, for on the other side of the valley Soakpak lifts its head into the sky—the mountain called after the great hunter who lived long ago.

A buzzing filled the valley; an aircraft came into sight, flew low over the tents, and landed on the ice a little to the north. The dogs were harnessed, the sledges sped off, and we were there in a twinkling. The Eskimos crowded about the plane, while the dogs lay stretched out on the ice around it. There were the hunters: Paniaq, Kakinnâq, tall stately Maptirâq, with his rifle slung over his back, and the rest—the wives, too, with babies peeping out over the wolfskin edges of their hoods, and the girls. And the children, my little tyrants: smiling Alasuq, of course, in front and dainty shy Sikiârjuk at the rear of the party. With all these friends I had shared good and ill for so long.

We rose into the air. I looked down toward the little group of skin-clad people on the ice, so small and poor against the background of savage mountains which extended in every direction. The last relic of a caribou-hunting people. All by themselves they maintain the struggle for life out in the wilds. Poor, but with unflinching courage and resolved to be happy.

The plane made a wide circle and then flew over Paniaq, who was driving his dog-team toward the settlement. As we flashed over him he threw his head back and waved his arm. His cordial smile was my last impression. . . . Then we flew on, southward over the blue mountain world of Alaska.

Spelling of Eskimo Words

In this book Eskimo words are quoted in a simplified phonemic notation. Among the consonant letters the following need special explanation:

g: (1) voiced spirant similar to German g in *Tage*.

(2) voiceless spirant similar to German ch in *Ich*.

j: between English r in *true* and z in *azure*.

l: (1) voiced like English l in *ceiling*.

(2) unvoiced like l in *Tlingit*.

(3) after i in some words palatalized like Italian gl in *figlio*.

n: (1) similar to English n.

(2) after i in some words palatalized like French gn in *digne*.

ng: like English ng in *singer* (g not separately pronounced), but both short and long.

q: uvular k, pronounced farther back in the mouth than English c in *car*.

r: (1) voiced uvular spirant, similar to Parisian French r.

(2) voiceless uvular spirant, somewhat similar to ch in German *Bach* and Scottish *loch*.

s: usually more like English sh in *she* than s in *see*.

Long consonants are written double, except in the case of ng.

Vowels are short: a, i, u, and long: â, î, û, and they vary according to the adjoining phonemes.

a may be similar to English a in *man,* but before uvular consonants it is more like English a in *father.*

i may be similar to English e in *equal,* but before uvular consonants it is more like American English i in *stirrup.*

u may be similar to English u in *yule,* but before uvular consonants it is more like English o in *or.*

BIBLIOGRAPHY

Andersson, Johan G. Hunting magic in the animal style.—Bull. Mus. Far East Antiquities. Stockholm 1932. Pp. 221–317.

Beechey, Frederick W. Narrative of a voyage to the Pacific and Beering's Strait, to co-operate with the polar expeditions: performed in His Majesty's Ship Blossom . . . in the years, 1825, 26, 27, 28. A new ed. in two vols. London 1831.

Birket-Smith, Kaj. The Caribou Eskimos. Material and social life and their cultural position. I, II. Copenhagen 1929. 306 pp., 419 pp. illustr. pl. map. fig.—Rep. of the fifth Thule expedition 1921–24. Vol. 5.

— Early collections from the Pacific Eskimo. Ethnographical studies. Copenhagen 1941.—Nat. Mus. Skr., Ethnogr. række 1.

— Ethnographical collections from the Northwest Passage. Copenhagen 1945.—Rep. of the fifth Thule expedition 1921–24. Vol. 6, no. 2.

Boas, Franz. The Central Eskimo.—Sixth Ann. Rep. Bur. Amer. Ethn. Washington 1888. Pp. 409–669.

— The Eskimo of Baffin land and Hudson bay. N. Y. 1901.—Bull. Amer. Mus. Nat. Hist. Vol. 15, p. 1.

— Second report on the Eskimo of Baffin land and Hudson bay. New York 1907.—Ibid. Vol. 15, p. 2.

Bogoras, Waldemar. The Chuchee. New York 1904.—The Jesup North Pacific Expedition, 1904–09. Vol. 7, p. 1. Also as Mem. Amer. Mus. Nat. Hist. Vol. 11, p. 1.

— Ethnographic problems of the Eurasian Arctic.—Problems of Polar Research. (Amer. Geogr. Soc., Spec. Publ. No. 7.) New York 1928. Pp. 189–207.

Brower, Charles D. Fifty years below zero. A lifetime of adventure in the Far North. London 1942. 254 pp. illustr.

Catlin, George. Letters and notes on the manners, customs and condition of the North American Indians. 2 vols. London 1842.

Chevigny, Hector. Lord of Alaska. Baranov and the Russian adventure. London 1946. 255 pp.

Collins, Henry B., Jr. Prehistoric art of the Alaskan Eskimo. Washington 1929.—Smithson. Misc. Coll. Vol. 81, no. 14.

— Prehistoric Eskimo culture of Alaska.—Explorations and Field-Work of the Smithson. Inst. in 1929. Washington 1930. Pp. 147–56.

Collins, Henry B., Jr. Archaeological Investigations at Point Barrow, Alaska. —Explorations and Field-Work of the Smithson. Inst. in 1932. Washington 1933. Pp. 45–48.

— Archeology of St. Lawrence Island, Alaska. Washington 1937.—Smithson. Misc. Coll. Vol. 96, no. 1.

— Outline of Eskimo prehistory. *In* Essays in historical anthropology of North America.—*Ibid.*, vol. 100. Washington 1940. Pp. 533–92.

— Eskimo archeology and its bearing on the problem of man's antiquity in America. *In* Recent advances in American archeology. Philadelphia 1943.—Proc. Amer. Phil. Soc., Vol. 86, no. 2.

Cook, James. Transactions amongst the Natives of North America; Discoveries along that coast and the Eastern Extremity of Asia, Northward to Icy Cape; and Return Southward to the Sandwich Islands.—*In* A Voyage to the Pacific Ocean . . . , Vol. 2. London 1784. Pp. 269–549.

Dall, William H. Alaska and its resources. Boston 1870. 657 pp., illustr., map.

Dufresne, Frank. Alaska's animals and fishes. New York 1946.

Early Man.—The Academy of Natural Sciences. Philadelphia 1937. Ed. by George G. MacCurdy. Lond. 1937.

Elliott, Henry W. Alaska og Sæløerne. Oversatt fra engelsk ved O. Storm. Christiania 1888. 462 pp. illustr. kart.

Franklin, John. Narrative of a second expedition to the shores of the Polar Sea, in the years 1825, 1826 and 1827. Including an account of the progress of a detachment to the eastward by John Richardson. With appendix. Illustr. by numerous plates and maps. London 1828. XXIV + 320 + CLVII pp.

Giddings, J. L., Jr. Dated Eskimo ruins of an inland zone.—Amer. Antiquity. Vol. 10. Washington 1944. Pp. 113–34.

Gjessing, Gutorm. Circumpolar stone age. Copenhagen 1944. 70 pp. fig.— Acta Arctica 2.

— Norges steinalder. Oslo 1945. VII + 527 pp. illustr.

Golder, F. A. Bering's voyages. An account of the efforts of the Russians to determine the relations of Asia and America. In two vols. Vol. 1. The log books and official reports of the first and second expeditions 1725–1730 and 1733–1742. New York 1922. 371 pp. illustr. map. Vol. 2. Steller's journal of the sea voyage from Kamchatka to America and return on the second expedition 1741–1742. New York 1925. 290 pp. illustr. map.—Amer. Geogr. Soc., Research series No. 1 and 2.

Hatt, Gudmund. Arktiske Skinddragter i Eurasien og Amerika. En Ethnografisk Studie. Copenhagen 1914. 255 pp., illustr.

— Moccasins and their relation to Arctic footwear. Lancaster, Pa. 1916. —Mem. Amer. Anthrop. Ass. Vol. 3, no. 3.

Hawkes, E. W. The Labrador Eskimo.—Mem. Geol. Surv. Can., no. 91; (Anthrop. ser., no. 14.) Ottawa 1916. Pp. 1–235.

Holtved, Erik. Archaeological investigations in the Thule district. 1, Descriptive part; 2, Analytical part. Copenhagen 1944.—Medd. Grønland. Vol. 141, nos. 1 and 2.

Hone, Elizabeth. The present status of the muskox in Arctic North America and Greenland with notes on distribution, extirpation, transplantation, protection, habits and life history. Prepared by . . . Cambridge, Mass. 1934. 87 pp.—Spec. publ. Amer. Comm. Intern. Wild Life Protect. Nr. 5.

Hrdlicka, Ales. Anthropological survey in Alaska.—Forty-sixth Ann. Rep. Bur. Amer. Ethnol. Washington 1930. Pp. 19–374, 61 pl. 29 fig.

Ingstad, Helge. Pelsjegerliv blandt Nord-Kanadas indianere. Oslo 1931. 245 pp. illustr. (= Land of Feast and Famine. New York 1933. 332 pp. illustr.)

— Øst for den store bre. Oslo 1935. 182 pp. illustr. (= East of the Great Glacier. New York 1937. xvi + 271 pp. illustr.)

— Apache-Indianerne. Oslo 1939. 324 pp. illustr.

Jacobi, Arnold. Das Rentier. Eine zoologische Monographie der Gattung Rangifer. Mit 6 Tafeln und 32 Abbildungen im Texte. Leipzig 1931. 264 s.

Jenness, Diamond. The life of the Copper Eskimos. Ottawa 1922. 277 pp. illustr. pl. map. fig.—Rep. Canad. Arct. Exped. 1913–18. Vol. 12.

— Myths and traditions from Northern Alaska, the Mackenzie delta and Coronation Gulf. Ottawa 1924. 90 pp.—Ibid. Vol. 13. Part. A.

— A new Eskimo culture in Hudson bay.—Geogr. Rev. Vol. 15. New York 1925. Pp. 428–37.

Jochelson, Waldemar. Material culture and social organization of the Koryak. Ed. by Franz Boas. Leiden 1908.—The Jesup North Pacific expedition. Vol. 6, p. 2. Also as Mem. Amer. Mus. Nat. Hist. Vol. 10, p. 2.

— Archaeological investigations in the Aleutian Islands. Washington 1925.—Carnegie Inst. Publ. no. 367.

Laguna, Frederica de. Eskimo lamps and pots. London 1940.—J. R. Anthrop. Inst. Vol. 70, p. 1.

Larsen, Helge and Froelich Rainey. Ipiutak and the Arctic whale hunting culture. N. Y. 1948. 276 pp. 101 pl. 4 tab. 60 fig.—Anthrop. Pap. New York Vol. 42.

M'Clure, Robert. The discovery of the North-west passage by H.M.S. "Investigator," Capt. R. M'Clure, 1850, 1851, 1852, 1853, 1854. Edited by Commander Sherard Osborne, from the logs and journals of Capt. Robert LeM. M'Clure. London 1856.

Markham, Clements R. Arctic Geography and Ethnology . . . London 1875. 292 pp.

Martin, Paul S., George I. Quimby and Donald Collier. Indians before Columbus. Twenty thousand years of North American history revealed by archeology. Chicago 1947. 582 pp. illustr. map.

Mason, J. Alden. Excavations of Eskimo Thule culture sites at Point Barrow, Alaska.—Proc. 23d Intern. Congr. Americanists, held at New York, 1928. New York 1930. Pp. 382–99.

Mason, Otis T. Aboriginal skin-dressing. A study based on material in the U. S. National Museum.—Rep. U. S. Nat. Mus. for the year ending June 30, 1889. Washington 1891. Pp. 553–89.

Mathiassen, Therkel. Archaeology of the Central Eskimos. I, II. (I. Descriptive part. II. The Thule culture and its position within the Eskimo culture.) Copenhagen 1927. 327 pp., 208 pp., illustr. pl. map. fig.—Rep. fifth Thule Exp. 1921–24. Vol. IV.

— Some specimens from the Bering Sea culture.—Ind. Notes, Mus. Amer. Ind., Heye Found. Vol. 6. No. 1. New York 1929. Pp. 33–56.

— Inugsuk. A mediaeval Eskimo settlement in Upernivik district, West Greenland.—Med. om Grønl. Vol. 77. Copenhagen 1930. Pp. 137–340.

— Archaeological collections from the Western Eskimos. Copenhagen 1930. 98 pp. pl. map. fig.—Rep. fifth Thule Exp. 1921–24. Vol. 10. No. 1.

Murdoch, John. A study of the Eskimo bows in the U. S. National Museum. —Rep. U. S. Nat. Mus. for the year 1884. Part 3. Washington 1885. Pp. 307–16.

— The ethnological results of the Point Barrow expedition. Washington 1892.—Ninth Ann. Rep. Bur. Amer. Ethn.

Murie, Olaus J. Alaska—Yukon Caribou. Washington 1933.—N. Amer. Fauna. No. 54. U. S. Dept. of Agricult.

Nelson, Edward W. The Eskimo about Bering Strait. Wash. 1899.—18th Ann. Rep. Bur. Amer. Ethn., Washington 1899.

Petroff, Ivan. Report on the population, industries and resources of Alaska. In U. S. Census Office, 10th Census, Washington 1884. Vol. 8, p. 8, H. Misc. 2d Sess. 47th Congress.

Quimby, George I. Aleutian Islanders. Eskimos of the North Pacific. Chicago 1944.—Anthrop. leaflet, Chicago Nat. Hist. Mus., No. 35.

Rainey, Froelich G. Culture changes on the Arctic coast.—Trans. N. Y. Acad. Sci. Ser. 2. Vol. 3. No. 6. New York 1941. Pp. 172–76.

— Discovering Alaska's oldest Arctic town—Nat. Geogr. Mag. Vol. 82. New York 1942. Pp. 319–36.

Rasmussen, Knud. Fra Grønland til Stillehavet. Rejser og mennesker fra 5. Thule-ekspedition 1921–24. 2 b. Copenhagen 1925–26. 464 pp., 415 pp. illustr. kart.

— Myter og Sagn fra Grønland. 3 b. (1. b. Østgrønlændere, 2. b. Vestgrønland, 3. b. Kap York-distriktet og Nordgrønland.) Copenhagen 1921–25. 375 pp., 354 pp., 340 pp., illustr.

Ray, Patrick H. Report of the International Polar Expedition to Point Barrow, Alaska, in response to the resolution of the House of Representatives of December 11, 1884. Washington 1885. 695 pp. illustr.

Reuterskiöld, Edgar. De nordiska Lapparnes religion. Stockholm 1912.—Populära Etnol. Skr., Nr. 8.

Schrader, F. C. A reconnaissance in northern Alaska across the Rocky Mountains, along Koyukuk, John, Anaktuvuk, and Colville rivers and the Arctic coast to Cape Lisburne, in 1901. With notes by W. J. Peters. Washington 1904. 139 pp. pl.—Prof. Pap. U. S. Geol. Surv. No. 20.

Simpson, John. Observations on the western Eskimo, and the country they inhabit; from notes taken during two years at Point Barrow.—*In* Arctic geography and ethnology. A selection of papers on Arctic geography and ethnology. Reprinted and presented to the Arctic Expedition of 1875, by the President, Council, and Fellows of the Royal Geographical Society. London 1875. Pp. 233–75.

Simpson, Thomas. Narrative of the discoveries on the north coast of America; erected by the officers of the Hudson's Bay Company during the years 1836–39. London 1843.

Smith, P. S. and J. B. Mertie, Jr. Geology and mineral resources of northwestern Alaska. Washington 1930. 351 pp. 34 pl.—U. S. Geol. Surv. Bull. no. 815.

Steensby, H. P. Om Eskimokulturens Oprindelse. En etnografisk og antropogeografisk Studie. Copenhagen 1905. 219 pp.

Stefansson, Vilhjalmur. My life with the Eskimo. Lond. 1913. 527 pp. illustr. map.

— The Stefansson-Anderson Arctic expedition of the American Museum: Preliminary ethnological report. N. Y. 1914. 395 pp. map. fig.—Anthrop. Pap. Vol. 14, p. 1.

— Hunters of the great North. N. Y. 1922. 301 pp. illustr. map.

Stoney, George M. Explorations in Alaska. Annapolis 1899.—Proc. U. S. Nav. Inst., Annapolis. Vol. 25.

Thomsen, Th. Eskimo archaeology.—Greenland. Vol. 2. Copenhagen 1928. Pp. 271–329. Illustr.

Trætteberg, Gunvor Ingstad. Handakledet og dets seremonielle tildekning av hendene. Oslo 1949.

Weyer, Edward M., Jr. The Eskimos. Their environment and folkways. New Haven 1932.

Wissler, Clark. Archaeology of the Polar Eskimo. New York 1918.—Anthrop. Pap. Vol. 22, p. 3.

(Wrangel, Ferdinand v.) Reise des kaiserlich-russischen Flotten-Lieutenants Ferdinand v. Wrangel längs der Nordküste von Sibirien und auf dem Eismeere, in den Jahren 1820 bis 1824. Nach den handschriftlichen Journalen und Notizen bearbeitet von G. Engelhardt. Berlin 1839. 321 pp.

INDEX

Fishing, 40
  inland Eskimo, 34, 84–89, 220
Flaying techniques, 95–96
Flint, 96–97, 157, 281
Flood, story of the great, 175, 257
Fog, 270
Folk-lore, *see* Story-telling
Folsom arrowhead, 160
Foods, 38–40, 77–78, 122, 276
  fish, 85
  importance of fat, 166
  maggots in, 102–103
  meal customs, 123–124
  meat diet, 120–124
  skins as, 235
  storing, 119
Footwear, 167–168, 226, 231–232, 274
Forests, 276
Foxes, 75, 149, 189, 191, 233
Frostbite, 208, 226
Fruits, 119
Fuel, 126, 211–212, 281
Funerals, 103–106, 260
  dancing at, 107–108, 110
  see also Burial customs *and* Death
Fur trade, 35, 251–252

Gadfly, 66, 120, 276
Games, 105, 143–144, 234–235, 265
Garlik, 73
Geese, 284
Giants' Valley, 76, 165, 274, 285–286
  sheep hunt in, 167–170
Gift dance, 112
Gilberg, Dr. Aage, 122
Glaciers, 28
Glands, as food, 77–78
Gloves, white, 107, 108, 110
Good, Eskimo attitude toward idea of, 184
Government Research Institute, 89
Grant's caribou, 63
Graves, 259–260
Gravy, as drink, 121
Grayling, 84, 87, 220
Greenland, 69
Ground squirrel, 73, 279

Groven, Eivind, 243
Gulls, 284

Hand covering, 110
Hare, 75, 223
Herring, 87
Herschel Island, 110
Hirshi, 132
History, Eskimo, 28–36
  see also Story-telling
Homes, 38–39, 213
  heating and cooking in, 206–207
  housecleaning, 280
  stone huts, 159
  tents, 206
  turf huts, 158–160, 265
  see also Families
Honour, attitude toward, 129
Hordaland, Norway, 110
Horns: as food, 120, 122, 271
  deer's, 123
  sheep's, 282
Howard, W. L., 35
Hudson's Bay Co., 252
Hunters, The, 210
Hunters' Dance, 108
Hunting: bear, 195–196
  caribou, *see* Caribou hunters
  hardships associated with, 208–209
  of mountain sheep, 72–83
  shoulder packs for, 72–73
  wolf hunts, 189–198
Husband-fishing story, 176
Huts, 39, 158–160, 265
Hydrophobia, 90–91

Igloos, 39
Iglugalûjaq, 129
Ikâksaq, 142–143
Ikiaqpak, 219, 220
Iliapaluk, story of, 180–181
Illaganniq, stories of, 181–182
Iluppak, 270
Imairniq, 148
Indians, 25, 29, 31, 47, 277
  adaptability, 211
  dances, 109, 110
  diet, 122

HARRISON COUNTY
PUBLIC LIBRARY
105 North Capitol Ave.
Corydon, IN 47112

Nunamiut : among Alaska's inland Eskimo
A 305. 897 ING   80766

Ingstad, Helge,
HARRISON COUNTY PUBLIC LIBRARY